PASTORAL CARE

IN HOSPITALS

PASTORAL CARE
IN HOSPITALS

Neville A. Kirkwood

MOREHOUSE PUBLISHING

Morehouse Publishing
P.O. Box 1321
Harrisburg, PA 17105

Morehouse Publishing is a division of The Morehouse Group.

Printed in the United States of America

Cover design by Corey Kent

Library of Congress Cataloging-in-Publication Data

Kirkwood, Neville A.
    Pastoral care in hospitals / Neville A. Kirkwood.
        p.   cm.
    Originally published: Australia : E.J. Dwyer, 1995.
    Includes bibliographical references.
    ISBN 0-8192-1790-5 (pbk.)
    1. Hospital patients—Pastoral counseling of.   2. Church work with the sick.
3. Pastoral medicine.   I. Title
BV4335.K57   1999
259'.411—dc21   98-35131
                                                                     CIP

FOREWORD

Jesus Christ told us in Matthew 25:36 that Christians, as followers of His, have an obligation to visit the sick.

This book will become a valuable tool in the training of pastoral carers for the hospital scene. The chapter "Know Yourself", is a great examination of conscience for those who are already practising in this field.

Rev Neville Kirkwood's use of language and his approach is a credit to him. His non-verbal communication indicators are among the best that I have read—covering facial expressions, appearances, voice, body posture, gestures and manners.

In the chapter "Jesus—A Theological Model", the author explains ten different theologies, looking at the way in which we, the readers, minister to our clients.

The experiences that Dr Neville Kirkwood relates, after sixteen years in the ministry of pastoral care in various hospitals, are enlightening and his anecdotes are full of interest.

I have used some of the principles expounded in this book in the training of laity for the role of lay pastoral workers. I wish it had been published previously because, being an eclectic, I find the information gathered here of tremendous value and use.

Ron Davoren CP
Coordinating Chaplain
Royal Melbourne Hospital
Victoria

DEDICATION

To the late Principal T.C. Warriner,
under whose ministry
my perception of our great God
and a love for all God's handiwork,
especially for men and women,
flourished and continues to do so.

Table Of Contents

SECTION 3 —
FOR CLERGY
VISITING HOSPITALS

PROLOGUE

Recently a church official boastingly remarked, "My chaplains have a sacramental ministry. They don't get involved in this so-called pastoral care, which is nothing more than gossiping in the wards." Such a comment brings a sense of deep sadness. Pastoral care shows Christ's interest in total persons in their various aspects: physical, social, emotional and spiritual. The shepherd of the Old Testament and the Good Shepherd of the New Testament reveal that God's touch goes beyond the spiritual into all aspects of life.

The absence of any significant mention of sacramental ministry here is not to denigrate or relegate the value of the sacraments in hospital pastoral visitation. Each tradition is expected to administer this form of care at the appropriate time and in the appropriate way. It is anticipated that the sacraments will have a far greater spiritual impact after the practice of the insights outlined in this book.

A general hospital is one of the most significantly helpful places of ministry available to the church today. Many ministers, religious and lay persons are becoming aware of the importance of this area of Christian service and witness.

There are three categories of visitors addressed in the book's three sections, although there is some overlapping of the roles of the hospital visitor from the church, the official lay pastoral worker and visiting clergy. (There could be a fourth section for hospital chaplains but the temptation to extend the scope of this work to include chaplains has been resisted.) It is recommended that each section be read and the information applied to your own particular ministry.

The purpose of this book is to help those who feel that they have a calling to hospital ministry. It is a specialist ministry. In the past and currently, many well-meaning pastoral visitors have not always been helpful to patients and their relatives. It has been my endeavor to highlight the need for training and preparation for this ministry. It is also important that the church make suitable provisions for the emotional and spiritual after-care and debriefing opportunities, so necessary for the hospital care team. Special attention should be given to the heightened anxiety levels that this type of visitation generates. The church owes this essential support to its appointees.

In the effort to make this advice as practical as possible, I trust I have also been careful not to make it appear as if hospital visitation is easy if you follow certain rules. I offer here what may be called a set of guidelines. The fact is that every person reacts differently to whatever malfunction of the body or mind is the cause of the hospitalization. Medical and surgical procedures also bring different reactions.

Appreciation is expressed to those who for over sixteen years in full time ministry in hospitals have taught me so much. Their patience, love and acceptance have encouraged me in this. Often those bedside encounters, dealing with relatives in the interview rooms and also with supporting staff are very exhausting and draining, yet satisfying and rewarding. Gratitude is expressed for the privilege of sharing the intimacy of such occasions.

To those who have typed and set up this book, to those who perused and offered advice, I express my thanks. Especially would I thank Dr. Bruce Peterson, who offered wise guidance in the preparation. Professor Bruce Rumbold's critique of the manuscript was positive and is reflected in the final presentation.

My desire is that this book will help others to provide a pastoral ministry which will be as caring and helpful as possible, enriching the lives of those to whom it is offered in Jesus' name.

Neville A. Kirkwood

INTRODUCTION

Visitation to a hospital patient's bedside appeals to many people as a fruitful and rewarding type of Christian service. A sincere desire to support and comfort an ill patient, bringing hope, encouraging faith, stirring optimism, lifting inner tension, relieving depression and, by being there, distancing isolation, is a Christ-approved ministry: "I was sick and you visited me" (Matthew 25:26).

It is intended that this will help you to clarify the types of hospital ministries that are exercised today by the church. Chaplaincy ministry is not considered here, as it is a specialized ministry as part of the therapeutic team working within the institution. Hospital visitation operates from without. Chaplaincy expectations and privileges are of different character to those of the Christian worker coming from the parish situation.

This book is divided into three sections in an endeavor to distinguish between the three different visitation roles of the church to the hospital bed. As we have said, these roles have an unavoidable overlap, so all sections will contain material which may be of benefit to all visitors. And there are some lines of etiquette which should be followed by all categories of church visitors.

Hospital staff have certain standards of expectation of church visitors. At the Central Coast Area Health Service, where I previously worked, each April the various denominations appointed chaplains who are an integral part of the hospital system. They are expected to minister in appointed wards for a minimum session each week, being responsible for facilitating pastoral care for all patients in the ward. They are issued with the normal staff photographed identification card. The hospital also issues an identification card without a photograph to "visiting clergy," nominated by their religious authority. A similar identification card of a different color is made available to church-authorized "pastoral visitors." The last two are revalidated each April upon receipt of updated lists from the churches. The pastoral visitors usually visit patients of their own denomination on a regular basis, reporting to their own priest, minister or chaplain. There is a further unnamed person, whom the local church calls the "hospital visitor," who is mostly untrained in specific hospital pastoral skills yet is faithful in ministering to the sick.

Lay pastoral visitors usually have undergone some pastoral care training at the parish level or beyond and have a proven aptitude for hospital pastoral care. They are able to provide a deeper level of pastoral care than the hospital visitor. Their training equips them to offer a wider and more perceptive ministry to the patient and their families and alerts the priest, minister or chaplain to any special needs observed.

The visiting member of the clergy is the local parish priest or minister who comes in to visit the church's own parishioners or the members of his/her own denomination, on behalf of that denomination. This role falls short of the type of pastoral care offered by the chaplain to the hospital and its community.

Hospital etiquette for visitors involves such questions as: To whom do I report in the hospital? Who am I allowed to visit? To whom am I accountable? What is the relationship with the Chaplaincy Department? When should I visit?

These matters will be dealt with here and may be reiterated elsewhere in the text for the purpose of emphasis.

THE HOSPITAL VISITOR

The unidentified hospital visitor comes to the hospital like any other visitor. The normal visiting hours are observed. The hospital visitor, like the pastoral visitor, is not permitted to visit people of other denominations or religions without the permission of the patient or their relatives. Where an adequate hospital security system operates, the ward staff may summon the security guard to escort the offending hospital visitor off the premises if he/she presses beyond those boundaries.

There are some hospital visitors who feel they have the right to visit every patient and leave literature with them. This is in breach of the Privacy Act and may cause offense to patients who do not wish to have a religious visit.

Hospital visitors visiting a member of a local parish congregation are not obligated to report to ward staff, although that is advisable, and are generally treated like other people visiting friends or relatives. Hospital visitors are accountable to their own parish clergy.

THE LAY PASTORAL WORKER

An official visit by identified lay pastoral visitors has deeper significance for the denomination. In some hospitals they may have access to denominational lists through the chaplain or visiting clergy. Where a chaplaincy department is firmly established, such lists may not be available even to visiting clergy. Organization and structure of each hospital varies. All pastoral care workers should, therefore, acquaint themselves with local hospital protocol before engaging in such ministry.

Lay pastoral visitors usually identify themselves to the nursing unit manager, or the ward clerk in some institutions. The staff will then know that the patient has community pastoral support and it will probably be assumed by the staff that the patient would appreciate a call to the chaplain or visiting clergy if the patient's condition should deteriorate or there develops some special condition (such as depression, for example) which is outside the normal course of the treatment or its side-effects.

Lay pastoral visitors generally are quite regular in their visits. The frequency is more readily noted when a report is made to the nursing station and staff; acquaintance with the pastoral worker often produces a warmer and more co-operative relationship. Staff who have built up confidence in the pastoral carer are likely to pass on information that may assist them in their understanding of the patient.

In most hospitals the visiting hours have been extended from 12 noon or 2.30 pm to 8 pm. Pastoral visitors are advised to work within those hours for the patients' welfare. There may be hospitals where special concessions are possible for lay pastoral visits outside these hours, but it is generally wise not to abuse privileges or make special demands. Depending upon the local arrangements, the visitor reports to the parish clergy person or the denominational chaplain, whoever is responsible for visitors within the hospital.

THE VISITING MEMBER OF THE CLERGY

Parish clergy are very busy people, trying to be ten specialists rolled into one, with an incessant clamor to be all things to all persons. For many, hospital visitation makes unpredictable demands on their time, necessitating a reshuffling of schedules and appointments. Visiting clergy are given wide privileges, such as access at almost any hour. They often know the patient and family intimately and will have the responsibility of follow up, after family ties with the hospital are severed. Visiting clergy are an important factor in the life of hospital patients and their families.

It is important for such members of the clergy to get to know and report to the nursing unit manager or other ward staff whenever they come into the ward and inform them of the patients they have come to see. The staff can then pass on helpful information or ask questions on some aspects of the case which are puzzling the nurses or the doctors. Such sharing builds up valuable rapport between the clergy and staff. Trust develops and many other doors for co-operation open. Opportunities for ministry to staff in their own personal and spiritual matters also may develop.

Where there is a working chaplaincy department, chaplains welcome contact with the parish clergy and are able to provide many forms of assistance to them. Chaplains have access to medical records and—within the bounds of confidentiality—are able to assist the clergy to understand what is happening medically, emotionally and even psychologically with the patient. The seriousness or otherwise of the case is able to be explained on occasions.

The chaplain may, for example, warn of manipulativeness on the part of the patient, thus saving the visitor from being trapped into game-playing. Contact between chaplains and parish ministers is thus of benefit to both. The chaplain may well be able to advise the parish clergy of the urgency or otherwise of a requested visit, and in an emergency, may be able to support the patient and relatives until the parish minister arrives.

In summary, it is wise to remember that visiting the hospital on behalf of the church, whether as a hospital visitor, pastoral visitor or visiting clergy, is a privilege and not a divine right. Therefore visitors should remember to respect the common rules of courtesy within the hospital.

Further procedures and protocol to be recognized will be discussed as we proceed.

SECTION ONE

For Hospital Visitors

1

Off to Hospital

So you are going to visit a patient in hospital? Before you go you should know the reason which prompts you to make the decision to go. The simple question to ask before you make any move is "Why am I going?" That perhaps sounds ridiculous. It is not. The motive for your visit is a gauge against which the value of your visit will be measured. Your reason for visiting will be reflected in your attitude to the patient, and in most cases that attitude will be obvious to the patient. Too often our decision is reached without any thought of how or why the visit is being made.

Too many visitors may have an adverse effect on the progress of a patient in hospital, as well as the nature of the visit. As those who move among patients daily, chaplains and staff frequently hear expressions of relief that a visitor or visitors have at last gone. Patients are sometimes more exhausted and weak on a Monday morning after a weekend of visitors. There are also the occasions when a patient becomes very depressed following the visit of a pastoral person who speaks inappropriately.

After visits by two clergymen to different terminally-ill patients, the relatives present at the time of each minister's call requested that those visitors not be allowed near the patient again. On both occasions it was the reading of the 23rd Psalm, and in particular the verse which refers to the "valley of the shadow of death," that caused concern and distress. In one it was the spouse who was not able to cope with the reality of the situation.

One must assume that in both cases the visitors went with the purpose of preparing the patient to face death. They had a purpose, a motive and most probably had thought out their agenda for the visit. However, it proved not only ineffective but harmful.

WHY AM I GOING?

Questionable motives
There will be many surprises if this question is faced honestly. The reasons for hospital visitation will vary and we shall see that many are of dubious character.

Out of duty
As a relative, friend or pastoral care visitor, the reason for going to the hospital springs so often out of a sense of obligation. The fulfillment of that sense of duty hopefully will make the patient happy. Is this a trap we fall into? Are we visiting in order to be released from the guilt of unperformed responsibility? All this has a ring of selfishness about it. It is satisfying our ego. Duty can help fulfill our desire to be needed and our sense of being a martyr for the cause. It promotes the concept that we desire other people to have of us as always being busy doing good.

Doing our job helps maintain the reputation and name we are building for ourselves. The greater the inconvenience, the greater the expected acclaim. The duty visit lacks the vital component of pastoral care: spiritual sensitivity.

The mantle's accepted
Appointed as an official hospital visitor the person assumes a certain performance framework. Lay pastoral care workers and clergy are the ones that frequently fall into this trap.

A parishioner is in hospital so a visit must be made to fly the flag. In doing so, an official church visitor presumes a certain expectation by the church to perform particular functions, such as reading the Bible and praying. As I will show later, these *may* be inappropriate at that particular stage of the patient's hospitalization.

The mantle that has been assumed is likely to color the method of approaching the bedside. Naturalness and spontaneity are sometimes forsaken in order to fit the role.

Role modelling as a parish visitor often presumes that religion will be raised during the visit. Such a preconception, particularly if you know little about the patient, is as subtle as pushing a bull into a china shop to catch the attention of the proprietor.

To cheer up the patient

It must be remembered that persons under treatment in hospital are not physically well. Their whole person, body, mind and spirit in most cases is affected by the illness or treatment. This means that they tire easily. Rest and sleep are two of the greatest components of the recuperative process.

A patient was three days out of major surgery. A good friend, a renowned pastoral visitor, came along armed with a small projector and slides of a recent holiday with the intention of providing something of interest to take the patient's mind off the pain. To entertain? To cheer up? The patient was in agony, heightened through the effort of trying to concentrate and not appear rude by nodding off for the much-needed rest. The visit lasted three hours. One wonders how many lengthy entertainment visits were made to other patients who were less understanding.

Out of curiosity or competition

Hospitals and illness hold an unusual fascination for some people. They seem to have an obsession about the symptoms that people are experiencing and the treatment they are undergoing. For this reason such people are eager to become hospital visitors.

Other folk love to know what is going on in the families of the community. The church calls for prayer for those in hospital. It is a topic for conversation. To have visited the patient in hospital is to have first-hand information and the bearer of such information becomes the center of news—that may be presented as data sincerely conveyed for the purposes of prayer. The visit and the visitor become the source for the church bulletin news flash!

Both these compulsions give rise to visits that are of little value because they are made out of curiosity, to satisfy a personal need: the need to be the center of news or attention, to be thought of as selfless and caring, to be near suffering, pain or even death, or just to be in the know as to what is going on. Such visits seldom bring support, comfort or strength to the patient.

A successful and respected pastoral carer was the envy of another person, who increased visits to a particular patient in order to out do the first visitor. The patient knew exactly what was going on and when the jealous visitor's calls became a source of anxiety and a burden, she conveyed her feelings to the carer she valued. To spare her the strain of too many visits, and because he detested competition in Christian service, this pastoral worker cut down on his own calls. In this case, the loser was the patient.

A visit to a patient in hospital must be offered in deepest sincerity and with a genuine desire to provide positive pastoral care. Curiosity and competition are evils that have no place in the context of hospital care.

CHAPTER

2

Visiting the Patient

QUESTIONS VISITORS NEED TO ASK THEMSELVES

Does the patient need a visit?

One hospital I know has a very strict protocol concerning visitors to patients in intensive care. Only members of the immediate family and only one member of the clergy associated with the patient's church are allowed to the bedside. The chaplain of the intensive care unit has the responsibility to verify the identity of that priest, minister or rabbi. This policy had to be brought in because a patient or family well known in religious circles had numbers of clergy popping in and causing confusion.

The wisdom of your visit at a particular time has to be considered in the light of the best interests of the patient. One patient may be too weak to see you and may need all the rest possible. Another patient may have sufficient people offering pastoral care. Remember, visitors may often unnecessarily tire and exhaust patients. At the height of the crisis you may encroach on the privacy which the family and patient require.

If your visit coincides with a patient's grief and hostility against God, your presence may increase that hostility. Your words and pious offer of prayer may do irrevocable damage, closing off all future opportunities for pastoral care. It may be the last straw which results in a total and final rejection of God. You must ask yourself seriously, "Does the patient need my visit just now or at any time?" The timing of a visit before or after surgery demands your consideration. Visits, unless there are special reasons, should be avoided until a few days after surgery. Sometimes a pre-surgery visit assuring prayerful support is appreciated, but at other times it may not bring any comfort. Many a deeply religious and active member in the church has said that they have not told their minister or priest about hospitalization because they want to be quiet and not be overwhelmed by parishioners. A private person may desire to share such an anxious time with the family only.

Would my visit be appropriate? Do your homework. Do not take it for granted.

Am I the appropriate pastoral person?

A patient had been transferred from a country hospital to the city by air ambulance. The patient's minister had contacted me, giving details of the family's journey and expected time of arrival by road. In the meantime, an aunt's city minister of another denomination appeared in the intensive care unit and gave an entirely different version of the family's movements to the nurses. That threw the staff into confusion. The fact was that the aunt's minister had it wrong. This type of situation can arise when inappropriate visits are made by pastoral visitors.

The city minister had not ascertained all the facts. While he must be commended for responding to the call, he failed to find out whether the patient had church connections, what they were, what the immediate family would have wished. He did not seek out the chaplains at the hospital for possible assistance, advice and information on the patient. It turned out that he was not the appropriate person to be involved at that time.

Even when someone is a member of the local parish, she or he may not be the ideal person to provide the most significant contribution. One church elder has a real commitment to the care and support of many people both within and without the church. Her contribution is valuable as an elder. She has a strong personality, is a good organizer, and knows what a person needs.

When it comes to hospital visitation, however, patients are often overwhelmed by her presence. Her kindly nature wants to mother and organize both patient and family. Sometimes that is good but not always.

Know your own strengths and weaknesses as a pastoral person. Endeavor to know and understand whether your gifts can be used with this case or whether an approach would be considered an unhelpful intrusion.

A willingness to accept that we cannot minister to all people is a major criterion for a good pastoral care person. With that principle established, it should be an automatic self-posed question: "Am I the most appropriate one to make this visit to this person or family?"

THE VISIT IS TO THE PATIENT

Having decided that you should make the visit, the next factor to concentrate upon is that the visit is *to* the patient and *for* the patient.

It is a truism that hospital patients are a captive audience. They are confined to bed. They have no means of escaping from visitors. Evangelical concern for the external welfare of the patient often places expectations upon the carer to say the magical words that will produce a desired spiritual decision. This can translate into pressure on a "trapped" patient.

Every chaplain is called numerous times a year with the "Will you visit Mr. X...He is in your hospital seriously ill. I don't know whether he is a practising Christian or not. Would you visit him and lead him to the Lord?"

It is such a common request. The chaplain usually replies, "I will see what the situation is and will act appropriately." More often than not, the raising of religious issues would have provoked strong negative reactions in the patient.

On one occasion I was asked to see a terminally ill retired postmaster on the terms just outlined. His two sisters were present. The whole conversation centered around his far-from-religious activities. It was one of his few lucid days. His sisters were taking advantage of it and were also receiving much comfort. It would have been most inadvisable to press eternal issues. After weeks of confusion and irrationality, he was revelling in reminiscing with his sisters. It was a memorable, comforting and happy time for all present—the last time they were to have communication with him in conversation.

Patients are very vulnerable to their spiritual needs at such times and are susceptible to any suggestions. Coercion, manipulation, and occasionally dishonest methods are used by pastoral visitors to obtain decisions and promises about which the patient has little understanding. Often patients are in a state of mind that is not receptive to theological pronouncements on spiritual matters.

Some so—called deathbed conversions are assents to pressure tactics. Affirmations are sometimes made to relieve the pressure and make the pastoral visitor happy. Patients have admitted "anything to shut them up." That is not pastoral care. A caring relationship is not built this way. The many who have come into a deeper and closer relationship with God through the bedside ministry have usually done so after bridges have been built.

If the aim of your visit is to build a caring relationship, then your visit must be *to* and *for* the patient. You are wholly concerned with the easing of his or her burden in the Spirit of Jesus. (See Chapter 10, "Jesus—A Theological Model".)

MAKE IT COMFORTABLE

For any relationship to be meaningful and helpful, each person must be at ease with the other. Signs of feeling uncomfortable must be recognized immediately. If that uneasy feeling is not dissipated, then the impossibility of a continuing relationship should be recognized. No one person is able to be all things to all persons. To persist in the face of a continuing hostile reception is unproductive. It can also be damaging for the ministry of other pastoral carers who have more in common with the person confined to bed.

There are occasions when a patient will deliberately make visitors feel uncomfortable in an effort to test their sincerity.

One young woman made it quite clear to me that she didn't want to see a chaplain. A visit the next day, in spite of the put-off, indicated my willingness to show care and concern for this patient. The ensuing daily visits elicited her story of a lifestyle of prostitution and many incidents in her past. At the end of her stay, with open arms and a kiss she expressed her gratitude for my concerned attention and sincere care, which had weathered the test.

It took grace to go back the day after when she made it obvious that the "Not Wanted" sign had been hung out. It paid to take the rebuff on the chin and then continue to make her feel comfortable. However, if evidence of a thaw had not ensued, then it would have been a mistake to have persisted. The zealot in the carer must be tempered by discernment of the right moment to pull out or to continue. For care to be helpful, a sense of comfort should be tangible to all concerned.

SHOW GENUINE CONCERN

Visitors very easily fall into the trap of letting the visit become a social occasion. There are other friends also at the bedside. Some you may know from the church or other quarters. Of course, you were all at a recent church activity, that is, all except the patient. The conversation turns to that occasion and you all reminisce. You recall Mrs. X's act, you share the humor of her antics. Oh! and the outfit John Wilson wore sends you all into peals of laughter—except the patient, who has no clue of what you are all talking about. So the conversation goes on with not a word addressed to the patient except, "Oh! you should have been there." The patient is silently fuming because none of you is interested in what should be the real purpose of your visit: to be a blessing to the one lying in the bed. The visit is marked by a lack of genuine concern.

Perhaps you have never met one of the patient's friends before. You are a keen pastoral worker. You are interested in all people. She lives in the parish area. Here is a person you may be able to get into the church's program, so you make the effort to get to know her. She used to be a physical education and aerobics teacher. You remark, "That's strange, our girls' club is looking for someone to teach aerobics. Would you be free on a Thursday night between 7 and 8?" So the conversation proceeds until you have arranged for her to see the girls' club leader and you go away feeling it was a profitable afternoon. The patient is quite depressed thinking, "The church is not really interested in me, only itself." Where was the *real* care in that visit?

All too frequently, you see visitors around a bedside with three or four conversations in progress. None is directed toward the patient, who is under tremendous strain trying to pick up the gist of each conversation. This can lead to greater and greater frustration, anxiety and a feeling of abandonment in spite of the presence of six or eight visitors. For the visitors it is a great reunion, for the ill patient, only torment and further headaches and pain.

Maybe you are the sole visitor. This is a golden opportunity for you. Instead, in the midst of your time together, your eyes wander across to another patient who is having a great time, like a king holding court with his loyal subjects. He is so amusing your eyes and ears try not to miss anything. Another patient is gasping for breath and looks very ill. The labored breathing troubles you so your concentration is on the next bed. Meanwhile your patient finds you saying "yes" and nodding when you should be saying "no." Frequently you are forced to ask that a sentence be repeated. Your eyes are not on the patient but elsewhere. The real sphere of your interest and concern is perfectly obvious to the patient. Pastoral care takes a holiday.

Why are conversations thus turned away from the patient? Often the reason is that it is easier to take in these diversions than to face the real issue of the visit, which is to offer pastoral support to a person suffering, bewildered, lonely and dependent.

The patient in fact has become an embarrassment. The visitors, pastoral family and friends avoid the real issues facing this person. They shun the purpose of the visit.

We will never know how many patients feel very hurt each day, demoralized and relieved when the visitor leaves. "They were not interested in me," they say, "only themselves."

The pastoral visit is *to* and *for* the patient. Keep the conscious patient the centre of your attention and conversation unless he or she is so debilitated that simply having family and friends near is enough.

DEFINING PASTORAL CARE

Hospital pastoral care workers can accept the definition of pastoral care given by Hulme:

"Pastoral care is a supportive ministry to people and those close to them who are experiencing the familiar trials that characterize life in this world, such as illness, surgery, incapacitation, death and bereavement"[1].

You are therefore to support the person experiencing the necessity to be hospitalized. Alister Campbell[2] introduces another term into such care: "pastoral relationship." This, he considers, is the key by which we enter the world of the person. Christians care because of their own relationship with God and they are able to bring an extra dimension to the bedside. Any pastoral care offered to the hospital patient involves entering into a concerned, caring relationship with that needy patient on the part of one who is effectively motivated by a pastoral relationship with God in Christ.

In genuine pastoral care the person visited becomes aware of this other dimension in the person of the visitor. At the time the patient may not identify that difference. However, it eventually will be acknowledged as God in Christ being present in the carer. That added presence gives the patient and the relatives a calmness and increased confidence of being cared for and valued as persons.

A pastoral visit which is properly patient-centered leaves peace and assurance in its wake due to the divine presence, expressed through the visitor.

NOTES

1. Hulme, William E. *Pastoral Care and Counseling Using the Unique Resources of Christian Tradition* pp 4–13.
2. Campbell, Alister V. *Rediscovering Pastoral Care*, p 10.

3

Respecting the Patient

Visiting the hospital patient often reveals more about you than you may realize. It indicates your thoughtfulness or thoughtlessness. It shows the depth of your care. It displays the magnitude of your sincerity and genuine interest. More importantly, it broadcasts the depth of your understanding of the feelings and emotions of one confined.

FEELINGS AND EMOTIONS

A hospital ward is packed with the widest possible range of feelings and emotions. Do you readily recognize them?

Exposed
Most people have their own domain where they are able to make their own decisions and do their own thing—how, when and where they choose. Others have greater responsibility of leadership and authority from the workplace, to school, home, church or area of recreation. All of us guard jealously our privacy and rights to privacy as individuals. In ordinary life we do not like being put down, mocked or being made to look like a fool. Our mistakes, if held up to public view, cause us embarrassment. Whenever we are embarrassed, it is a blow to our dignity. Our sense of personal dignity is the measure of our self-esteem.

In hospital a patient loses many of these cherished rights. Autonomy is gone. The freedom to decide when to get up, dress, or take a shower is stripped away. For many, the ability to perform natural functions depends upon when a nurse is able to bring a pan or a bottle. The executive streak in all of us is effectively blocked for the duration of the hospital stay. Doctors, nurses and therapists are the ones to make the decisions. The patient becomes the subservient one who must obey or risk deterioration of health and sometimes the effectiveness of treatment.

The curtains are pulled, the consultant, registrar, the resident, perhaps a student and a nurse gather around the bed as the patient lies bare while a thorough examination is undertaken. The patient's own feelings to such exposure are secondary to the necessity for the examination. When medical or nursing students also are present, those dozen or so pairs of eyes on you seem to pierce every part of your torso. It feels as though every mole is being counted and every private organ is being charted for shape and size. There is nothing that is sacred to the person of the patient, who feels like screaming "Exposed! Exposed!" Self-respect is often in tatters. Dignity has been stripped. The shameless cloud of inhumanity seems to be overshadowing this victim of the institution.

Useless

The man who controls a professional office, now publicly exposed at midday in his pyjamas without the phone ringing to seek his direction and decisions, may feel emasculated. His self-image of always being in command and productive is destroyed. In the hospital his cherished work ethic lies in tatters. This applies equally to the union organizer, who expects his word to be followed without question; the bricklayer who takes pride in the straightness and neatness of his walls; or the apprentice bent on accurately reassembling the motor he has stripped.

For the woman who is principal of a renowned high school to be taking orders from nurses only a few years older than her students is a challenge to her authoritarian role. Her controlling personality and sense of appropriate dress for her status in the eyes of her pupils are abandoned as a hospital gown reduces her to equal status with the other patients. Unable to complete the reports for her administration board, the enforced idleness torments her.

The mother who bears the anxieties of a family's welfare is struggling against the separation caused by hospitalization. All the mending and ironing that is mounting up because she cannot do it weighs heavily on her mind.

The popular lass who works in a government department finds no rewards in the hospital for time spent on a perfect make-up job. Her delicate nighties are not the type usually worn in a hospital. She cannot look her feminine best. She cannot do the things she normally does.

Many patients are bogged down in the despair of uselessness. Idleness does not lie easily with most people. Each hour seems to drag.

The patient you are about to visit may be in that state of feeling worthless. Life in hospital holds few achievement challenges.

Patients are conscious of having had taken from them that precious gift of a democratic society's independence to do and to be. This adds to the bodily "insult" which resulted in the admission to the hospital in the first place.

A burden

Independence can be a factor militating against recovery. An independent person finds it difficult to accept any help or care from others. As the word suggests, an independent person detests being dependent upon anyone. For these people, dependence implies a necessary obligation. Even though they may be paying full hospital rates through a medical insurance fund, they still feel an obligation to those providing health care. They develop a misguided awareness that they are a burden to society. Their occupation of the bed is precluding someone else, who may be sicker, from receiving treatment. The reasons mount as they try to find ways to prove that they are an encumbrance to others.

This feeling in some respects has the effect of firing scatter-shot into an empty sky: it does not target any particular person or thing. However, when the sense of being a burden to family members is voiced, complications in relationships are possible. One patient had exhausted all possible treatment for cancer and was told it was a matter of weeks. He began talking about nursing homes.

His independent nature assumed that he would be too much of a burden on his wife, that she would not be able to cope. I noticed her hurt expression as she repeated to her son, "He says that I would not be able to manage him at home." His condition had so deteriorated by the next morning that it was impossible to take the matter up with him. Was it a sense of obligation or the guilt of being a burden that he shrank from? In any case it denied the wife the privilege of caring for the one she loved, even for a few days, before he died.

This phobia of being a burden does affect the patient's ability to be able to relate to loved ones, friends and others who want to devote themselves to caring. To repeatedly have had your efforts spurned makes natural grieving following the death more difficult. Unrectifiable hurt, even when mingled with forgiveness, remains unpalatable for a long time.

Threatened

From earliest days, our culture has conditioned us to associate hospitals with death. This association stems from the days of limited medical knowledge during which many people admitted to hospital died. Presently, hospitals cure and successfully handle many illnesses. The risk of death associated with surgical procedures has been reduced dramatically. A longer life-span is now possible for some cancer patients through medical treatment. Yet, the old fears still persist. There is still a majority of people who on being hospitalized see their existence threatened.

Life is the one thing on earth that has no price about it. Life is a precious commodity to be cherished and maintained at whatever cost, sometimes at the expense of quality of life.

Hospitalization poses a threat to a patient's continuing to live a normal life. It shouts "change."

In a normal society any suggestion of a change stirs a certain amount of resentment. Church services can be cited as an example. The adverse response to any move for change hinges upon an ignorance of conditions that are likely after the innovation. When life is threatened, a fear of the unknown beyond death becomes mind-absorbing. Most people in the Western world have few ideas of what any future life will be like.

An eighteen-year-old remarked, after being told he had less than a week to live, "I'm not afraid of dying, only afraid of being nothing when I die." According to Christian belief, he was well astray. Yet many practising Christians find it difficult to cope with the thought of their own death, simply because they do not know what lies on the other side.

Any threat to life raises all the fears of the unknown, of separation, of loss of mobility, independence, and friends; of pain, mutilation, unfinished business; fears for the welfare of loved ones; fears of being unable to cope with the illness, of being unable to express feelings and love; of suffering the side-effects of the treatment, and so on. We shall look at these fears in detail later.

Your visit may be to a bedside where a combination of these fears are raging in the patient's mind. Consideration needs to be given to your sensitivity to such mental torment so as not to add to it inadvertently.

WHAT THE PATIENT NEEDS

Any of these anxieties can lead the patient into varying depths of depression. He or she has three basic needs: to be restored to health, feel cared for and to be reassured. Hospital visitors may be able to assist in meeting some of these needs although they may be limited by the nature of the patient's mental health, the trust relationship between the visitor and the patient, lack of medical knowledge of the case, or inappropriateness of the time for developing the issue.

RESTORATION OF SELF-RESPECT

Where the self-image of patients has been shattered, they require a vision of themselves as having worth in spite of their illness or threatened death. Recalling the many positive, happy and helpful things that have characterized their lives deflects the mind from the present hurt. Helping patients to recount family experiences, holidays, business or spiritual highlights begins to brighten the picture and reaffirm them as persons.

TO BE REASSURED

Reassurance can be given in many ways. There is the reassurance, for instance, that the patient is not forgotten but remembered, prayed for and respected by many others. To name names of those who enquired after them, or those who are praying for them lifts their spirits.

Where there are doubts about treatment and its effects, it is often not possible for the visitor to personally make any medical contribution. However, he or she may leave word with ward staff that the patient wants further explanation. Remember that the patient often exercises "selective hearing" for coping. That means that although the medical personnel may have repeatedly explained clinical conditions and prognosis the patient's coping ability did not permit absorption of such information. Some call this a form of denial. Often the fact is that the patient is so overwhelmed by what is happening that he or she cannot comprehend the implications of what is being said. The benefits of treatment need to be emphasized or, if no treatment is possible, then the sick person needs to hear that adequate pain control is possible and will be given. With current palliative care programs, pain can be minimized and well controlled.

There are times when confidence in the staff and the specialist is low. The boosting of such confidence often turns an unhealthy passive attitude to the treatment into positive, optimistic co-operation with the doctors. Because of the deflation of personal ego as a result of the diagnosis and treatment, the patient needs to express stored-up anger at anything that can be conveniently blamed for unnecessary pain. After allowing for some ventilation of these feelings, strong efforts should be made to reassure the patient that there are good grounds for anticipating the best care possible.

It is at such crisis times that people imagine God has abandoned them. To demonstrate that God still cares, in the manner of Jesus, raises the person's spirits immeasurably. The "Jesus manner" is seen in his dealings with Zaccheus, the woman at the well in Samaria, and blind Bartimaeus, or in parables such as the prodigal son or the good samaritan. An understanding, gentle approach to fostering an awareness of our loving, caring God can bring the reassurance the patient needs.

WHAT THE HOSPITAL VISITOR CAN DO

Accept patients as they are
If there is one way in which patients can feel the genuineness of care, it is when they are accepted as they are, sick, wan, depressed, irritable, exhausted, unsociable, unloving and difficult to love.

Respect patients in your own conversation
A patient doesn't want to hear *your* gripes. To talk or gossip about another person or mutual acquaintance further depresses. In any conversation with the patient a positive approach should be presented without stretching reality.

Relating your experience with your own operation or about someone else who died from the same complaint will bring an antagonistic response. Your subsequent visits will not be welcome.

One hospital visitor revelled in the opportunity to talk about the number of times she had faced death's door with a clot in the lungs. Whilst she was able to say, "Look I'm alive," it proved to be very alarming for patients threatened with that condition. It was not appreciated particularly by one young mother with five children, who thought of the ramifications if she should die.

Watch your dress

In modern times formality of dress is very optional. Patients are sick, however, and respect shown to them is reflected in the style of your attire. A person in evening finery, "showing off" like a parading model in full array, may further crush the patient's spirit. The invalid situation is rubbed in. On the other hand, dirty jeans, revealing tops and thongs shout disrespect for the patient: "I'm not worth much, look how they dress."

Dress moderately, cleanly, tidily and in keeping with your role as a person visiting a hospital patient. The staff also will pay you the respect you deserve as evidenced by your manner of dress.

Don't do the things that patients can do for themselves

When patients have dropped their bundle, and defeat stares them in the face, they need to be encouraged to do things for themselves, such as simply pouring a glass of water. Don't emphasize their weaknesses, incapacity or invalidism by being too helpful. The sense of achievement gained by doing something for themselves is great therapy.

Where the condition is terminal, causing business or personal accomplishments to be restrained or even abandoned, the question is often asked, "What have I done to deserve this?" Drawing attention to those achievements and days of happiness helps lift the vision from the depression and enables her or him to see that the question is irrelevant to the situation.

A patient may sink lower into depression if there is a trace of dishonesty or patronizing insincerity in efforts to restore self-respect. Genuineness and honesty must characterize any relationship and conversation. To be patronizing or condescending destroys even further the patient's self-esteem.

To feel cared for

This is where a visit out of a sense of duty or responsibility is detected. Your visit should be made out of deep concern for the patient. The one on the bed needs tender loving care, not the breezy "I'm here to see you, buck up and get on with the job, get better, let's read a prayer and I'll be off" attitude. When the patient is exhausted, in pain, or just confused as to what is happening, a truly gentle approach is necessary:

"I see you are weary and just want to sleep and rest. I've come to let you know I really care and am praying for you. I'll continue to do it. You just get as much rest as possible and I'll come back when you are not so exhausted."

A visit of such short time and few words may be one of the most valuable visits ever made to a hospital patient. Conversely, much time and many words may only show just how insensitive a visitor is to the patient's condition and need.

The hospital visitor is able to do much to bring encouragement and support into the lives of the ailing, and recognition of their personal value.

CHAPTER

4

Observe

You have thought about the motive for the hospital visit and are convinced that the call should be made. You understand a little of what the patient's attitude to his or her illness may be and what may needed from you. The next question is "What more can I do?" The first essential of any approach to patients is the ability to observe all you can as you enter the hospital and the ward.

THOSE HOSPITAL SIGNS

Look for hospital notices. The first signs the visitor should heed are the ones relating to traffic. One-way and parking signs, like all laws and regulations, have been installed out of experience and necessity.

Being in a hurry and having an exaggerated view of the importance of the visitor's role can lead to the temptation to park in a disabled drivers' zone. Or a space in a 15-minute parking spot is looked on as convenient and time-saving. Parking close to the hospital is often considered an essential prerequisite by visitors. Sometimes the accident and emergency parking areas have empty spaces that are appropriated on the grounds, "I'm a hospital visitor doing my good deed. I'm doing this voluntarily, therefore the authorities won't object. They will understand."

It is very convenient to rationalize our action of parking illegally but would we take such liberties with signs outside the police station? Signs outside the hospital building are placed there for the ease and welfare of our fellow human beings, as are the signs inside

Most hospitals have clearly marked notices on every floor as to the visiting hours, and some hospitals are more strict with such hours than others. Whether the policy is rigid or lenient for the hospital visitor, it is courtesy to respect it. The patient's own parish minister or priest may be exceptions to the visiting hours rules, but generally speaking, these privileges should not be misused or abused.

Visiting hours are recommended for the good of the patients. In the average hospital patients find it difficult to get a good night's sleep and some use sleeping tablets, only to find that the sedation and dopiness can take most of the morning to wear off. When this is the case, the struggle to keep awake for the hospital visitor adds stress, anxiety, embarrassment and further exhaustion. The arrival of the relatives during the approved hours often finds the patient too tired to appreciate the visit.

Non-visiting hours are generally in the morning when doctors are involved in rounds or when treatment, tests and dressings are attended to. Pastoral visiting at these times may be interrupted by medical personnel so that meaningful involvement with the patient is not possible.

Other signs such as "Restricted Visiting," "Please See Nursing Unit Manager" or "No Visitors" are for the protection of the patient whose condition may be such that there is a risk of visitors increasing harmful stress when rest is interrupted. In some cases the patient may not want to see certain visitors and requests a monitoring of callers. If you are an official church hospital visitor, it is appropriate to see the nursing unit manager to introduce yourself and confirm the convenience of your visit.

"Isolation" may be the word that is prominent at the patient's door. This particular sign is in place for two reasons. Firstly the patient may have an infectious disease, so the visitor needs protection. In the second case, the patient's immune system may be so low that he or she runs the risk of being infected by any germ or virus the visitor may introduce into the ward. Such infection could develop into a major set-back.

"Nil by mouth," and "restricted fluids" are warnings or instructions for patients, staff and visitors. Prior to surgery, an empty stomach is essential. Even a sip of water may have its effect upon the patient either in theatre or after the operation. Or the patient's kidneys may not be able to rid the body of excess fluid; hence the need to be on a severely controlled fluid intake. (Often the fluid intake is measured against the output to keep a check on the effectiveness of the drug dosage or kidney function.) It has been known for the unwary visitor to be conned into relieving the poor thirsty sufferer without the nurse knowing. I recall a case where the visitor was asked to help clean the patient's teeth, and then the patient gulped down all the rinsing water.

If staff co-operation is expected, or your role as a pastoral visitor is to be accepted in the ward, then obviously signs must be heeded.

OBSERVE THE PATIENT

Your observation of the patient is critical to the success of your visit. A correct assessment of the patient's condition and mood should permit you to make the most appropriate introduction.

Looks provide the key to condition. Is the patient wan, listless, sleepy, or alert and smiling? depressed or pleased to see you? indifferent to your presence or teary, flushed, breathless? worse or improved since your last visit? The "hail-fellow-well-met" approach to a depressed or extremely weak patient brings an unverbalised reaction of "get out of here." Such a visit will be considered as insensitive and insincere. Similarly a patient struggling and slowly making improvement is not impressed by being told they look dreadful. This may break their spirit, particularly if they were just starting to feel a bit better. To the same patient equally inappropriate are words such as "you're looking splendid."

Your observation of the patient's physical condition will give you clear leads as to how your meeting will develop. One important decision that should be a result of your assessment by observation is the length of time you should stay (see Supplements 1 and 2).

Patient showing weakness

This calls for a short visit with few words. Concentration on conversation may load further strain and stress onto the patient, which can accelerate fatigue and debilitation.

Patient looking depressed

The need may be for a quick hello and goodbye or even a long, silent time of just holding hands and an effort to assess the reasons for the despondency. The assessment may have to be reappraised as the visit develops or on subsequent visits.

Patient showing signs of pain

Seriously ill patients, both medical and surgical, may experience much bodily discomfort and pain. Their condition can be so agonizing that they are on pain killers such as pethidine or morphine, and they may be unable to cope with much beyond their own concerns. Their concentration span is extremely short. In fact the need to concentrate on anything but their condition is distressing, and the discomfort is aggravated by a hospital visitor coming in with a smiling face and words such as, "Well, the Lord knows and understands your condition. Leave it in his hands and just trust." At this point, patients could feel like screaming but have to bottle up the anger, which only increases the pain and trauma.

Patient's reaction to the visit

The patient's first sighting of you frequently produces facial expressions or bodily movements which indicate that your visit is welcome or otherwise. Be sensitive to that initial reaction. The length of your stay should be determined in part by those indicators. One day the patient may not be up to a visit. The next day or next week it may be different. Hostility toward God, with its recoil back onto anyone from the church, needs to be considered as a possible reaction. It is unwise to take the attitude, "They are angry. I must reconcile them with God. This is my mission." You will only drive the wedge in further against God.

A good look at the patient should reveal much concerning what you should do. To think that you have the answer for them and that this is your mission may be out of touch with God's plans for ministry to that patient at that time. Your need to help people should not get in the way of correctly observing the patient.

OBSERVE THE WARD

Whether you are meeting the ailing for the first time or are well acquainted, the perusal of the ward is likely to provide indicators of what's happening for the patient. A bare table and a shelf with no flowers or cards may point to a lonely person requiring lots of attention. It may also declare that this well-known person has not publicized the hospitalization to church or friends and is seeking quiet. Except where there are clear contrary markers, the visitor should not be presumptive and outstay the welcome or tell others that the patient is in hospital. The patient's right to confidentiality and privacy must be respected.

Lots of cards and flowers shout out for all to see: this patient is loved and well cared for. It is possible that your attention to him or her is not as necessary as to some other sick folk. On the other hand, that show of popularity may indicate that the person is a great game player, a very gregarious, life-of-the-party person, whom no one really knows. Perhaps nobody can get very close. Hospitalization may be the one opportunity for a skillful hospital visitor to ease the clam open and discover the real person. Such revelation, if handled rightly, may be an instrument leading to real growth and development for the patient. However, it is unwise to start something you can't handle. With permission, refer to someone else.

More frequently the multitude of cards and flowers do tell what kind of support patients have. Religious cards possibly indicate good prayer support. Cards and flowers provide the opportunity for the patient to share something of themselves, their family and friends. Flowers not from the florist may indicate the patient's own love of gardening or a spouse's keen gardening pursuits. The degree of companionship in the marriage may show through.

A hand-made card by an offspring or grandchild may provide some family background upon which the relationship with the visitor is developed. An expensive card may become a focal point of the conversation, with the sender described as a significant person in the patient's life, who provided support at a point of earlier crisis. The telling of that crisis episode may trigger current feelings, attitudes and relationship issues which can be poignant matters. Here the visitor's ministry may make a vital contribution.

Photographs of either family or friends are sometimes on the bedside table. These can tell stories and give indications of the family dynamics. If there is sufficient trust, these are often shared.

Observation of the ward when it is a multiple-bed one may reveal an intensely depressing spectacle. The nature of the surgery, the degree of the illness of the patient, the noise of other patients' relatives and friends, the groans and moans of another, or the lonely patient who wants to be part of your conversation, perhaps listening to all you say—all this often strains your patient's patience. Your adeptness in allowing a ventilation of these feelings may prove to be of invaluable assistance.

The perceptiveness of the pastoral caller in the initial minutes of the visit are crucial factors in hospital visitation.

The effectiveness of any relational development depends upon the patient's ability to detect in you genuine care and not merely the spirit of the "do gooder." The visiting person has to earn acceptance and trust. Often that right is gained through those early moments of observation. Where adequate care is being offered, be Christian enough to bow out without feeling hurt, letting others do the job. You may not be God's choice for this particular person. Care where God wants you to care.

OBSERVE THE UNSPOKEN

Vulnerable, helpless, dependent feelings often overwhelm patients. They want to give the impression of coping and not needing the sympathy being offered. Accepting sympathy or pity is a demoralizing experience. Many independent folk who are now confined, restricted and incapacitated have their pride and ego seriously dented by their illness. In order to avoid further self-conscious humiliation, masks are put on to distract the visitor from their real suffering.

The feeling of the injustice of the illness promotes anger. That anger is often turned Godward. "Why me?" "I've done nothing to deserve this." "I've been faithful in my church activities." These may be expressed openly or otherwise. When verbalised, the sentiment may be uttered in a placid, accepting tone. The stoic sufferer is the front put forward by many, including those renowned for their self-control, initiative, drive, coping ability and leadership skills. It is important to them that the public image be maintained.

Detection of such stoicism is important. It may be possible for you to delicately let your suspicions be known. This may allow a degree of self-disclosure. Lack of subtlety may force up irremovable barriers, so caution is needed in handling such cases. The observant visitor is alert and able to detect whether the words coming from the mouth match the communication from body and facial movements. The unspoken may be evident in the way the patient parries questions on certain subjects, deflecting the conversation into another direction. Those thrusts that come too near to the core of the truth are threatening, causing observable protective measures to be taken.

On some occasions, when there has been a good rapport established with the patient, it may be appropriate to face the issue head on. However, seldom does such a confrontation prove profitable on an initial visit. Rather, it tends to put up shutters that remain closed to the visitor. Tuck the observation into the mind's computer, to be recalled and developed at the appropriate time.

If the temptation to rush in too soon is not resisted, there is a greater need to observe the more pronounced positive and negative vibes issuing from the patient. If they are negative here is a second chance to avoid a fouling of the lines of communication. This second opportunity to act aright should be accepted. In my experience patients have often complained that they have been forced too soon to face issues for which they were not ready. There is a tendency for social workers and others to prematurely open up the subject of death and dying. Pastoral visitors must be observant enough not to do the same.

Nor should they prematurely raise the issue of the patient's preparedness for the future life while the negative, disinterested or denial signs are being flashed. The visitor must be courteous enough to respect and react appropriately to these unspoken warnings. In many cases they would be wiser to leave such issues to trained pastoral care workers.

5

Relatives and Friends

The nature of the illness and the condition of the patient elicit a range of emotions and responses. The patient is not the only one experiencing such reactions of heart and spirit. Relatives, friends and even staff become involved in emotional expressions—from elation over a healthy birth to grim forebodings at the bedside of an intensive care patient comatose from septicemia.

At this point it is wise for us to recognise that these people also require pastoral care. As a hospital visitor, it may be your privilege to provide a supportive, understanding, caring touch to others as well as the patient. In fact, your nurturing of relatives or friends may be of real value to the patients, who sense that their loved ones are responding with less agitation, more confidence and less self-pity.

That supportiveness is best recognized and appreciated when you share their feelings of gladness or sadness (see also Appendix 1). The ability to enter into the feelings of others is termed *empathy*. Empathy stands distinctly apart from sympathy. When anguish or depression is deep, it may be beyond the limits of your expertise or training. Do refer such cases to a better-equipped pastoral person. It may not necessarily be your minister or priest.

When the patient's condition is serious, the various family members display some of the typical dynamics of grief, such as fear, guilt, anger, bewilderment, denial, depression, frustration and withdrawal. It is good therapy to allow them to verbalize or even physically express their grief. In encouraging such behavior, the visitor should not be trapped into over-involvement with the anger, guilt etc. It is our responsibility to maintain a position from which we, at all times, are able to view the situation objectively.

Take, for instance, a case where a man had been involved in an industrial accident. The hand had been crushed. The forearm had been severely lacerated, with ligament and muscle damage. The doctor provided the relatives with a straight forward description of the nature of the wounds, and told them that Tony was going to have surgery to remove the four fingers and part of the palm. Every effort would be made to save the thumb. It depended upon what was discovered in the operating room as to exactly what would be done. The consent form for the operation was signed by Tony's father.

During surgery it was revealed that there was greater damage to the wrist bones than the x-ray had showed. Also, the ligament, muscle and nerve damage was more extensive than had been observable in Accident and Emergency. Reluctantly they had to amputate the hand just above the wrist.

On hearing this news, Tony's father, mother and one brother started screaming abuse at all who came near. "Incompetent doctors! They fouled things up! Through negligence he has lost his whole hand! We will sue the doctors!" and so on. A hospital visitor could have been manipulated into taking Tony's parents' side. They sounded so convincing. The atmosphere was emotionally charged. The empathy would have become unsoundly based on a one-sided version of events.

A visitor can no longer provide real care for a family if he or she is being controlled. The perspective would be lost. The staff might also lose respect for the visitor because of the unreasoned stance being taken. Listen, support and care without becoming the family's crusader when the ground is thin. Refrain from adding fuel to a futile fire. Keep your lips sealed, free from taking sides, until the facts are confirmed from other information.

In each family, the closeness and depth of relationship varies from person to person. The nature of these relationships needs to be understood during a traumatic hospitalization. One family member may be talkative; another moves away in withdrawn silence; others just weep and cling to each other; there may be the defiant one or two with a chip on the shoulder concerning the patient or other family members present. In some cases, they may snap at one another, trying to apportion blame. It is unwise of course to get into family feuds. Perhaps the self-isolationist needs a silent arm about them, away from the others. Oftentimes in such circumstances, a non-verbal presence is all that is necessary. The twin ministeries of presence and touch convey the concern of the God we represent under these circumstances.

Unless you are well skilled in ministering to the grieving, the fewer words said the better. Along with this, the acumen to discern whether or not you are treading on private ground needs to be sharpened. If you stay around when you are not appreciated, it makes the grieving harder and aggravates the already-sensitive, angry emotion. There may be family friends who are more acceptable to the family at the time of your visit. Acknowledge it to yourself. Excuse yourself, assuring the family of your continued interest in them.

Family relationships are intricate and, as I have already said, vary from family to family and between members of the same family. It is unwise to take any family situation for granted. Some family members may be active church folk, others may be far from sympathethic to the church. The ability of pastoral people to maintain the confidence of all family factions requires perception as well as divine wisdom. If both are liberally exercised, a valuable healing and unifying ministry is possible. The bedside provides opportunities for reconciliation between family members, and family members and God. An acceptable, sensitive hospital visitor or other pastoral person may be the catalyst for such reconciliations.

Ministry to the family should be treated with awe. It is a task filled with responsibility. There may be resentment, feelings of intrusion, accents of guilt, or the warmth of glad acceptance. With the concurrence of the family, the hospital visitor, with the genuineness of true pastoral care may be able to generate a harmony and strength previously lacking.

During times of distress the visitor will be privy to some very personal matters and understanding of family dynamics. In times of crisis, the pastoral carer becomes like an unofficial adopted family member. Intentionally, I am repetitious here. Whatever you hear at the bedside or with the family, consider it as privileged confidential knowledge.

Healthy family and social relations are important at any stage of hospitalization. Whatever a hospital visitor or other pastoral person does to maintain and encourage such family solidarity is a major contribution to pastoral care.

It cannot be stressed too much that any person who makes hospital visits in the name of the church should avail themselves of every opportunity to participate in pastoral care training programs. Appropriate seminars or workshops are very helpful in forming more effective visitors/carers. If your church does not have regular pastoral care training sessions, enquire what can be done to fill the need. If you intend to be a regular hospital visitor, who has an acceptable ministry, equipping yourself for the task is essential. Later chapters will give you further insights.

SUPPLEMENT 1—NON-VERBAL COMMUNICATION INDICATORS

In many cases communication between individuals involves words which carry less influence than bodily movements and expressions. Non-verbal signals, as they are called, are communicated by each person in any encounter. In visiting the hospital patient, irrespective of role, the visitor needs to observe these tell-tale pointers to understand the real message that patient, relative or staff is really sending. Outlined here are some of these message-carrying signs which you should observe at the bedside.

Both during and after visits, try to recall those indicators. Remember that *you also* relay messages with your own voice and body. At the time of each visit, be aware of the counter-messages you may be signalling. Assess how you think the patient is reading you.

POSITIVE	NEGATIVE
Facial expressions and appearance	
Warm, inviting, smiling	Cold, stiff, distant
Appropriate dress	Too formal, too casual dress
Groomed appearance (hair, make-up)	Careless appearance
Good eye contact	Roving or staring eyes, or no direct contact
Voice	
Warm, natural	Dull, monotone
Circumspect tone	Embarrassingly loud or too soft
Understandable rate of speech	Too fast or too clipped speech
Fluent language	Stuck for words

Empathetic (understanding, supporting tone)	Artificial, false, insincere
Audible responses (*hm, hmm, aha,* etc;)	Hesitant, with many *ers, ums* and *ahs*
Appropriate silent gaps (for reflection)	Embarrassed silence with fidgeting
Interrupting to clarify or reflect before proceeding	Saying "yes, yes" when it should be "no"

Body posture

Leaning toward person at eye level	Sitting side on (discouraging to relationship and interaction)
	Cold, rigid, impersonal attitude; remaining standing in an authoritative position; looking ready to leave momentarily
Comfortable and relaxed position, settled, making it obvious that time is no problem	
Where possible, being three to four feet distant	Too distant or too close

Gestures and manners

Extended, accepting arm/s	Arms by the side, in an indifferent manner
Firm handshake if appropriate	Limp hand shake
Keeping head and body turned toward patient to indicate full attention; making patient the center of conversation	Talking to others, ignoring patient, yawning, fidgeting with anything, looking frequently at clock or watch

SUPPLEMENT 2—
VOICE CHARACTERISTICS
AND THEIR MEANING

Your tone of voice and the tempo of your speaking often indicate sincerity or lack of sincerity behind the words you utter. Become alert to these factors in your own bedside visits. Your hospital awareness may be sharpened by observing voice characteristics in television programs.

Voice characteristics and their meaning

Monotone	Boredom
Slow speed, low pitch	Depression
High voice, empathetic speed	Enthusiasm
Ascending tone	Astonishment
Terse speech and loud tone	Anger
High pitched, drawn-out speech	Disbelief
Short guttural sounds	Impatience

SUPPLEMENT 3—DEATH AND YOU

1) How many deceased persons have you seen? Have you been present when somebody drew their last breath? Recall your feelings at the time.

2) Describe your last encounter with a dying person or a person who nearly died. What anxieties were raised in you? Are you more or less confident about sitting with a dying patient now?

3) What do you understand when Paul calls death an enemy? Do you see death as an enemy? How does your answer to (2) affect your attitude to a dying person?

4) Kubler-Ross entitled a book *Death—The Final Stage of Growth*. Does such a concept help you in your ideas about death?

5) Have you thought about your own death? Are you frightened, anxious, very anxious, apprehensive or accepting of thoughts about your own death?

6) How would you feel if you were told you had one hour to live? Are you prepared for your own death?

Your serious consideration of these points will identify your suitability to minister to terminally ill or dying patients and their relatives.

Allow sufficient time to work through each question. Write down your thoughts and share them with another pastoral care person or an active Christian, who is experienced in bereavement counselling or in the care of the dying in hospital.

SECTION TWO

*For Lay
Pastoral
Workers*

6

The Patient's Needs

Susan Williams was involved in a road accident. With fractured legs, she was given a six weeks' sentence in hospital. I use the word "sentence" because that is what it seems like to a very mentally alert and athletically active young lady. Her netball team was leading the competition. Now she will miss the final, including the coveted trophy for her shelves.

George Arnold, fifty-two years of age, a good, honest battler, lives an ordinary quiet suburban life. He is a storeman and packer so his income does not allow for many of the luxuries of life. His teenage children, some still at school, are demanding and hard to discipline. His serious heart attack looks like forcing him to take an invalid pension. With still three years to complete his house mortgage repayment, George has many concerns on his mind.

Karen Reid has the most adorable children, aged seven, five and two, and at thirty-two she should be at the prime of life. Instead, an ultrasound has shown a sizeable mass in her abdomen. Is it cancer or fibroids, or perhaps a cyst? Malignant or benign? That is her great question. Will she live to see her children through school, marriages, and grandchildren? Everything has that terrible cloud of uncertainty hanging over it.

Mark Brown has been told he has leukemia, a very acute form, and the doctors warn him of the consequences if he does not have treatment. They have also stated clearly that the only option is chemotherapy, with its possible and unpredictable side-effects. And even with chemotherapy there are no promises, only "maybes." To have chemotherapy or not is an extremely hard decision to make. His wife, Joyce, has always been so dependent on him; the children are married and scattered in the country and interstate.

The hours of lying in that bed are hours of loneliness and mental torture for Mark, not made any easier by his wife's holding his hand. He cannot express his feelings to her. He wants her with him yet it hurts just to see and feel her there.

John and Cheryl are elated that they have a beautiful baby daughter, after 9 years of marriage and unproductive previous attempts to conceive. Their dreams have come true.

Mrs. Wilson is doing well after having bunions removed. In fact, she is enjoying being waited upon.

Young Craig has come in to have his appendix out as it has been causing him problems. He is bouncy about it, although somewhat apprehensive. The first time in hospital for him is like the mixed feelings of a first trip of white water rafting.

Anne is in her eighties and in hospital for chronic obstructive airways disease. She is gasping for breath. Having to wear that uncomfortable oxygen mask is exhausting. Her family are not game to tell her that her daughter was killed in a road accident.

Shirley Davis' concern is not unlike Joe Ferguson's. Shirley has breast lumps and is to have a mastectomy. Joe has prostate problems and also requires surgery. Both are worried that their respective femininity and masculinity are to be excised by the surgeon's knife. They have logical explanations to the contrary but their emotions suggest otherwise.

All these individuals, along with the diabetic, asthmatic, renal, pneumonic, neurosurgical patients—and scores of other types—are the people whose bedsides you approach as a pastoral worker. They are all experiencing different needs, feelings and sensations.

As a lay pastoral worker you should always inform the hospital staff of your presence. The patient may have spoken to the staff concerning spiritual needs (or a lack of desire to have a pastoral visit). Your speaking with staff also helps them to understand the patient's support network.

SENSITIVITY

Above all else, patients need your sensitivity to their particular needs and circumstances. Pastoral workers often mistakenly consider they have an unchallengeable right to be at a bedside. On the contrary, our right to be there depends on whether the patient is comfortable with us at that time. When the patient comes to feel the need to make conversation and entertain the visitor, then the visit is a failure. The visitor is an embarrassment.

The patient is often too polite to ask you to leave. Your ready ability to assess the situation and feelings of any one of the above types of patients is a necessary skill to be developed by you as a hospital pastoral worker. Such sensitivity, of course, comes with training and experience.

APPROPRIATENESS

Your developed powers of observation enable you to be more sensitive to the patient's condition. That ability to read and act appropriately to the unspoken will enhance the chances of your acceptance.

Mary had just been told her condition was terminal and that further treatment would not be possible. She would receive only palliative care to keep her comfortable. Mary was lying there shattered. "Mid-forties is too young to die" was the thinking behind the sad, lethargic, depressed look.

The recently retired, spritely, happy Mr. Brown, the Church pastoral visitor, bounced in and chirpily asked, "How's my bright girl today?" Mary, the patient, started to sob saying, "The doctor told me there is no more treatment possible."

"What nonsense! What would he know?" was Mr. Brown's opening salvo. "We will have you out in no time. It won't be long before you will be into your bikini and having those hilarious pool parties at your place. We can't have you losing your reputation now, can we?" All this seemed to hit the midships of Mary's emotions. Her tears flowed broken-heartedly.

"Now, there is no need to cry. Come on, dry those tears!" Mr. Brown blundered on. "You should not upset yourself too much. What would your husband think if he saw you crying like this?"

Such a type of conversation is not an isolated instance. It happens daily in any major hospital. It reeks of inappropriateness. The only thing the patient does not do is to scream out, "Get out of here, you insensitive buffoon." To be smart, or to try to be funny in the presence of a despondent and deflated patient is simply inappropriate. Considerable skill is required to appreciate when and how to promote brightness. The right times are rare and only a few people can successfully do it with an anxious, depressed patient.

A young trainee pastoral care person learnt a significant lesson when reflecting to a group upon what he considered a successful pastoral encounter. This patient, Mrs. Connor, had been diagnosed as having cancer a few hours earlier and was scheduled for emergency surgery the next morning.

"When are you going for the operation?" was a suitable question to ask. It showed concern and interest. It could have been intended to see whether it was possible to visit her and pray with her before she went.

On hearing that she was scheduled for the morning, the trainee's response was inappropriate. Uttered with a smile, it was an endeavor to be bright: "So you will be first cab off the rank tomorrow." The lady was probably still in double shock: she had been told she had unsuspected cancer and then told of immediate emergency surgery. A person trying to come to grips with both blows certainly would not appreciate being compared with a cab going for a ride.

APPROPRIATE RESPONSES

Mrs. Connor would have responded positively to the visitor if she could have taken in anything he was saying, if he had said something along these lines:

"You have been hit with two hammers," or, "You feel like you're dreaming and you are going to wake up and find that it's not true" or, "It must seem like the rug has been pulled from under you by the doctor," or, "To be told that by the doctor must be devastating".

There is not a question in any of those responses. They leave the way open for Mrs. Connor, if she is not in too great a state of shock, to start expressing what she is feeling deep inside. The door is left ajar for her to push open and share her bewilderment and shock if she feels trusting enough to do so. She is also able to let the matter rest and close the door.

Sensitivity leads to appropriate responses which you should respect.

JUST TO BE

Both terminally ill Mary and Mrs. Connor were in a state of shock. Conversation would not have been acceptable. When such news is conveyed to a patient, there is a need to be quiet and try to collect thoughts, to come to grips with the situation. In such circumstances co-ordinated thinking is difficult. Often a multitude of concepts, people, consequences and what now may seem like vain aspirations float around in a confusing mix, with no one idea becoming firmly anchored.

The pastoral worker's conversation, however bland, may add to the turmoil going on within. Just to be with the patient in silence is often preferable.

A young adult had a motor cycle accident and was brought in with major head injuries—suspected "brain death." For two and a half hours the doctors worked on him. I sat with his wife during that period. She was silent. The only conversation concerned periodical reports on what was happening in the emergency receiving room. After the declaration of death it became a coroner's case. The police took another hour before arriving for identification of the body. Again, in that hour, less than one hundred words passed between us.

When I escorted the wife to her car, she broke down, sobbing, thanking me for my help, support and comfort. I had sensed that all she wanted was to be alone with her thoughts in order to come to grips with what was happening. I had been content "to be" there for her. Her thoughts were interrupted only with essential information.

Sensitivity enables the pastoral worker to be the right type of support at the right time (as long or short as necessary) with as few or as many words as fit the circumstances. That is true pastoral care—"to be". Patients need to be able to find their own coping mechanisms and the carer needs to be the type of person the patient requires at each visit. To be the one who recognizes those coping needs is to be a pastoral carer.

TO SEE THE CHRIST IMAGE

Surely the most effective pastoral care person recorded in history is Jesus. His sensitive handling of each and every encounter has provided the perfect model. He astounded people, bringing comfort and peace to folks such as the woman at the well, the widow of Nain, Zaccheus, Jairus, Mary of Magdala, Mary and Martha, his tormentors at Calvary, Peter and the Emmaus disciples. (See Chapter 10, "Jesus—A Theological Model".)

A person enduring hospitalization needs the care of someone like Jesus. They need to recognize a person of the Jesus mold at their bedside. That same gentle discerning touch can provide the soothing warmth and relief that was experienced by the people of Galilee and Judah so long ago. Jesus promised that his disciples would do greater things than he did after the Holy Spirit filled their lives.

The pastoral carer must be recognised as one bearing that same touch. It is this that speaks of Jesus, not our scripture reading or our offered prayer. Our prayers become meaningful and valued only after the Christ has been first discerned in the carer.

The best textbooks for pastoral care are the four gospels. Studying Jesus and his attitude to each person is essential. Our minds, thoughts, lives and actions should be so filled with Jesus that, like light, we bring the Jesus image and way to the bedside.

A carer becomes Christ to the patient. This is our responsibility: to be a modern-day reincarnation of Christ to the patient. Presumptuous? No! It is an awesome responsibility which emphasizes our own humanity and dependence upon Christ.

If we are diligent to know him more, our efforts to naturally model him in our lives, both within and outside the hospital, will bear fruit.

Whether patients acknowledge it or not, they need to see the Christ image and touch reflected in the pastoral care workers at the bedside. Paul suggested that we become living letters, able to be seen and read by the community around us. This should be more evident at the bedside, where people are often longing for such a sighting.

TO COMMUNICATE

Pastoral care of the sick may now be understood as something much more than a social call, more than a friendly visit, more than just a wish to cheer the patient up. A pastoral visit to the bedside should hold an aura of responsibility, not of a duty to be discharged. The first visit should never be taken as a last visit. The patient may expect from you henceforth a commitment which may mean demands on your time, energy and emotions.

The outcome of your visit is unpredictable. Some visits will be encouraging and full of blessing. Others will leave you with a sense of failure, whether that truly be the case or not. In actual fact, the assumed failure, may have created such a good impression that your next appearance at the bedside will be eagerly anticipated, and the assumed "sucessful" visit may have actually been an absolute disaster in the patient's view!

The object of your visit is to communicate. There are many ways of communication. For face-to-face encounters, the ancient Epictitus gives us a clear hint: "Nature has given to man one tongue, but two ears, that we may hear from others twice as much as we speak". The patient should be the one allowed to do most of the talking.

Joseph Zima[1] takes this up further in his chapter on "Listening". He says, "Listening involves eyes and ears." So he takes communication one step beyond Epictitus. Hearing, sight and speech are involved in communication. He develops his case by stating that listening is a complete process involving hearing, understanding, judging, storing and responding.

Ole Harlem[2] in his advice to the medical profession on dealing with patients analyzes communication as having three integral parts:

- To make known one person's thoughts or ideas to others
- To do so with as much ease and as quickly as possible
- To convey knowledge of things

He says language is abused when it fails on any of these points. When we are a hospital pastoral visitor, our role is to allow the patient or the family to communicate with us. For the pastoral scene the word "feelings" should be included in the first point above, making it thoughts, feelings or ideas.

Likewise, the third point could be rewritten: "to convey knowledge of attitudes and feelings".

Often the best communicators are children. They are able to fulfill all the above criteria. Yet we usually take little notice of them or ignore the knowledge and information they are communicating. By so doing we prove to them that we cannot be trusted with their communication. Consequently, we may see them talking with their dolls, pets, a tree or themselves in a special hide-a-way. This continues until they feel ready to test our trust again. Patients and their relatives need to have their confidence in us, too, as accepters of communication, to be respected and actively honored in the appropriate way.

A person's real need in hospital as elsewhere is for someone to listen to them as a fellow human being. Lake makes some significant observations:

"If present loneliness can induce neurotic anxiety, then its opposite, namely genuine company, can combat neurotic anxiety."[3] An attentive listener can put to flight an army of irrational fears. "By offering to be an attentive listener...we draw (the patient/relative) back into a place of safety...". Any pastoral visitor who cannot listen hard and long will very quickly become irritated and fidgety. He or she will take over the conversation and the patient will become the passive, disinterested and hurting listener.

Zima identifies two components of any communication, namely:

- The content of the message—information value
- The feelings of the message—the underlying attitudes and emotions

In this he suggests that there are two strands of conversation going on in communication, one verbal and the other non-verbal. In our communication with our patient, we should be the gatherer of offered information and at the same time the identifier of the feelings that are being emitted.

Sensitive listening is hard work. It is active, not just sitting passively, it is reflecting on the contents of what is being said and the feelings of the patient or relatives to deduce meaning. These meanings are similarly reflected upon to discern the implications.

Suppose a man has been told that he has cancer and that the only treatment is chemotherapy. The patient recalls the situation of a relative who had received chemotherapy and had long and uncomfortable side-effects.

The knowledge of the cancer has been reflected on. Then the feelings are reflected on to discover meaning. If you suggest, "You must be frightened (or some such feeling word) *because* of your relative's experience," this remark promotes further reflection.

The reason for the fear is now acknowledged. The implications of that fear must be recognized through further reflection: "You are therefore scared to agree to have the chemo." The implication of the knowledge and the feelings is that the patient is negative in attitude toward undergoing such treatment.

Simply, it may be said that sensitive listening is able to reflect content, feelings, meanings and implications. The patient knows that the communication is being heard, resulting in deeper perception of what is happening personally within and without.

It has been already pointed out that listening involves the eyes as well as ears. As the patient speaks, the body posture and movements are revealing. The genuine feelings and truth which are difficult to express in words are being transmitted. This is commonly called "body language" and was referred to in the last chapter and Supplement 1.

There is also a hearing with the third ear. Effective listening involves hearing with the first ear the words that are being said. Hearing with the second ear is hearing what the words are not saying but what the non-verbals are telegraphing. The third ear is that which discerns what the patient cannot express—maybe because the real situation is not fully understood. Relationships, loyalty, or fear may be prohibiting overt revelation. In other words, there are times when words and body language together are inadequate; that is when the third ear is required.

Reflection is the opposite of expressing an opinion. Once you have passed judgment, that is, an opinion, whether critical or favorable, it makes patients' free expression difficult. They need all the friends they can have, so they will not offend you by disagreeing with you. Even the positive and encouraging evaluations you offer make it difficult for people to talk about fears, faults or failings that may be distressing them. To reveal these or even harbor them within, in the light of your good comments, may cause the patient to develop or increase feelings of guilt. Pastoral communication's aim is to release the person from fears and guilt, not to increase them.

Two patients from the same parish objected to their minister's visits. He was uncomfortable at the bedside so he resorted to a good sprinkling of pious talk, Bible reading and prayer. He became a religious man and ceased to be a Christian...Every pastoral worker must wait until there is a freedom to speak of holy things, a freedom which the Holy Spirit gives. Dietrich Bonhoeffer's advice[4] well applies to the bedside visit when he says that we should listen with the ears of God that we may speak the word of God. Maybe this is a fourth ear which we should develop as a pastoral worker with the hospitalized.

Thus we should not enter a hospital with a preconceived idea of the issues we want to raise with the patients. Such will pollute any effort at sincere listening. Our preoccupation will be with waiting for a suitable time to intrude our own agenda items into the conversation. Our ability to permit the patient to reflect and to discover the meaning at the back of the communication will be destroyed. Perhaps our agenda items are our own perceived concern and totally irrelevant for the patient.

After your visit it may be rewarding to evaluate your listening skills against the checklist below:

Negative

Was there any one-way conversation (the patient being the silent one)?

Were there any negative interruptions by you which changed the conversation?

Did you ignore attempts at understanding?

Did you notice your own negative emotional reactions to what was said?

Did you miss any opportunities to use reflection?

Positive

Did you encourage the patient to explore and clarify statements?

Was reflection used effectively?

Were there few "yes"/"no" responses to interruptions?

Were there positive interpretations of what was happening?

It will pay to do such an evaluation after each significant encounter. Supplements 1 and 2 are intended to help you evaluate your personal efforts.

NOTES

1. Zima, Joseph P. *Interviewing, Key to Effective Management* pp 39–58.
2. Harlem, Ole K. *Communication in Medicine—a Challenge to the Profession* pp 30-32.
3. Lake, Frank *Clinical Theology—a Theological/Psychological Basis to Clinical Pastoral Care* pp 1–28.
4. Bonhoeffer, Dietrich *Life Together*

7

The Patient In Crisis

ILLNESS IS A CRISIS

It is rare that a person is admitted to hospital without some justifiable reason. The patient has gone to the local medical officer, or the hospital emergency department with certain complaints about some physical or emotional functional change. Weighing the evidence of verbal description, physical examination, obvious symptoms, x-ray and other tests, the doctor deems that there are grounds for a hospital admission. Things are not right. When the body is not performing as designed, the person is living below normal efficiency and therefore is suffering some deprivation. The sufferer is in some form of crisis. And crisis produces anxiety and uncertainty: a threat hangs over the normal living of the person, the family and maybe even a wider circle.

Illness, however mild, raises the specter of mortality. Human finiteness, the weakness and frailty of human flesh become more evident. Unless a pastoral worker is able to understand some of the personal dynamics and enter into the feelings of the people being visited, the visit is of little consequence. Many times patients request that a minister or pastoral worker not come again. Without sensitivity they have probably pontificated and made presumptive, even dogmatically pious pronouncements as to how the patient should react. They have squashed and driven inside the patient's natural emotional reactions.

In any crisis situation, such a reaction is that which is appropriate to the temperament and nature of the person to cope with the situation. It may be stunned silence, talkativeness, a questioning of God, self and others, shrinking from reality; it may be panic, tantrums, the expression of anger, or self-blame. These are all coping reactions. They are right reactions for that person at that time. We must accept them as such and not judge them by the way we ourselves would react or how we think they *should* cope with the circumstances.

Elisabeth Kubler-Ross identifies them in her general classification of stages[1]. Her term "stages of death and grief" is not useful as it has been interpreted and applied differently from the way she intended. A more lucid perception of all the emotions of grief is obtained, I believe, when we speak of them as "the coping mechanisms of grief" and there are many more than Kubler-Ross' five. The question that we should hold in our minds as we observe some of these reactions around the bedside is, "What is triggering off these reactions?" There are a number of different things that a patient in crisis meets that cause fear and panic to develop. We shall look at some of these fear reactions separately, recognising that each case is different and that there may be even more than the types of fear and their causes we discuss here.

SYMPTOMS

Before the patient even comes into hospital the stage has often been set for fears to start snowballing. The lethargic feeling that has been creeping on for months has meant curtailing some activities and even missing out on others. Maybe the resulting lack of concentration has been producing decreasing efficiency at work. The back pains which were once put down to heavy lifting are now getting worse. It is getting harder and harder to pass a stool and now there is a show of blood. Those chest pains passed off as indigestion are now accompanied by a shooting feeling down the left arm. These symptoms cannot be ignored.

Still the sufferer endures however, because of fear of what the doctor might reveal. The family is noticing the changes. The loved one tires more readily. Bruises very easily. Is more quickly irritated and uncharacteristically snaps back. Asking if anything is wrong means getting your head bitten off. The symptoms are denied and put to one side. What is the basis of this denial? Is it the fear of what these signs might reveal?

Thus the patient may have been beset with this fear for a considerable time before arrival at the hospital.

THE LANGUAGE OF DIAGNOSIS

The reason for the initial admission to hospital is to perform tests which are intended to identify the cause of the presenting symptoms. The language of diagnostic tests creates the major fear of the early days following admission: "We'll send you for a CT scan." "I think a liver biopsy is necessary." "An endoscopy is called for." "An electroencephalogram (EEG) is the order." "We have to give you an angiogram." New terms—new words—the patient does not know what is involved with the procedure. Often doctors do not tell the patient why a test is being done or what they are looking for. Whatever it is, it sounds ominous. Patients put on a brave front that seems like a mask, as they fob off on relatives' questions. They try to recall the stories they have heard from others about relatives who have had similar tests and later died from an incurable disease.

Unless there is denial, the tendency is to dwell on the most pessimistic interpretation of the results of the tests. Thus the second tier of fears is the mention of tests in the language of diagnosis.

The third tier, still relating to diagnosis, is added a day or two later when the doctor returns with the result. Here the powerful language of diagnosis may create severe anxiety, even panic, in the patient. Cancer, leukemia, a mass in the bowel, a cardiovascular accident, chronic obstructive airways disease, blocked arteries, stroke and so on. These are all terms which are not fully understood. Even when the doctor tries to explain what a term means, the mind is so full of dread of the worst possible consequences that the words come across as garbled sounds. *The mind absorbs only what it can bear and it may hallucinate as to the course of the disease,* or simply shift into neutral.

Where the patient cannot face the truth or adversity, the coping mechanism of denial really begins to take control. We must accept that such denial is a sanctuary to which the patient flees for shelter and protection. For the present it is a very adequate coping mechanism for the fears which the language of diagnosis has caused the stricken one. To destroy that haven prematurely is to increase a flood of those fears, and drown the emotions with hopelessness and despair.

TOO MUCH TOO SOON

The patient may have been ill for some time at home waiting for the doctors to come to some conclusion. During that period he or she frequently is forming a personal opinion of what the problem is. Surprisingly, these unscientific self-diagnoses often prove to be accurate. A fact to store away in the memory is that eighty percent of terminally-ill patients know of their condition before doctors tell them, according to Kubler-Ross and others.[2] Nevertheless, many such patients fear being told too much, too soon. Again that coping mechanism of denial comes into play allowing the mind and emotions to absorb sufficient information without breaking the spirit.

A father of two early teenagers, a fit, healthy-looking man, went for exploratory abdominal surgery. He was closed up again without anything being done. The abdominal cavity was riddled with cancer. The surgeon told him, "You have a fifty percent chance of living two years and a twenty percent chance of living five years." This wise surgeon was giving him scope to accept what he was most comfortable with.

Three minutes later I asked him, "What did you understand the doctor was saying to you?" In a confident voice he replied. "I've got a ninety percent chance of getting completely better and a ten percent chance of dying." He wasn't lying, his coping mechanism released to his mind and emotions all he could take at that time.

It would have been cruel to indicate that it was not so. We cannot torture patients by trying to force on them too much knowledge about their disease if they are not ready for it. It is best simply to answer the patient's questions and nothing more. A medical person is the person to give the medical information. Therefore, the wisest course is simply to say that you are not able to give medical details. Suggest that they write down their queries so that when a doctor comes, the direct questions may be asked.

It is amazing how many times patients will ask the question of a non-medical person and fail to ask the doctor. In some cases, they genuinely forget to ask, being overawed by the doctor's presence. Others are frightened of learning too much, too soon.

Remember that the patient does not have to know the full details of the prognosis for the disease to run its course. The patient has "the right to know" about the illness and its implications and can insist on that right. The patient also has the "right not to know." A patient may die much happier if unaware of the full extent of the spread of the disease.

Reiterating the full information against the patients' wishes may mean that they fret, develop anxiety and undue fear which can mushroom, causing unbelievable stress and mental agony. One of the harmful aspects of the Kubler-Ross contribution to death education is the popularity of her five stages of dying. Every medical practitioner, paramedic and the general public has become aware of her bereavement reactions. If the patient is in denial, or has not shown anger, or cried, then the social worker or some other bereavement counsellor is called in by the nursing or medical personnel to talk about death. These counsellors are often guilty of imposing too much too soon. They literally try to coerce the patient into premature tears or anger. The patient in crisis has needs which relate to personality and temperament and these must be considered when it comes to the speed by which the patient's perception of the condition is informed and reinforced.

Remember that every human being is unique. Reactions to physical and emotional pain differ with each of us. The pastoral person's awareness of such uniqueness should result in an effort to understand just where a particular patient is at the time of the visit.

NO NEWS GOOD NEWS?

Many people have taken comfort in the adage "No news is good news." The patient is lying in bed waiting for results of tests to determine the diagnosis or a decision on the nature of the treatment. The longer the doctors delay relaying the awaited information, the more the uncertainty and doubt fuel their fears. No news is usually perceived as bad news by patients in crisis. A common complaint is that the doctor has not told them anything, yet some of those selfsame doctors have a reputation for being open and honest with their patients.

"They know something and they are avoiding me." "They don't want to tell me." "I'm sick of being kept in the dark." The inference here, of course, is that the doctors are shielding themselves from unpleasantness by not passing on bad news.

The visitor needs to be aware of two real possibilities: firstly, the patient may have been told the situation very clearly by a doctor and had it confirmed on other occasions by the nurses, chaplain or social worker. Innumerable times the chaplain has reported such complaints only to hear from various members of staff, "I've told them the score myself." As we have already said, patients often exercise selective hearing and selective recall.

Secondly—and this is the likely cause—the doctors just don't know and cannot give a definite diagnosis. The tests are inconclusive. The patient is showing mixed, atypical symptoms and the tests are confusing. It is often difficult for the haematologist to isolate and identify the infection which is playing havoc with the treatment protocol of a leukemia patient. Medical staff usually endeavor to be honest and responsive to the patient's anxiety over "no news." Again, let it be stressed that it is not the pastoral care visitor's role to pass on medical information or criticize doctors' methods and treatment.

Sometimes the doctors are forbidden by the relatives to inform the patient, due to special circumstances which may be unknown to the pastoral person. This is an ethical issue the doctor has to come to grips with before dealing with such a patient. If the pastoral visitor is concerned over the "no news" anxiety, a word of explanation to the nursing unit manager would be proper and sufficient for any necessary action. An aggressive attitude to hospital staff for the lack of communication is not, of course, an appropriate response.

THE PROCESS OF DYING

In one generation a whole change of outlook has taken place. Hell-fire and brimstone preachers are now seldom heard. People's indifference to God and the future life has grown. Scripture for the majority of people holds little influence. Although many believe in God and Jesus and still say their prayers at night, almost like wearing an amulet, theological and ontological considerations are irrelevant for great numbers of people in their day-to-day living.

When the news of terminal illness or a threat to existence comes, there is seldom a fear of "What will happen to me when I die?" or "Will I go to heaven or hell?" In many years of chaplaincy work, I have seldom been asked this by the patient. For most there is a basic fatalism: "What will be, will be." "When your number comes up you cannot do anything about it." This attitude tends to lead to the acceptance of the inevitable. Again we see in this evidence of a spiritual indifference.

There is, however, a fear of the process of dying. An accepted fallacy is that a person must always suffer prior to death, that death must be an agonising experience. Proper medical care should relieve pain and physical distress for the terminally ill patient. Palliative care, as it currently is, aims at a comfortable, pain-free death. This means the medication is monitored and immediately adjusted to meet the pain tolerance of the patient.

Popular notions of the likely trend of the disease are often more influential than the medical staff's explanation. So much mental torture is unnecessarily endured in anticipation of what might or might not be.

The various reactions of relatives and friends, such as over-protectiveness, apparent rejection of the patient and the disease, the decreasing regularity of visits, only escalate the patient's fear of the dying process. The message that is being received is, "It is going to be terrible to see you suffer while you are dying."

In the early stages of the disease patients with normal mental health are alert to such reactions. They are likely to interpret what they see as the visitors' abhorrence of their condition. As mentioned they often fear the worst and are looking for every indication that will confirm that fear. Illogical? Yes! But a frequent reaction.

A weekly support group for leukemia and lymphoma patients spends most of its time dealing with these fears. Long-standing patients or ex-patients in the group who share experiences are able to quell, to some extent, those terrifying, rest-disturbing thoughts.

In a paradoxical way, the sick may try to mask that fear by an apparent denial of the seriousness of the diagnosis. The brave front may hide deep internal turmoil caused by churning over possible future experiences. Thus denial appears as a coping mechanism to counter the fear of the dying process. This denial must not be mistaken for the positive attitude of the person who acknowledges the condition and is determined to beat it. Frequently, it is the person with the strong, positive attitude who responds better to treatment.

Much of the anger and violence sometimes encountered in patients is a reflection not so much of their concept of death itself but of the pain and suffering being experienced, about to be experienced, or imagined as yet to be experienced. Protestations of unfairness often relate to this anticipated process of dying. When pain is cruel, nurses in particular may be very rudely castigated. Those dedicated to the care of the terminally-ill are not offended by such outbursts. They understand and expect patients to occasionally be demanding in this way.

Mr. Watson, who was very demanding, was encouraged in this attitude by an uptight family. One hectic Saturday morning when a death had occurred in the ward, it took two of the three registered nurses on duty three hours to cope with the persistent oozing of blood after death. The only other registered nurse on the ward was involved with a transplant patient in isolation. Because of Mr. Watson's intolerance he was the only patient on the ward who was given a sponge before 1 pm. However, in the midst of the emergency, Mr. Watson's relatives were incessantly coming out and demanding the staff's attention. Although Mr. Watson's condition was terminal, he was the healthiest in the ward at that time. The relatives reported what they perceived as the staff's negligence to the administration. The other more needy patients did not raise a voice, appreciating the dilemma the staff had been in.

Mr. Watson and his relatives were behaving inconsiderately because they knew the dying process was going to be difficult and they hoped by their demands it would be made easier. The anger they demonstrated emphasized this underlying fear.

The family's demands may sometimes be a response to guilt over past bad relationships or neglect of the patient. The visitor must be aware of such reactions. When the likes of the Watsons behave so selfishly, rather than getting more staff support, they may get less—the staff may try to avoid abuse by keeping away. Good pastoral care workers have the opportunity to detect such irritating behavior and are able to provide support by trying to make positive observations about the care offered by the staff. They may tactfully point out to the relatives that their angry demands only cause greater anxiety within their loved one. This may, in fact, help ease their own tension and the patient's stress.

An unemotionally involved pastoral person can help to restore a more balanced perspective to the family. The discerning carer is able to assist the patient, relatives and staff, resulting in a more relaxed and helpful environment in the ward.

SEPARATION

When we consider terminally ill patients we should recognize the magnitude of what they are soon to experience. In most cases, excepting sudden death, of course, the patients are aware of the impending outcome of their illness. They therefore are able to reflect upon the fact that they are soon to leave everything behind. There is little they can do to alter the situation. The doctors may continue heroic efforts to prolong their lives, but deep down they know it will be of little avail. Ultimately, they will have to let go of home, assets and all their loved ones.

Lying in bed the terminally ill person has all the time to think. Particularly in the restless night hours, the mind turns to the various members of the family—father, mother, spouse, son, daughter. Where the family is loving and close, the thought of being cut off from them is like a nightmare. The fear of this separation generates more and more unrealistic hopes for their condition.

Family and other loved ones are so much the center of most of our lives. The destruction of this bond threatens the whole group. The fear is even greater when the patient is under sixty years of age; in our modern society death at such an age is considered untimely. Life has not been able to realize all its projections. Many of the pleasures associated with a growing family are not going to be witnessed and enjoyed. Who will look after this family? Although the patient may have encouraged the partner to remarry, what type of person will be the children's stepparent? This is the nagging question that remains and will remain unanswered. To imagine the children in the care of another who may have different ways and standards is a tortured exercise of the mind.

We often see children crying when a mother leaves them at a child care center, kindergarten or primary school for the first time. This fear in children is increased when a permanent separation is envisaged. Therefore children, whether patients or relatives, need especially attentive tender care.

Great sensitivity is required when we meet people facing such loss. The patient either allows these fears to be expressed without feeling guilty or withdraws almost to the point of refusing to speak. The hurt and aching heart needs to find release and bring into the open those tormenting fears.

In any grieving situation, emotions rule the mind. It is often difficult and sometimes unwise to try to impose rational thinking on such a patient. A patient who is withdrawn and depressive is most likely to be absorbed with the thoughts stirred up by fears of the loss of loved ones. A gentle, supportive attitude often produces positive responses.

Any effort made to allow an opportunity for the expression of such fears will be helpful. To verbalize them aloud in front of someone else assists in bringing the situation into the right perspective. The magnitude of the event can never disappear. We must remember that and provide all the love, care, and understanding attention that we can. Only those of us who have been near death ourselves can understand something of the depth of this fear, remembering also that each person's experience is unique.

UNFINISHED BUSINESS

Most of us take life very complacently. We do what we want when we want to do it. We often go about life with the philosophy that there is plenty of time, or that tomorrow is always to be. When the doctor's pronouncement is received the truth dawns that there is not plenty of time. All the things that had been planned now may not be done. Even the things that needed to have been said, and repeated often, now no longer can be recapitulated in the same way.

A man in his early fifties had a severe heart attack. His wife had been nagging him to paint the kitchen for the previous two years but her persistence raised his stubborn streak. Now he was forbidden to get up ladders and stretch. This man worried and loaded himself with guilt because he would not be able to do the kitchen. He had let his wife down. He now also would be forced to accept the invalid pension, which meant that the hiring of tradesmen would eat into their meager savings.

An older gentlemen visited his son overseas. There was a very emotional scene at the airport as they said their farewells. They both embraced, wept and told each other for the first time in about twenty years that they loved each other. A few weeks after he arrived home, the father was diagnosed with advanced lung cancer. That father wept as he realized all that he had missed out on over the years.

There are many others who do not have such an experience before they die. They cannot make amends and fear overtakes them as they begin to dwell upon what might have been, but more so on what damage and harm will continue to exist in the hearts of the survivors because they thought there would be plenty of time. Sometimes angry words are spoken that cannot be retracted. That inability to make amends arouses guilt over the incident. This may cause the terminal condition to be looked upon as a punishment, sending the patient into great fear of possible repercussions in the after life.

Possibly financial, emotional and relational factors are among the causes of reactions of fear in the patient, fear for the surviving relatives who may be adversely affected by the previous procrastination, plain apathy, or simple lack of planning for the future.

Such fears, created by the guilt of unfinished business, are increased when the survivors express anger at the early death of their loved one. This piling on of guilt only hastens the deterioration in the patient as the emotional torment comes into full focus. The pastoral visitor requires patience to allow these guilty fears to burst out from time to time. In fact, encouragement to voice them is necessary.

After allowing such free expression, some sense of assurance, if that is possible without blatant untruth, should be presented. Sometimes the patient is far beyond the stage of conscious recall of the past or of communication with those being left behind.

Others just have never been able to express their true feelings all their lives.

The father of nine living children had not spoken to half of them for more than thirty years. Only three spent much time with him in the final stages of his illness. An apparently godless man who had lived rather selfishly all his life and seemed incapable of showing love was in a semi-comatose state, not able to respond. Two daughters each held a hand while I prayed that this man might discover and experience God's peace in these final hours of earthly life. At the close of the prayer these two sisters, over forty years of age, looked at each other and with great emotion said, "He squeezed my hand." They concurred that it was the first sign of affection he had shown in their lives. They were overjoyed and tears flowed.

A few minutes later he sat up in bed, stretched out his open hands before him with a smile on his face and lay back on his pillow. He died within half an hour.

That experience of hand squeezing was spoken of at the funeral to give comfort, or rather, to ease some of the bitterness felt by most of the children toward their father. It was explained that he had the capacity to love, but was not able to show it because of some of the sad, lonely and hurtful experiences of his younger life, including four years as a Japanese prisoner of war. This flicker of light in a gloomy world of unfinishable business was seized upon and brought comfort.

ISOLATION

A stinging remark is often hurled by the terminally ill patient at would-be caring friends and helpers: "You don't understand how I feel." "You have never been through it, so how can you know?" In many respects the patient is right. Unless we have walked a similar path we cannot fully understand.

Now the patient will perceive, and to a large extent rightly so, that no one else has trodden that path in exactly the same way. Each patient's illness is unique. As our bodies look different, so do they react to disease and its treatment differently. I observe this daily with patients who have a terminal condition. Different people receiving the same drug protocol experience widely varying pain and other symptomatic side-effects. Their response to the treatment also is widely diverse. So each individual's sickness is unique.

Each patient will experience the care and attention at home or in the hospital in different ways. The gentlest care may be deeply appreciated or received with bitter criticism. The patient's reaction to what may be termed their death sentence varies from day to day, according to the prevailing emotion or degree of pain and discomfort. Our caring ability is demonstrated by the way we adapt to the changing emotions and state of the patient. Terminally ill and other patients are perceptive. They are acutely aware if we really do not understand. This increases within them a sense of isolation.

Most people, when faced with the situation, are embarrassed at having to talk to a person who has been told they have a short time to live. The average visitor's ability to handle this situation is not very good. They may:

- Ignore any reference to the patient's condition, which highlights the isolation. That is, the patient's condition is a taboo subject.
- Try to deny the situation by saying that the patient looks much better. Or the very isolating remark "Go on, you are not going to die, you will live for years." Such a remark is the biggest blow to the patient's integrity you can offer.

The best way to help people who are feeling isolated is to allow them to talk about their condition, their fears, their past years. Turn on the nostalgia. Let them see that you are interested in them.

Often the staff become very close to the dying patient. Doctors as well as nurses, male and female, have wept as we have watched a long-loved terminal patient gradually slip from this world.

Isolation tears at the patient when, because of their low immune responses, they are placed in "Isolation". This means reverse barrier nursing. The restriction on visitors may stir feelings of being equated with a leper.

The specialist made a referral to the chaplain because he was concerned over the emotional instability of an HIV patient's son and his inability to cope with his mother's condition. I phoned the mother, offering to go to her home rather than have her come to the hospital. Sitting with her in her lounge room on the same lounge helped to establish the fact that I had no fear of catching AIDS. She was a normal human being and was accepted as such. That was the message she received.

Similarly, when patients are in isolation we should obey isolation ward instructions but let patients see we are not scared and that our love and concern is real and genuine. If visiting is restricted, phone calls should be made to reassure them of our concern and prayers.

When a patient is swamped by feelings of isolation and ostracism, our assurances should be like casting a life belt to someone splashing in the water, struggling to be rescued.

The loneliness of isolation in any form can be eased as we show that we are prepared to willingly give up our time, convenience, and even sleep to be with others.

In some respects, modern medicine is cruel. It can prolong life when sometimes the quality of that life is very questionable.

Chemotherapy, radiotherapy and surgery are marvellous developments. In innumerable cases they have added years of happy life. The physician and surgeon must be guided by the success of so many patients and he or she cannot refuse to treat a patient while there is some hope of positive response to therapy. There are many cases where doctors and others have concurred that there could be virtually no chance of a reasonable life for the patient. But the prognosis has been proved wrong and the patient has recovered to go home and resume a normal life.

There are occasions, however, when these treatments with their side-effects turn life into a living torture. They can stretch for a period of months. One patient experienced eight months like this during which he enjoyed his wife, family and home for only about three weeks. He fought on, hoping for a permanent cure. His wife regretted that he had gone through the treatment procedure.

There were times when he was more than fed up with what was going on, day in, day out, week in, week out. He lay in discomfort and agony, being relieved with pain killers. He could not support his wife. They were on an invalid pension, although he previously had his own business. He could not even do the simple things: taking his boys to soccer or the family to church. In fact, even in hospital the children exhausted him after a few minutes.

He felt that his life was utterly meaningless. Such thoughts bring a great amount of fear and that sense of fear stirs up a desire to die quickly rather than face a drawn-out process.

Such thoughts may in turn promote a sense of guilt. The patient interprets them as a selfishness which shows little concern for the feelings of the spouse and family that will be left behind; so guilt mounts up and adds to the fear. Frustration and impatience develop. This development leads to either irritability and lashing out at friends and loved ones or the reverse: withdrawal, depression and non-communicativeness. The relatives become more depressed and anxious as their own sense of helplessness is magnified. All this further intensifies the feeling of isolation.

All these are logical, expected responses to the situation. You should affirm that these are natural feelings. Give them the assurance that it is all right to have those thoughts; confirm that these feelings are the human part of us coming to the fore. Suggest that even with enforced physical inactivity and suffering, a person can still bring blessings into the lives of their family and others. Their love for their family and loved ones needs to be received and known.

THE UNKNOWN

The allegorical picture of heaven being a city paved with gold and hell as a place of fire and brimstone, which were believed literally by so many a generation or more ago, has brought about a reaction of doubt and disbelief. The biblical literalists have done more harm than good on the average. They have brought scepticism and ridicule upon the church and its teaching, causing added confusion to the impossibility of knowing exactly what lies beyond death. This is no more evidenced than at the bedside of the average nominal Christian who is terminally ill.

This person does not really believe in anything. Is there such a place as heaven or isn't there? Increasingly people, particularly the young—those without church or Sunday school backgrounds—are accepting the position that there is nothing beyond this life. This is the finish. Among dying people, there are generally three types in my experience:

- The enthusiastic believer, who believes in a hereafter with God or Allah or whoever;
- The person who says there is nothing else, death is the end;
- The person who does not know.

It is these last two categories that hold to themselves the fear of the unknown.

An 18-year-old patient had been told he had less than a fortnight to live. (Actually he lived another seven days.) In conversation with him, just a few minutes after he was told the news, he said, "I'm not afraid of dying, I'm just scared because I don't know what it will be like to be nothing".

There are also those who say that they are not afraid of death but are frightened of the process of dying. What will it be like to die?

This is the fear of the unknown. It can haunt the terminally ill patient. The night hours are often spent thinking and worrying about this great unknown. Patients may be given sedation to help them sleep, so fear is suppressed until the daylight hours. To whom can they express these fears? They think people would laugh at them. Some try to get over it by saying, "God is a God of love; you don't have to worry about it." "You have led a good life—you have not been bad." This advice is cold comfort for a person with such fears.

The unknown is a frightening thing. Often patients are too sick and sedated to be involved in the kind of theological discourse designed to assure them of the fact of heaven.

The pastoral carer can, however, stress the reality of God and invite them to communicate with him even if it is only through prayers offered as the patient's prayer. To present the four spiritual laws for salvation or some other packaged evangelical approach would possibly be damaging. It might be rejected or produce further anxiety because the patient's condition will not permit them to follow logical argument.

PAIN

It is not only the terminal patient who fears the physical pain of illness. Most hospital patients experience pain to a greater or lesser degree. The ability to tolerate pain varies from person to person and often depends upon background and experience. Very insecure people will find the degree of their reaction to pain brings a corresponding degree of attention from staff. If overdone it can bring an opposite reaction as when the boy in the story called "Wolf, wolf'" too often.

There are those people who create a lot of fuss over a simple intramuscular injection. Others hardly feel the prick of the needle. When a terrified patient does not see the needle and it is surreptitiously injected, it is possible that the patient may not flinch. Even if a pain is largely psychological in origin, we must accept the reality of the pain to the patient. It is real. Naturally there are those whose pain is directly proportionate to the nature of the illness, the severity of the injury, the organs or nerves affected by the condition, or the treatment being received. That pain is real. Even the most stoic show it at times. Tough, hard, "devil do-all" characters have been observed to shed tears of agony when pain from a spinal injury, for example,

ROUTE ITEM

Title: Pastoral care in hospitals / Neville A. Kirkwood.

Author: Kirkwood, Neville A.

Call Nu 259.411 K599, 1998

Enumer

Chronol

Copy: 1

Item Ba

3 4 7 1 1 0 0 1 5 1 7 2 1 0

Route T ILDS Delivery
ILLINET Libraries
ILLINET Libraries

[various]
IL

Callslip Request   10/19/2011 5:30:47 PM

Pick-up Location:

Location: stx
Call Number: 259.411 K599, 1998
Copy Info: c.1
User Comments:

Title: Pastoral care in hospitals
Item Barcode:

Patron Category: UBIN
Patron Barcode:

Request Date/Time: 10/19/2011 11:41 AM
Request ID:

has electrified the body. Having once experienced such pain, the patient dreads the possibility of recurrence.

People experiencing pain are preoccupied with the pain. The caring visitor will not try to engage them in conversation unless they specifically initiate the talking. Presence is the important factor for some, while others prefer to be alone. The visitor needs to be aware of the patient's preference.

MUTILATION

Along with pain there is a fear of mutilation by the surgeon in the operating theatre, or disfigurement caused by an accident, or the effects of the stroke, arthritis, muscular atrophy, burns and so on. Disfigurement affects one's public image and acceptability, in the view of the patient, who is looking at the longer-term prospects of being disabled or incapacitated. This is the fear of being less than a whole person. Mutilation may not necessarily be an outward condition. A teenage or young married person may be told that chemotherapy or radiotherapy to be undertaken will result in the destruction of the reproductive capacities. Simply put, they will become sterile. They see it as the destruction of part of their manhood or womanhood. The loss of the ability to become a parent is a major and devastating loss for a young person to contemplate.

Disfigurement often brings rejection by one's peers, or spouse and even children. It is noticeable how often young people will tend to stop visiting a friend who is wasting away with cancer. Older folk tend to do this too in some cases.

A mastectomy often causes a woman more anguish than any other operation. Her very body image is destroyed. She feels herself to be unattractive and unacceptable to her husband or other men. She feels herself to be less than a woman. Some women cannot bear to look at their body full length in a mirror following such an operation. Many a husband has separated from his wife because for him some of her sexual appeal has gone. Other husbands have slept in another room and abandoned any physical intimacy with the wife. After surgery, a woman suffering such feelings of mutilation is apprehensive about leaving hospital. What will the home response be to her disfigurement?

Surgeons are aware of these responses and are continually adjusting their surgical techniques to eliminate as much disfigurement as possible. Reconstruction surgery also is amazingly successful.

Surgeons are more thoughtful these days as to where they make the incision for an operation. They try to make it in crease lines or wherever it will not affect the wearing of beach clothes.

Amputations are a most obvious form of mutilation. The loss of a foot or the leg to the knee or thigh is an horrendous thought. Many resist or delay to the last possible moment before agreeing to such surgery, much to the frustration of the surgeon. In so many cases a prosthesis or artificial limb can ensure that the patient resumes a more or less normal lifestyle, including some sporting activities.

In the ward there was an 84-year-old evangelist of amputation. He had feared and refused the doctor's advice until he was 82 years old. There was then no other option: he had to have his leg amputated above the knee, or die. An artificial limb was fitted. He regained a lot of his previously lost activity. Above all he was free from pain in that limb. He came in for a second amputation when his remaining leg showed similar symptoms and because he did not want to suffer unnecessary pain, as he had done before. This 84-year-old was moving around his fellow patients as an enthusiastic advocate of the success of modern artificial limbs, urging these other men and women not to hesitate having surgery.

A young man who had his wrist torn off in an industrial accident was a sporting and fitness fanatic. He saw his whole world shattered. Life wasn't going to be worth living. We talked about the possibilities of the future, including a vision of participating in the disabled Olympics. The biography of Dr. Mary Verghese was given to him. This book described how she developed her reconstruction surgery skills after having both her legs smashed. She had character. At one stage in the conversation it was suggested that a whole new world was opening up to him. During a later visit his remark was exciting: "I'm better off now, I've got two worlds—this one and the one as a disabled person.". He was seeing life from the two experiences. This resulted in personal growth and a positive stance toward his traumatic experience. The life-shattering became life-enriching.

Many fears of pain and mutilation are unfounded. Hospital treatment in most cases relieves pain. Mutilation and loss of parts of the body, whether internal or external, again can lead to greater personal growth and development as well as making life much more bearable physically. We can encourage these patients to acknowledge this fear, recognize its reality and then look to the positive gains physically, emotionally, and for them as a person.

LOSING CONTROL

Living in a democracy the words "liberty" "civil rights" "freedom of speech" are part not only of our thinking, but of our way of life. We are taught to be independent. Schools teach our children to do their own thing, think for themselves and to make their own decisions. When a person is hospitalized they come into an institution which is regulated with a system where staff are under constant surveillance to see that hospital protocol and treatment orders are efficiently carried out. Into this environment, independent individuals are introduced as patients. They have to obey instructions and often be subjected to a young student nurse attending to their personal hygiene. Frequently, they are stripped of their freedom even to get out of bed. They have to do as they are told.

For a business person, a woman who runs her household and children, or even a child used to being able to go out to play, this produces a sense of incapacity, loss of dignity and status. For many people there is humiliation, particularly when they are not permitted to even go alone to the toilet. The fear of this loss of independence and loss of control of various faculties due either to medication, surgery or an accident, raises inner anxieties which work against bodily healing. The patient's dignity and personal confidence are scurrying from their sight.

This fear of the loss of control is very real and the person can feel imprisoned within their own body. A young woman developed a rare disease which paralyzed her from the neck down. Even her breathing had to be assisted. She remained in hospital. She could not have existed without constant hospital supervision and facilities. Her two young children only saw her on Saturday afternoons. During the twelve months before she died, it was interesting to see her manipulation of the staff including pitting one against the other. She had to be removed from her original unit to another, the staff of the first unit forbidden to visit her. She had lost control of so much that she made efforts to control others in another way.

Patients do experience a loss of control. Patients whose condition is critical fear even greater loss of independence the longer their treatment continues. Our efforts should be to encourage them to do the things that they can. To rush to their aid and, for instance, pour them a drink which they are capable of pouring, only reinforces dependence. Any attempt to restore to them a sense of dignity and self-worth is important. "Overcare" can become overwhelming. Dignity is further eroded.

The combination of uncertainties, confusions, fears, anxieties, information and misinformation, fact and suppositions is never the same in any two patients, nor is it the same on any two visits. Effective pastoral visitation in hospital depends upon the minister, priest or lay visitor being fully aware of this. It requires time to sense where the patient is at. It must be remembered that the patient is often acting out of character due to the illness. Perhaps, for example, the church-going religious facade is not providing the same camouflage that is maintained outside the hospital. This revelation may be startling for the visitor.

The necessity to try and understand the complexity of feelings highlighted in this chapter cannot be overstressed. Begin your visit by assessing these. A similar time for assessment must be taken each visit and issues half-concluded in the previous visit should not be taken up until the appropriateness is ascertained. It may not be relevant on this visit.

Simply put, good advice is, "Get to know your patient's state of body, mind and spirit first on each visit." This leads to good pastoral care.

NOTES
1. Kubler-Ross, Elisabeth *On Death and Dying*
2. Stated by Kubler Ross at a workshop in Sydney 1979

8

Temptations

There are a number of eager people who seek opportunities to visit hospitals as a form of Christian service. Frequently such people come up and say to me "I love hospital visitation. You are able to get alongside really needy people." To love hospital visitation is an inappropriate expression. Hospital visitation is exacting: it demands concentration and so often is physically, spiritually and emotionally draining. Often it can appear unrewarding. Such times are compensated for by those very fulfilling, positive, even if vitality-sapping, traumatic ministrations to distraught, frightened, angry, or hurting patients or relatives. There are also those visits to some of God's saints, who minister more to you than you do to them.

The reception of the offered cup of water in Christ's name is often treated with suspicion and even sometimes scorn, but others will drink and Christ will be honored.

To hear a person say that they love hospital visitation is to hear warning bells concerning that person's effectiveness around the wards. Most experienced, trained workers, as well as hospital pastoral workers new to visitation, all face temptations when they come to the bedside or are dealing with relatives. Some of the more common temptations will be covered here. Some of these may find earlier echoes in this book. They are reintroduced here in another guise to reinforce an awareness of our need to be conscious of the pitfalls. All of us face them, all of us will continue to succumb to them on occasions.

TO SET A PROGRAM

Is this a familiar scenario? A hospital visit is planned. The pocket edition of the New Testament and Psalms is taken, after carefully selecting the passage that will be read. The same reading is used for each patient. Of course, the traditional passages are trotted out. One day a partly deaf lady at a nursing home loudly explodes, "Why is it that you ministers always read Psalm 103?" The lesson is learnt!

If a visitor goes along with a set program for four patients—allowing twenty minutes each—subconsciously there is recorded that after about 15 minutes there must be the Bible reading and prayer before leaving. The offer of these is the indication that the visit has ended.

Such set programs take no account of the circumstances of each patient. It can be safely assumed that the same passage of scripture will *not* meet the needs of all four patients. They will be in differing stages of hospitalization. Their needs, physical and spiritual, will require different touches.

A set program or agenda will not provide an effective ministry. One chaplain, who developed a set routine, boasted of visiting over one hundred patients each day. His ministry was considered worthless by patients and staff of the hospital. The staff would call others in an emergency rather than send for him.

Those who set agendas are more preoccupied with self-achievement than the welfare of the patient or family. Self-achievement as a goal can be a threat to hospital ministry.

PAUSES IN CONVERSATION

Whether it be in a prayer meeting or at a hospital bedside, it is surprising how we are embarrassed by silence. There are many situations when silence is so necessary for the patient. The patient may be unable to concentrate through debilitation, tiredness, drug effects, or sheer pain and discomfort. Your silent presence on such occasions is the most appropriate form of care at that point of need.

A patient may be so bewildered and confused that a multiplicity of thoughts are rivalling each other for the mind's attention. Your chatter may add further distraction to an already-overcrowded mind.

Your presence or something you may have said may have raised issues about which there is a desire for discussion. The patient, recognizing the need to open up, is also reticent to make the disclosure. The struggle to find the opening gambit is disturbed if the pastoral visitor's uncomfortableness with the silence is obvious.

Pauses in conversations may indicate many things. They often provide the opportunity to regroup thoughts or to allow what has just been said to be fully applied and digested. Rushing in to break the silence may squash and repress the very thing which might have made the visit productive.

TO BECOME THE FOCUS

A minister or an official pastoral visitor has a special status and position. There is a certain expectation by the patient which the visitor feels must be seen to be fulfilled. They must be seen to be doing their job and making sure that conversation flows. To keep the conversation going it is easy to talk about personal experiences. The whole meeting then becomes centered on the visitor. The patient's needs and circumstances are fully put aside. It becomes a lively, happy, interesting and perhaps even informative time. The visitor has become the star, the patient the ignored.

Visitors sometimes delight in talking about their own periods of hospitalization and their own close encounters with death. It is an almost irresistible topic. At other times the visitor's illnesses become the depressing focus of the visit, which is even more disastrous.

The visitor probably departs feeling elated that everyone was responsive. Prayer was offered. The visit was successful. The patient when alone might think it was nice of the visitor to call— but! He or she may also smart at the slight shown during the visit.

So obsessed was the visitor with making the visit a success that the real reason for it was lost in the parade of self. When self comes to the fore, the wrong motivation becomes evident.

TO "OUT TALK" THE PATIENT

A variation on the temptation for the carer to do most of the talking is the person who is a compulsive talker. This type of person is a chronic interrupter of conversation, who "talks over" other people. Such persons have real difficulties with truly listening to others. Very often they volunteer for a hospital visitation role, where they find a captive audience with little reserve or energy to put them in their place.

They are often kindly people who have an open heart. They are anxious to help but their need to be accepted is greater. It is generally recognized that this need to talk, to help and to be accepted has its origins in unsatisfactory childhood relations.

This type of person should be recognized when a lay pastoral team is being selected. It is not easy to cull such people from a hospital visitation program without hurting the already-sensitive feelings which are the cause of their compulsive talking.

Patients may become deeply distressed and anxious when a person is talking over them all the time and they are not being heard. The priest or minister or lay pastoral team leader should be ever-conscious of the possibility of such a person being in their group. This is where supervision and feedback from the group is so important in hospital ministry.

TO COMPARE PATIENTS

At times, chaplains as well as other pastoral visitors find themselves guilty of likening the patient's condition to that of similar and even dissimilar cases. Some visitors have a penchant for describing every like diagnosis they have experienced or heard about.

The odd illustration of a case may be made to help a patient deal with a particular situation, to encourage hope. Sometimes it may be necessary by this means to prepare the patient for the reactions that may be expected from the treatment. A comparison may be the balm to soothe unrealistic fears.

The danger in citing other cases is that firstly you do not have the full medical facts of both cases to justify making comparisons. Secondly, the other case may be that of an identifiable person. It is unethical to use the case without that person's permission. Thirdly, it is likely that the patient is so immersed in their own situation that reference to anybody else indicates that you are not really interested in them. Fourthly, you are likely to be judged as one interested only in airing your knowledge.

TO PROVIDE SOLUTIONS

One of the most abused terms today is the word "counselor." It seems that anyone who completes some short course or attends a number of seminars or conferences feels justified in calling her or himself a counselor. We hear of telephone counselors, bereavement counselors, family counselors and so on. Unless they have done several hundreds of hours of supervised counseling they have no right to be called counselors. Lay pastoral care courses and even most theological college courses do not entitle a minister or a visitor to be classified as a counselor.

Many bedside encounters see the visitor coming in as the counselor like a ferret trying to find a problem or difficulty needing solution. Some pastoral care workers feel as if their visit has not been successful unless they have been able to be the knight in shining armor riding to the rescue of the patient.

Pastoral visitors have no brief to prove that they are counselors extraordinaire. The attempt may satisfy the ego needs of the carer (placing a question mark on the title "carer" in such circumstances), but does little for the confidence of the patient. The perceptive patient recognizes that the visit is most probably to fulfill those needs.

There are the occasions when patients are seeking some comfort, help and advice. More likely the need is to sort matters out themselves with a little guidance. The carer becomes the facilitator for the patient to begin to view events less subjectively. The patient is given room to think out aloud, to reappraise and to change mental, emotional and spiritual attitudes.

Mrs. Jones had just been told of the need to have urgent surgery. Her disease was life-threatening and she was told that surgery might give her two or three more years. She didn't want her children upset by the news. The doctor had left her to talk it over with the family and let him know the decision the next day. I was called to Mrs. Jones because she was very depressed and feared surgery. She pleaded with me to tell her what to do. This was my first visit. After having the above scenario outlined to me prior to the visit I said, "Well, let's look at the situation."

I got her to talk about her children and her grandchildren, the nature of their relationship, what their hopes and aspirations were. Mrs. Jones also outlined what she wanted to do and looked at the possibilities.

She was asked what she understood the doctor had said. She reported that the doctor had said if her heart stood up to the surgery and she came through, there was every chance of no further trouble although he would commit himself to no more than two or three years. Prior to my seeing Mrs. Jones, I had ascertained that the prognosis following surgery was reasonably good.

Mrs. Jones shared her feelings about an early death. She also became excited about what it would mean if the operation were successful. Without expressing my own mind, I continued to let her talk until she came to the decision to go ahead with the surgery. It was worth the risk, she decided.

We prayed for a right attitude of mind and spirit by Mrs. Jones as she went to theater, as well as for her to experience God's guidance through the surgery and after. She told the family of her decision that evening.

Mrs. Jones came through the surgery successfully, having entered theater with a deep peace, which came from her feeling of having made the right decision.

It was her decision, she was not coerced into it. This fact was possibly a significant factor in the success of the surgery. The chaplain facilitated the decision.

TO ORGANIZE THE PATIENT

Enfeebled by illness, the patient often presents a picture of help-lessness and forlornness. The pastoral carer in an image of health and vitality, might come marching in, mistakenly thinking to produce in the patient a better state of mind, a smile on the face, a happier and a more peaceful disposition.

Helplessness may stimulate maternal or paternal instincts in the carer. The need to smother the patient with overconcern becomes a distinct possibility. The patient begins to visualise the carer as a type of old-fashioned matron, who busily fluffs up the pillow, fills the water jug with fresh water, redoes the floral arrangement, tidies up the bedside locker, reads the get well cards, asks who they are from and orders tea or even holds the cup or props up the head to enable the patient to drink the afternoon tea.

The visitor is thus in control, organizing the patient—yes, and even at times ringing for the staff to do this or that for the patient. This looks very good to the visitor. The feeling of doing something worthwhile is exhilarating. The visitor is on a high.

The patient, however, may not be up to being fussed over. Rather than appreciating this fuss, he or she may resent it. The dominating visitor may seem to be tightening the screws of help-lessness. The spirit of the patient may be crushed even further. A domineering pastoral visitor wearies and saps away a little more of patients' dwindling physical reserves. Encouraging them, instead, to do something for themselves is often more helpful.

TAKE OVER THE ROLE OF THE RELATIVES

A pastoral visitor may not be an overpowering person but, driven by the demand to be a good pastoral worker, she or he may feel a strong desire to become an indispensable figure to the patient. There are a number of things which are the prerogative of rela-tives or other closer friends to see to. These include washing the patient's clothes, mowing the patient's lawn and watering the garden, paying accounts (such as telephone and electricity) which cannot be deferred. The offer to pay such accounts, like many other manipulative approaches of this nature, may become more than offers. The patient may feel obligated to give permission to proceed to do these tasks.

This type of role assumption and the need to feel indispensable may not only cause distress to the patient but also lead to friction between the relatives and the patient. The relatives' position must be deferred to by the pastoral worker.

Hospitalization of a sick relative provides the opportunity for some relatives to make up for previous neglect and lack of communication and concern. Such relatives are resentful of a visitor who appears to usurp their role. That antagonism increases if they are thwarted from assuaging their guilt for those years of disinterest by not being able to make these practical efforts for the ease and comfort of the patient's mind.

Where patients have no interested relations or friends, such help may be very appropriate and appreciated. Other members of the church family may be involved to further encourage these patients, showing that people are interested in them and care for them. If you are a busy pastoral person, then other people with practical skills and time should be given the opportunity to exercise them.

TO FORCE LOGICAL AND RATIONAL POSITIONS

We have already noted that one of the coping mechanisms of patients facing a difficult prognosis is to hear only as much as they are able to bear at the time. It is extremely difficult to listen to a patient talking about resuming athletics training when you know of mutilated tendons and calf muscles. This particular patient had been on his way to the top. The Commonwealth and Olympic games had seemed a real possibility. Now there was no way that track events could feature in his future.

"How kind it would be to snap him back to reality." "We can't let him keep going on with this delusion." "He must begin to face reality and try to think positively about life without athletics." These thoughts entered a lot of John's visitors' minds. The fact is that John had been told about his condition by the doctors and it had been confirmed by nurses and physiotherapists. John at that stage was unable to grapple with the thought of a life without physical prowess. The blow of the accident also affected study and employment prospects.

Impatience on the part of the pastoral care visitor can rival family pressure to be the one to put the patient right. The pressure to force John to accept a logical and rational appraisal of his position was hard to resist. What I did was encourage him to maintain hope for a fulfilling and satisfying future life. I spoke of the "Disabled Games."

There may come an appropriate time to reinforce the true situation. However, it would have been unwise to lock into John's subconscious the conviction that he would never again be useful. That would be a very depressing prospect for a virile youth to tackle. His denial of this gives him something to fight to regain.

Much response to hospital and other treatment is due to a positive mental approach. To destroy that approach by coercing a patient to accept reality prematurely is likely to impair the will to recover. It is likely to be presumptuous on the part of the pastoral care worker to assume the responsibility to press the issue. Where it develops, after a long period, into a pathological issue, then more professional help may need to be sought.

This applies to all hospital cases where a radical lifestyle change apppears the only option or where there is a terminal diagnosis.

As a postscript, since writing the above, I have received news that John has won gold at a World Disabled Games in Japan, in the discus event.

TO TAKE UP THE CUDGELS

The patient and the family sometimes are overwhelmed with the magnitude of their impending loss and the current circumstances. They are all in a state of shock. They feel they must be seen to be doing something for the patient. This is particularly true when the patient has always been mollycoddled by the family. Equally so, at the other extreme when previously the patient has been neglected—the need to assuage the guilt of that indifference is keenly felt.

In such cases, the patient in the relatives' eyes becomes the only and most important patient there ever was. Service is expected beyond the consideration of other patients and staff responsibility. When that is not forthcoming, the staff are castigated for presumed inefficiencies, such as the 12 noon medicine rounds not coming till 12.15 pm or a nurse taking 10 minutes to answer the call bell.

It is the basic assumption that the person from the church should carry more weight than relatives. The pastoral visitor is drafted into taking up the cudgels on behalf of the patient. The family often accompany the carer to see that he or she says and does what they have tutored him or her to say and do! The staff, however, are likely to treat the church visitor as one being manipulated by the family and so take little notice.

It is easy to be overwhelmed, like the relatives, at the loss being envisaged. The pastoral carer, through closeness to the family, may lose objectivity and become the defender and champion of the patient. Yet not always are the relatives' assumptions correct. Doctors' communications are not always interpreted accurately. The patient's and relatives' expectations of what should be done or what can be happening may be unrealistic given the nature of the case.

If you are tempted to take up the cudgels on behalf of the patient or family, it is wise to go alone to the hospital staff, and ask quietly about what is happening. It may be diplomatic to say you think there may be some misunderstanding and you would like to clear it up with the family. Such an approach will often bring co-operative responses and give you a much different picture. The staff may then seek your co-operation in helping the relatives to understand. The warning is: be sure of your facts before you become the champion of an alleged underdog.

TO DISSEMINATE KNOWLEDGE

Hospitals are involved with the lives of people. From the hospital's side all barriers are down. The patient's privacy in many areas no longer exists. The staff know the condition and often the cause of the condition. In some cases, such as sexually transmitted diseases, for example, it is a very personal affair. A person's bodily ills are their own personal matter yet they become necessary knowledge for the hospital and all too often this knowledge becomes available to the church, too. The church bulletin can become a serious offender in this regard...

Unfortunately, the source of information for those newsheets is sometimes the pastoral visitor. Yet to pass on such information without the permission of the patient and the relatives is a breach of confidentiality and is therefore indictable. A vindictive person could take you to court. These days the laws are very strict.

Requests have come from some patients who are active in their churches not to inform their parish minister of their stay in hospital. The reason is basically that they do not want the nature of their illness broadcast. It is sad that people have to forego spiritual comfort and help because pastoral people breach confidentiality sometimes .

Be worthy of the confidence placed in you during your hospital visitation.

TO ASSUME THE SOLE
PASTORAL ROLE

As an official visitor—priest, minister, sister, brother, deaconess or other religious leader—you are the one recognized by the church to offer pastoral care to a particular patient or family. You may not be the only pastoral person to call upon the patient regularly. Others may be a personal family friend of long standing, or a Christian work colleague who has shared many confidences over their long association. It may be a minister who married them or shared earlier life dramas. It may be the acquaintance who introduced them to the church scene. The person may be a trained person or an ordinary church member with no great claim to previous pastoral ministry.

Where pastoral care has become an ego-dominated ministry; where pride in being able to get on with people is projected; where there is a feeling of being better than others at visitation, and where personal status is important, then the temptation to adopt the role of *sole* pastoral carer becomes strong.

The patient or the relatives may have a greater rapport with another pastoral worker. It then becomes an embarrassment, confusing and disturbing for the patient, if the official church visitor subtly takes over. The patient and family may be hurt. The preferred visitor feels frustrated and angry, being thwarted in their efforts to provide the pastoral care the patient desires and needs. Competition in these circumstances is destructive for the patient, visitors and carers.

The grace to recognize and to defer to another, more appropriate person is a demonstration of your fitness to be involved in pastoral care. An inflated sense of ego is not needed in the hospital scene.

TO EXPECT A PATIENT'S OUTPOURINGS

Sometimes professional health care workers are referred to a patient whom nursing staff may consider to be acting inappropriately under the circumstances. They see the patient. They probe and delve until they get the emotional or other results they expect. Such tactics are often resented strongly by the patient and family.

Similarly, pastoral care workers can fall into the trap of considering that unless the patient has revealed something of their inner selves and feelings, the visit has been of little value. Such role expectation falls far short of what pastoral care is. It may take weeks, even months, before any free sharing may be possible. It may be that personal sharing of deeper feelings never occurs. This does not mean that the previous pastoral visits have been failures.

Patients may have no need to bare feelings and emotions. They are coping and have the very strong supportive care of family and friends. They may be having considerable drug treatment or recovering from an operation and finding it a struggle to concentrate on anything. To be forced to try and stir up even dormant feelings is just too much effort. It may be completely unnecessary. It is an intrusion of privacy in such cases.

A pastoral care worker who considers that care is not being given unless a "deep and meaningful" conversation has eventuated is putting role expectations above the best interests of the patient. A patient is under no obligation to accept the pastoral care visitor or to reveal more of themselves than they wish.

TO CONCENTRATE ON SOMETHING ELSE

There are two aspects of this temptation which need to be understood. The first is patient-initiated. Patients may not desire to be involved in any discussion about themselves or their illness with you as a church representative. This is their right. In exercising this prerogative they may deliberately turn the conversation to every other topic to occupy the time and save embarrassment. Attention is often deliberately directed to another patient for this reason.

To understand the real reasons for these diversionary tactics you should be alert. Possibly it is an indication that the patient is avoiding any serious involvement with the church. Or there may be something about you that is providing a barrier to confidence. An earlier unpleasant experience with the church may contain the embers of resentment and possible bitterness. Again, the patient may be still denying the seriousness of the illness and would not be able to cope with reality at this stage. Another possibility is that the patient is harboring some guilt feeling toward church and you have become a reminder of the spiritual ulcer within.

The second aspect is the initiation of the diversion by the pastoral visitor, who finds it difficult to come to grips with the patient's condition. Rather than face the uncomfortableness of talking about the illness and concentrating on the patient, the carer sees other subjects as safer. However, although the conversation might be interesting, informative and even spiritually uplifting, when the patient is struggling with his or her own doubts, anger and grief, such otherwise grippingly-important themes fall flat. And the patient is patently aware of the large detour the carer is taking.

Again the pastoral visitor must be aware of what is happening within the patient. A helpful line when the side-tracking is being done by the patient is to accept it. Other times it should be noted that the guilt or fear being experienced is what the patient is desirous of facing, yet hesitant personally to open out on the subject. Perceptive skills, adeptness at gently lifting lids, and empathy make the combination needed. The pendulum must swing.

TO STAY TOO LONG

Sometimes there is a tendency to stay too long. The patient may be the only one you have to visit in the hospital. The thought arises, "I've taken the trouble to come, so I may as well make it worthwhile." Depending upon the illness, the stage of its development, and the condition of the patient, a long visit may be the last straw. Your visit may become a further endurance trial for the patient.

On the other hand, your presence for a long period silently sitting there while the patient dozes, may be just the comforting assurance needed to relax enough to get some of that elusive sleep. Time and again as a chaplain I have found it possible to support a patient until they have fallen into a deep sleep and their grip on my hand has loosened, allowing it to be slipped out. The next call may then be made. Time spent like this is of immense value to the patient. For this to happen the patient must feel comfortable in your presence and be given full permission to sleep without any offence. The length of stay is assessed by your own sensitivity to the patient's needs.

There are pastoral workers who have assumed that the object of their visit is to cheer the patient up. There is a seemingly subconscious acceptance of the entertainer's role. It is viewed as a time of filling in the lonely hours for a patient. A pastoral visitor's role in a general hospital is not that. There may be some very lonely or frightened patients who may need and appreciate your presence, but not as an entertainer. Rather they would prefer you as an understanding friend who is able to listen to them without being advice-giver or counselor and who is able to appreciate true companionship at such a time. The entertainer seldom realizes when enough is enough. A showman is rarely welcomed by a very sick person.

Another reason for a prolonged stay may be that the visitor is waiting for an opportunity to say goodbye. Other visitors are monopolizing the conversation—you are sitting back and listening. It would appear rude to interrupt. In such cases your visit is not very productive. Your time might be more profitably spent with someone else. Politely excuse yourself, unless the patient requests you to stay in the hope that the other talkative people will depart instead.

Sometimes a carer might find it hard to conclude a visit because of a sense of not having accomplished what was intended. The agenda-setting fallacy is producing guilt feelings. Consider that a visit committed through prayer to the Holy Spirit's guidance *has that guidance.* Your own agenda may be most inappropriate at that time. Accept the situation. To prolong the visit waiting for your opportunity to do your thing may be closing those doors of opportunity to you forever.

Let it be repeated, sensitivity is the key in determining the length of time spent at each bedside.

TO BE THE EVANGELIST

There are those, both clergy and laity, who believe they as Christians must present the gospel or be assured that the patient is right with the Lord every time they visit a bedside. If the patient should die that night, they would feel responsible for his or her eternal status, good or bad, the latter being the greater fear.

There are some very basic theological and ethical flaws in this attitude. Without the Holy Spirit being able to break through and prepare a person's spirit for any sort of spiritual impact in their lives, all our talking is of little consequence. If the Holy Spirit does the work, we must be working in partnership and co-operation with that same Holy Spirit. Not every person is ripe for the harvest. In normal experience the Spirit would not give carte blanche to any individual to approach any and every patient in this way. Every patient is not ready for, or in a fit state to be able to comprehend the message of the gospel. Experience proves that with many the attempt to preach it drives an even bigger wedge between the person, the church, God and the carer. It also can cause a sudden deterioration in the patient's condition.

Any approach to the patient in this way should be with the patient's permission and when the patient is not too distressed with the progress of the disease. Partnership with the Spirit will enable the carer to detect the right moment—if there is to be one—when the Spirit wishes to use him or her for such an encounter.

A rigid and fixed agenda is likely to be cold, clinical and mechanical. It is similar to the door knocking routine of certain religious enthusiasts. The acutely perceptive patient is apt to switch off, hearing little of what is being communicated. Elsewhere it has been pointed out that God is able to use many avenues and resources beyond the theological methods we cling to so dearly.

The visitor has to earn the right from the patient to raise spiritual matters. It is seldom in a first visit that sufficient rapport is built up to launch into selling the gospel. Even if the patient was previously known to the visitor, circumstances have changed. The cause of hospitalization may be concealing many matters unknown to the visitor. To assume a right to know under such circumstances may be counter-productive. Time is required to ascertain if that is possible, where the patient is spiritually. Probing into the personal may be a breach of privacy.

Similarly, uninvited spiritual delving is breaching privacy. If your visit has been committed to God's guidance, allow the Spirit to open the door for you. A jemmied entry is unappreciated.

There is so much that we have to learn about God; we should not place limitations and expect God to conform to our ideas. Hospital visitation requires a great trust. We must believe, along with Job, that our just God will do what is right.

TO BE UNNATURAL

A hospital is an unnatural environment. People tend to act unnaturally there. The patient is treated unnaturally by relatives and visitors. For most people, medicine carries the feeling of the mystical. The doctors' language is often hard to decode. The nurses are rushing, busy, busy, busy. Pastoral carers likewise tend to approach the bedside differently from the way they handle other situations. There must of course be a difference because of the circumstances, but that difference should not interfere with your being yourself with the patient.

An artificial voice, whispered tones, nervous body language, stilted conversation, taboo subjects, wary responses, or exuberant laughter and loud talk are signs of the unnatural. It is all part of a game: the "Conspiracy Play," the "Near Death Drama," the "Panic Opera" or perhaps the "Marilyn Melodrama." There are times when the pastoral worker gets sucked into this unnaturalness.

Basically the patient requires you to act naturally when all else around is seemingly unnatural. There are certain normal restraints required in hospital visitation. To go beyond that is to indicate the unnatural.

In being yourself, you are being true to yourself and honest with the patient. In the midst of the artificiality around, the patient will be more likely to respond to you if you are yourself, and your ministry will, therefore, be more acceptable.

TO COERCE THE PATIENT

In any ministry we expect results. Hospital ministry can bring with it an air of urgency. The patient may or may not survive. The shortage of time can put pressures upon the pastoral person to try to get the patient to complete as much unfinished business as possible. Perhaps some relationships are strained.

Suppose the patient and another person in the church have had a running feud over the years. It is desired that they accede to some form of reconciliation. The obstinacy still continues in spite of the threat to the life of the hospitalized parishioner.

With all good intentions, the pastoral carer sets out to find a solution. The temptation is to manipulate the patient to admit wrong attitudes, to express regret over what has happened, to seek reconciliation. This is all in order that the patient might die in peace. In one way or another the visitor tries to force words out of the patient, words which the patient does not want to say. Or, even more unethical, to offer a prayer on behalf of the patient using the words the patient refuses to utter. (Confrontation is considered in Chapter 10.)

To coerce the patient into speaking or to say the words for him or her, implies that the patient is forced into a position or meaning which the visitor desires him or her to adopt and not what may be best.

The manipulative deceit of this type of move generally causes adverse reaction and hostility within the patient. At other times, being so debilitated and not wishing to get further agitated, the patient acquiesces to the visitor's maneuvers but unwillingly. The whole exercise is a falsehood. The patient often gives in just to get the visitor to depart more quickly. The zealous evangelist is prone to succumb to this temptation.

Manipulation is a temptation to which zealous evangelists are particularly prone. Coercion of a dying patient or critically ill person is morally and ethically wrong and cannot be accepted as Christian behavior.

TO HIDE BEHIND THE SCRIPTURES

The hospital is the place to hear questions and doubts about God that are unanswerable. Challenges to faith are seriously made. Even the most devout find it difficult to accept the unfairness of some of the pain and suffering experienced. Job-like situations are faced.

Many pastoral care workers, including theologically trained clergy, find answers that are logically integrated hard to come by. It is difficult to discover responses that satisfy theologically acceptable norms. Theology and practice seem poles apart.

It is tempting to produce a copy of scriptures and read some of the promises therein. The patient is told that God's grace is sufficient. The words of Christ, promising never to leave or forsake them, are expected to provide comfort. Psalms urging "trust in the Lord with all your might" stir scepticism. The scriptures are offered as a blanket cover to challenges to faith, and to question them is considered a sin. The guilt associated with doubt is added to the heavy burden already imposed upon the patient.

Some pastoral care workers hide behind scriptures as a ruse to avoid the unanswerable embarrassments. The patient, however, requires direct personal communication. To read scriptures in such circumstances seldom is effective. In my view it more often destroys communication. If scriptures are to be used, they should not destroy the eyeball-to-eyeball communion. Scriptures should flow sincerely from the heart, out of your own experience. The scripture should be made vital and alive, not at odds with the current ordeal the patient is experiencing. The printed page kept in the pocket, while its truth flows out of the mouth relevant to the practical needs of the patient, is the ideal. Where this is not possible, it is best to reserve the scripture for a more acceptable occasion, if it arises.

WHERE THERE IS DOUBT AND READY ANSWERS ARE NOT FORTHCOMING, BE HONEST, ADMIT YOU DON'T HAVE AN ANSWER.

There are other temptations facing the hospital visitor. Chaplains, visiting clergy and lay pastoral workers all, in varying degrees of frequency, fall into these snares. It is training, experience, empathy, awareness and sensitivity combined that will reduce the rate and regularity of the falls.

True pastoral care is hard and demanding work. We can take heart from the knowledge that the Holy Spirit has promised to give wisdom and understanding for each circumstance.

9

The Place of Prayer

An innate trait of the human race is the ability to pray. For many it has been suppressed by social pressures, scientific scepticism or the current growth of humanism which sees God as of little or no relevance to human existence.

"Immortalists," a relatively new philosophical group, are waiting for medical science to advance to the point where humans will not die. They want to live on earth forever without ageing and firmly believe that in the next generation this will be quite possible. It will make God and the need for prayer irrelevant, they say.

Yet, in spite of religious apathy, agnosticism, or antagonism, that inherent tendency to pray in a crisis remains. Across the millennia there have been those who have been set apart to communicate with the deity or deities on behalf of other people. All religions have had their shamans, priests and ministers to intercede for others.

Since the advent of Christ, the individual's right to pray directly to God has become a distinctive feature of Christianity. With education and the general liberation of access to theological knowledge and experience in Christianity, prayer individually, in small groups and corporately, has become more generally practised. In hospital, the patient is often longing to hear a prayer offered to God on their behalf.

In their pastoral duties in hospitals fewer chaplains are using manuals in their visitations. Lay pastoral workers are increasingly using prayer as a means of bringing spiritual assurance, comfort and hope at the bedside. Personal prayer becomes for many the focal point of the pastoral visit.

The two big questions that we will deal with in this chapter are: when and how to pray?

WHEN TO PRAY

Prayer "is a most powerful tool and requires care in its use.." These are potent words from Richmond,[1] who warns that it is possible to abuse prayer. It is sometimes used as a weapon, by busy people, to get away from the talkative patient. Others may use it as a means of avoiding issues the patient is raising.

Two traditional concepts

There are two traditional concepts as to when a visitor on a pastoral call should pray:

- on every visit
- only when asked

1. Praying on every visit

Whether a home or hospital visitation, it was always expected that a priest or pastor should pray with the person or family on every visit. This has become a tradition. Some lay pastoral care courses even promote it. Thus there are those pastoral workers who have ticked it off as a regular "to do" of pastoral visitation.

Not only is there a sense of expectation that a hospital visit must include prayer, but pastoral visitors may use prayer to maintain a role, to project an image. In such cases whether the patient desires it, or would like to reject it, prayer becomes the essential ingredient for the successful visit. We should ask, "Whose need is being met?"

There are dangers in making prayer a fixed rule for every visit:

Ritualization. Prayer becomes ritualized when it is part of the agenda for every visit. The tendency is to carry a prayer book or one of the minister's manuals which has prayers for the visitation of the sick. If these are said by rote, almost without reading the words, they come across to the patient as lacking in sincerity and real interest in the patient. The visitor is just fulfilling the role expected.

Even the administration of sacraments, such as the anointing of the sick and holy communion, may be interpreted in a similar vein. Prayer and the sacraments must contain more personal meaning for the patient than the mere fulfilling of a ritual obligation. The inclusion of the patient's name does not of itself indicate a personal concern by the carer.

Generalization. When prayer is expected to be offered at every bedside it is possible to detect a pattern in each prayer and visit. The prayers become generalized: a bit of theology; thanksgiving for the hospital staff, for the patient's healing, even when the prognosis is poor; and finally a prayer for the patient's family (usually vague on details). It more or less is a prayer where God is asked to bless them all—whatever that would mean to a patient feeling particularly unblessed!

The sigh of the patient on seeing the visitor enter muffles an inaudible "not again" or "for goodness sake, go away." Such feelings about the pastoral visitor are sometimes relayed to the full-time chaplain or staff.

Superficiality. A ritual or general prayer may also be perceived as being superficial and shallow. Visitors who always pray are either very confident of their ability as pastoral care workers or, at the other extreme, are very nervous and do not know what to say. The confident ones breeze in as if in control and offer prayer without much thought, because they have done it so many times before. Let the reminder be sounded again—patients are very perceptive of superficiality.

The nervous person, on the other hand, usually prays in the familiar language of the church, to cover up the awkwardness of inexperience, embarrassment or even a fear of identification with the patient. This results in an inability to become involved. The relationship and the prayer remain at a superficial level. The patient feels little comfort from such a visit which may in fact, stir up anger.

Piety. Even the most conscientious visitor steeped in his or her religion is often bound by theological upbringing from early childhood. Language has changed. The younger generation is more realistic about life and religion. If the old pious talk at the bedside is repeated in the prayer, a sentimentalism is detected which in no way suits the patient's condition. Even active church-goers are sometimes irritated by such pietistic praying. Much of the meaning and intent is garbled because of the mix of religious language. The patient may begin to wonder whether the visitor knows what the prayer really means.

Self-righteousness. The role of a pastoral care person in a hospital should carry with it a sense of responsibility. Very often visitors have little training and experience. Sometimes they interpret experiences wrongly and, like Little Jack Horner, say "What a good boy am I!". In fact he was a naughty boy for putting his thumb in the pie. These people have an underlying feeling that they have to prove to the patient and the church they are competent for the task of pastoral care. Their prayers they see as a means of advertising that they are spiritually right. The prayers are flowery, showing their wide range of scriptural knowledge and reverence of God. They are an avenue for the display of self-righteousness. Of course the report goes back to the church of how well accepted they were and how their prayer was very much appreciated. Whether this really was the case or not is beside the point. The appearance of being sincere and faithful in ministry was maintained.

Authoritarianism. There is a tendency to accept that if a certain act, procedure or ritual is performed, the one officiating has a function elavated above the others. An inner tension is often there until the task has been performed. The officiator perhaps is aware of this and assumes command until the duty is complete. The need to orchestrate procedures and the timing of them is a matter of prestige. Frequently that pressure rises until the order comes, "Let us Pray," or, in a more patronising way, "Would you mind if I prayed with you?" The latter really gives no option for the patient who, feeling like a captive, is obliged to keep this authority figure from the church happy.

The patient is in an inescapable trap. The prayer which follows is often accompanied by seething inner feelings at this further whittling away of the patient's independence and dignity. This, of course, goes completely unnoticed by the carer who has apparently fulfilled his or her appointed responsibility.

Even a polite "May I have prayer with you?" puts patients on the spot. To refuse outright leaves them open to the judgment of being unspiritual. What Perry and Sell wrote of the depressed patient may be equally said of many other kinds of patients we visit: "*Sometimes when you feel down, you don't need more prayer... You need a good night's sleep...*When there is adequate cause for feelings of depression we should not feel an urgent need to get right with God or to restore the joy of salvation."[2]

Heretical as this may sound to people of the "always pray" tradition, it carries much sound Christian counseling wisdom. People need to work through some of their bitterness and anger —perhaps even toward God—at being hospitalized, before prayer should be contemplated. But the authoritarian visitor insists it be done his or her way.

Where prayer might be an appropriate offering, an enquiry such as "Would you like me to pray with you today or some other time?" is fitting. This saves embarrassment and gives the patient the freedom to say "Some other time."

Even so, the patient may feel guilty in refusing. If this is likely, a further release clause is possible: "Sometimes the last thing we want to do is to pray. God understands when we feel like that. It's okay if you don't desire me to pray."

2. Praying only when asked

This tradition is the easy way to fulfill the responsibility of being tuned in to the patient.

It avoids the awkwardness of not knowing what to pray. You meet a person whose child is in intensive care with severe brain damage. Or maybe a man in his forties with leukemia or AIDS. What and how do you pray in such circumstances? To be able to pray, or to know if prayer is needed, requires a lot of concentration on what the person is feeling. What if the patient is withdrawn and the relatives are doing the talking?

Do you respond more to the relatives' needs or the patient's desires? If there is no request for prayer, the policy of praying only when asked lets the pastoral visitor off the hook.

There would be many an occasion when the patient and family would welcome the support and comfort that a few well-chosen words of prayer bring.

AIDS patients, irrespective of the manner in which they contracted the disease, often have an overwhelming sense of ostracism and rejection which is real and hurting. Church folk in particular may be ignorant and judgmental when it comes to the question of AIDS. For such patients, to be accepted by the pastoral visitor is unbelievably reassuring and spirit-boosting. For some, a prayer to God on their behalf can promote faith in God and the church. It may require a little initiative on the part of the visitor to assess the possible acceptability of prayer and then make an open-ended offer.

It avoids embarrassment . The embarrassment of having an offer of prayer refused extends both to the visitor and the patient. To refuse someone from the church is a courageous thing to do. The possibility of being labeled and branded by the church is likely if the carer reports back to the pastoral care group. Usually the patient knows this. Some patients, of course, do this to test the sincerity of the pastoral visitor. If genuine, the pastoral visitor will come back again and again, quite unperturbed by the refusal.

All the same, pastoral visitors do not expect to be refused. In their own opinion they are making a sacrifice in visiting the hospital and may feel hurt and rejected and look upon the patient as an ingratiate. This, of course, does not add to the confidence or the willingness of people to remain in pastoral care ministry.

It avoids dishonesty in praying. Some sections of charismatic and pentecostal movements place a priority of emphasis upon the ministry of healing. A pastoral visitor is expected to pray for healing and a complete cure.

There are also unchurched families. Their language and behavior indicate their irreligious stance. Yet these people, as patients, often welcome the pastoral worker as if they were staunch believers. The pastoral care worker may be faced with the need to minister to them and may be expected by the family to do so, almost as though to provide and ensure a place at the heavenly table.

The need to care for all people with all sorts of expectations is acknowledged, but your ability to fulfill all those expectations is not realistic.

Calls come sometimes in the early hours of the morning to say that a patient has died and the relatives are not coming in but they would like a chaplain or pastoral worker to go and offer a prayer over the body. These requests often have an ulterior motive: they are meant to assuage the relatives' guilt over not coming in themselves.

Integrity and honesty must be maintained. Where prayer has not been requested but it is evident that it is expected, it must be offered sincerely and in faith. Many a time I have been expected to pray for a miracle, which I believed I could not do with a clear conscience. I have also been expected to give a one-way ticket to heaven by prayer! These pathways I have declined, offering prayer for what I could honestly present to God.

Prayers may be said for strength to cope with whatever may happen in the next few days, or that the patient may reach up to God seeking the peace which God alone can give, or that inner healing may be experienced, or that patience may be given to bear the pain or that relief may come from the unbearable.

There are times when I am comfortable in praying for healing. Such prayers are offered when I can pray with integrity. It emphasizes *listening and understanding*.

Listening and understanding may help the patient or relatives to modify some of their attitudes and perceptions, thus easing some of their tensions.

Pastoral care where possible should not stop there, however. Soulen categorically states that prayer is invariably appreciated, but experience compels me to disagree. A more accurate statement would be "prayer is in most cases appreciated." But I do agree with Soulen when he says: *"It (prayer) should arise, whether expressly requested or not, out of the natural development; if it does not, then it should never be forced." ³*

There are times, as he acknowledges, when prayer is not requested but is the natural progression in the pastoral visit. The blanket ban—that unless it is requested there should be no prayer—truncates what might have developed into a fruitful faith ministry in the life of the patient. The patient's expectations may be dashed. Doubts about the visitor's own motivations in hospital visitation may be raised, alongside the question of the visitor's spiritual qualifications.

The visitor needs to feel free and flexible enough to assess what is happening and respond accordingly. The unshackling from the rigid and inflexible enables her or him to adapt to whatever develops.

Soulen's warning should be underscored: prayer should never be forced.

The question for the pastoral carer in a general hospital is, "How do we know when we should pray?" Here are some clues that may indicate the patient's sympathetic attitude to religion and prayer.

INDICATORS FOR PRAYER

Open talk about prayer. The patient actually mentions prayer. It may be only a simple remark like "there are many people praying for me," or "my daughter goes to church and she has her church praying for me," or "I'm not a religious person but I have prayed since I took ill." It is reasonable to assume that such folk will appreciate an offer for prayer. There may be a rebuff occasionally because of their own embarrassment. It may need to be clearly explained that you will do the praying and they will listen.

On many occasions the patient responds by saying, "I don't know how to pray." This is a good opportunity to say that prayer is simply talking to God. When you pray, you tell God what your gut feelings are. After one such explanation the next day a mother said, "I told God how angry I was with him over my baby's condition. It works. I feel so much better now. It seems as if I know God now." Often people are reticent to pray because of anger toward God (see Appendix 6).

Christian literature at the bedside. A Bible, a daily Bible study program, Christian magazines or other Christian literature on the bedside table indicate a person's active Christian life. Such people seldom refuse the offer of prayer. In fact they often anticipate it.

There are occasions however, when such literature may lead to a misunderstanding. A religious mother or neighbor, concerned about the patient's spiritual welfare, have piled up this material, hoping that he or she might (with time on their hands) pick it up, read it and be converted. Such pressure stirs antagonism against religious people so that you may have to work harder to earn the confidence of the patient. Before any consideration of prayer, that literature may become the focal point at some stage of the visit. If there are indications of embarrassment or uneasiness, then drop the subject and avoid the suggestion of prayer until, if ever, the appropriate time arrives.

It is for this reason that I have emphasized *observation* when you first enter the ward. On your next visit you may find that the Christian literature has been put out of sight. This indicates that the shutters are still up for any religious talk or prayer. In such cases it will be your continuing acceptance of the patient as a person and not as a possible church statistic that may prove most fruitful.

Some religious conversation. The irregular or nominal church person often welcomes a visit, if they are not overwhelmed with visitors. Expect the possibility of a range of excuses for not being regular in church attendance. They may declare their faith and even remark that they have said to their spouse they must start going to church again now that the children are older. Such expressions help to relieve their own guilt feelings over their religious inactivity. It is unwise, however, to accept such talk as evidence that prayer is desired.

Hospitalization can provoke sincere consideration of where a person is at spiritually. Initially it may not be overtly expressed. The occasional, if not surreptitious, probing enquiry (sometimes relating to a hypothetical friend) is made. Such probes must be taken seriously and dealt with honestly and meaningfully for the patient. Discernment is required as to the opportune time to offer prayer as it is seldom asked for. The offer made too soon may stifle the search. It is in such circumstances that we must hold our balance. Religious earnestness must be tempered by patient judgment of the developing dynamics.

There are other people, of course, who by their ready conversation on spiritual matters, you automatically know would appreciate prayer. In such cases it is expected and desired. But there are those who would prefer someone from their own cultural background or denomination to pray.

With the exceptions noted, patient-initiated, uninhibited religious conversations are generally a good indication of the suitability of offering prayer.

Sharing of an immediate anxiety. Some, whether religious or not, have deep-seated problems or anxieties. Being a person representing the church, you are considered to be trustworthy and able to keep what is said in confidence. Your identification with the church presupposes that you have some access to God. The situation may require more than human solution. When it has been explicitly revealed, an offer of prayer may be accepted or the patient may simply request you to "remember it in your own prayers." The latter response is often from a religiously non-active person. If such a request has been made, you need to comply because the patient will certainly enquire as to whether you've kept your promise!

Information from family or staff. There are times when the patient is so low or in such deep distress that they open up to the nearest person, such as relatives, nurses, doctors, or other hospital staff. Some of these worries may pertain to spiritual issues.

The relatives or staff may express these matters to you, asking if you would be able to take them up or try to have the patient talk about them. When such circumstances arise, always ascertain if the patient's permission was received to relay the matter of the conversation. If such permission was not given, either ask the informant to seek such approval or go to the patient as if nothing has been said, while at the same time trying to provoke discussion in the area of concern.

The information received from the relatives and corroborated by the patient may give sufficient opening for prayer to be offered, even if not requested.

Spiritual intuition. I hesitate to list this indicator. It relies solely on the carer's personal relationship with God. I firmly believe that hospital ministry is one that requires a heavy dependence upon awareness and direction from the Holy Spirit.

Unfortunately, such direction is claimed by many who are more anxious to prove their spirituality and right living before others. The Spirit has been held responsible for too many questionable things.

There are times when you become highly sensitive to an inner prompting to introduce the spiritual dimension and prayer to patients. These times I like to call "holy moments." They are not everyday events, although some people would claim such experiences as being common occurrences. Holy moments are reserved for those times when human wisdom is notably unrevealing and when it is difficult to know whether prayer or other spiritual ministration is required. The holy moment of Holy Spirit inspiration is a cherished privilege coming at the exact moment of need.

When one or more of the above indicators are recognized, the question is, "How do I pray?"

HOW TO PRAY

There are several basic rules to be kept in mind. The first and most important one is:

Be brief. Seriously ill patients have a short concentration span. The prayer with such patients should be only thirty seconds to one minute. That allows for no flowery introduction to God. The Lord knows who the patient is and doesn't need to be told at such a time. The petition should be short and direct so that the patient will be able to understand. The prayers for patients not so seriously ill may be longer but kept meaningful and relevant.

A minister's family had been called to his bedside as death was imminent. A senior minister arrived with the family and offered prayer. This good man gave a recital to God of the patient's Christian service and repeatedly thanked God for his life. With eyes closed the senior minister prayed for almost ten minutes, completely unaware of the effect the strain of concentration was having on the patient. The family watched their loved one's weakening, painful struggle. The chaplain and the nursing unit manager behind the glass screen of the nurses' station watched and were about to intervene when the prayer stopped.

The good man died a few minutes later, having undergone stress that he should not have experienced. The senior minister made it obvious that he felt good about having prayed with his colleague just before he died and at having been able to "minister" to the family at such a time.

Pastoral care workers are often oblivious of the added strains and burdens they heap upon a patient because of insensitive and inappropriate behavior, as in this case.

Mention the patient's name and the names of relevant associates. The patient is often traumatized. The essential concerns are their own personal welfare and that of loved ones and close friends. When a person is heavily sedated, often only the names register and nothing else about the prayer. To hear those names means that all are brought under the umbrella of God's care. This is most comforting. Generalizations are irrelevant, meaningless and counter-productive at such times.

Summarize the salient points of the encounter. This should be done without interpreting or running contrary to the feelings of the patient. The prayer at the bedside is incarnational prayer.

You are praying the prayer that patients cannot pray for themselves because of their weakened powers of concentration. "Incarnational praying" means that the patient's mind and thoughts are being born in you and presented to God. This highlights the need to listen to the patient and the relatives without a personal commentary on what you think is going on.

Words such as "Lord, you know how (name) feels about what is happening to him or her," or "(name) has expressed the desire to quickly pass into your presence. Hear (name's) cry at this time," or "(name) has been talking about his son (son's name) who seems far from you. (Name) wants him and his wife (wife's name if known) and their children to be under your care" and so on. The emphasis is upon what the patient has expressed in the conversation.

This ability to reflect the patient's mind back to God exactly as expressed proves to the patient that:

- you were listening
- you understood
- you accepted the patient's feelings
- you shared in those feelings
- your concern for the patient is sincere
- you have empathized
- you truly demonstrated pastoral care.

Avoid trying to put into the patient's mind anything which is not there. In contrast to the above there are those visitors who do not agree with all the patient's theology and feelings, and they try to use the prayer to put the patient or the relatives straight on a few points. To expect a person to assent to a prayer with which they cannot agree is the easiest way to invite rejection and build tension.

Avoid religious jargon. Bedside praying needs to be simple, in plain understandable language. The religious jargon of previous generations is not understood. The words may carry the meaning of the King James era (1610 AD) and have different connotations today. It is most probable that any relatives present have not used such words for decades, if ever. Idiomatic language of today conveys the meaning more appropriately, without ambiguity. The use of simple colloquial language equates you with the patient. An air of "down to earth" reality and meaning is engendered by using everyday language.

Bring a sense of God's compassion. What is the purpose of prayer at the bedside? It has many facets. It presents patients' feelings to God so that they have a sense of relief that their feelings have been expressed. But this is insufficient. Patients need to feel that God's concern, love and compassion are available to them.

To know that the future—which is clouded due to a diagnosis, a test, surgery, or a psychiatric drug or radiological treatment—is somehow being watched over by a loving God is one of the greatest comforts and assurances that a patient may receive. That is consolidated when the prayer includes reference to the doctors and staff. Bringing an awareness of the presence of a compassionate God is one of the main purposes of the bedside prayer.

Encourage hope. A person without hope becomes suffocated by a forlorn feeling. Their condition usually deteriorates very rapidly. The pain and physical distress appear to become more intense. The patient withdraws even further. The pastoral care person seems almost to mock them by their righteous, healthy presence.

Prayer should encourage hope. Here the prayers must be nothing less than honest, not encouraging false hope. Paul Irion suggests that in cases where a patient has been told that it is a matter of days, hope may be expressed for some good days with pain control, and the support of staff, relatives, friends. He adds that a "deepening faith" is integral to this.[4]

There are times when prayers for physical healing are valid. I have prayed for healing of the body and the Holy Spirit has responded positively. I refer to healings which cannot be classified as psychological. But these occasions are rare. Many petitions for physical healing have not brought the same result. A healing prayer should only be offered when you have a strong inner spiritual conviction that such a prayer must be made.

Dobihal and Stewart see hope as distinct from wishing for better circumstances. Wishing is a passive emotion and not hope. Hope, they say, *"is a goal-directed vision that enables one to live effectively in the present and move trustingly toward future possibilities."* [5] Hope for a physical restoration which has become unrealistic can be turned into expectation of a new and better relationship and experience with God. Prayer, as well as the conversation before (if appropriate), should speak of and include such possibilities. The vision or hope must have some solid grounding in reality. Patients instantly express appreciation for prayers that provide realistic hopes.

Care with words and information. Be careful not to divulge privileged information that staff may have conveyed to you. Care should also be taken not to misread or exaggerate the patient's condition. Depressing wrong impressions may be conveyed by the prayer, including too many words about being "in glory with God." The patient may be denying the seriousness of the condition or there may have been no suggestion and no reason for thinking of death. Under such circumstances to mention eternal peace and glory, or even Heaven's anticipation, may give rise to despair, depression and mistrust of relatives and staff because it is assumed that the real condition is being kept from the patient. Patients have lost their will to survive, become a difficult management problem and slowly deteriorated for no medically apparent reason, following a pastoral carer's prayer.

Manipulative prayer is unethical. If the zealousness of some pastoral care workers to see the patient "right with God" before they die becomes the motive for praying, prayer becomes a manipulative tool to obtain their confession and commitment to God. It is blatantly dishonest and unethical. Its effect upon the patient is to increase hostility. For a cardiac patient, in particular, it can raise stress levels and affect blood pressure, predisposing a premature fatal episode. Time that might have been available to the patient to face spiritual issues has been sacrificed because of evangelical enthusiasm.

Breath prayer for the seriously ill. Ron DelBene has produced a helpful series of resource booklets (published by The Upper Room). In these he introduces "Breath Prayer." His method is to select a word or phrase expressing need and a favorite name of God. Those two combined into a sentence prayer and repeated throughout the day become a source of great comfort and strength. I have found this to be of immense value to seriously ill patients whose powers of concentration are limited. The following are examples of "Breath Prayers":

- "Dear Savior, ease my pain."
- "Be close to me, loving God."
- "Gentle Jesus, touch my body and spirit."
- "Glorious Father, fill me with peace."

Patients may carry such prayers with them throughout the day or for several days.

The blessing prayer. In many bedside situations I have no lead as to the patient's religious affiliations, activities or feelings. No indication of any kind has been conveyed as to their desire for prayer or otherwise.

In such cases I simply use a blessing prayer. Touching them, on the hand or arm for example, I depart with the simple words, "God be with you" or "May God bless you." On numerous occasions the next visit has elicited words like "You don't know how much your touch and blessing meant to me when you left." One patient claimed being healed through it. Scans later that day showed no signs of the suspected diagnosis. Pain and the other symptoms did not recur from the moment of that spoken blessing.

The short four-word blessing may be the most effective prayer you can offer. It is also not intrusive upon the privacy or the stance of the patient. It can be accepted or ignored without adverse reaction toward the pastoral visitor. The patient can be comfortable with it in front of non-religious visitors. This blessing prayer I invoke on almost every patient I visit. It needs to be offered sincerely and not simply as a farewell line.

Prayer is an important aspect of ministry at the bedside. On many occasions when I have prayed, trying to give the patient permission to let go and be free to die, the patient has actually died during the prayer with my hand on the forehead or other appropriate part of the body—all in about a minute. On the other hand, prayers of hope have lifted patients to fight for life. Prayer is one of the most important communication networks available to us all and must be used lovingly and correctly.

Kubler-Ross wrote:

> What amazed me was the number of clergy who felt quite comfortable using a prayer book or chapter from the Bible as the sole communication between them and the patients, thus avoiding listening to their needs and being exposed to questions they might be unable or unwilling to answer.[6]

Sometimes it would be wiser to leave your prayer book at home. It often makes the prayer irrelevant and impersonal. It is highly unlikely that the prayer read will equate with the needs of any particular patient. Unless the prayer is centered upon the patient and his or her needs, emotions and hopes, it is of little consequence. The prayer must also affirm God's caring love, concern, and vital interest in the patient.

To balance the above there are some folk who are more comfortable with the old, tried and familiar liturgies. They would be lost without them. Often they are able to recite them with the priest. That ability to do so brings immeasurable comfort. They feel the church of history is with them and functioning for them in their need. For them the prayer liturgies are immensely valuable and we should not deny them. Of course, with the diminishing percentage of active churchgoers the number of patients familiar with such liturgy is also decreasing. Therefore, it is essential again to become aware of the patient's needs concerning prayer. Prayer always must be for patients in a form which is not only acceptable to them, but in which they can participate and respond.

Bedside prayer ministry requires a developing sensitivity to where a patient is, a deepening intimacy between you and your God and a growing ability to utilize these in tandem.

NOTES

1. Richmond, K. D. *Preaching to Sufferers—God and the problem of pain* pp 91-6.
2. Perry, L. M. and Sell, C. M. *Speaking to Life's Problems* p 111.
3. Soulen, R. N. et. al *Care for the Dying* p55.
4. Irion, P. E. *Hospice and Ministry* p 102.
5. Dobihal, E. F. Jnr. and Stewart, C. W. *When a Friend is Dying* p 84.
6. Kubler-Ross, E. *On Death and Dying* p 118.

10

Jesus—A Theological Model

Pastoral care in the hospital is not a ministry for the person who is looking for something to do, who wants to just feel accepted within the church, who sees it as a means of fulfilling personal needs, who uses it as an escape from unresolved personal problems, or who is merely anxious to please God. Hospital ministry is as much a call of God to a specific area of Christian service as is a call into the ordained ministry, a religious order or a missionary challenge. A person so called must clearly possess a theology of hospital visitation.

Any call into Christian service, either clerical or lay, requires a theological perception and motivation. This provides the foundation and stability which helps to shape the character, the approach and the dedication to the task. When a person receives a phone call from a friend to come for a visit, that person's busy routine is not dropped unless there is some definite sense of urgency which demands an altered schedule. Theology provides the criteria whereby each situation is assessed and action taken. It determines the attitude the carer should have toward the patient and the situation of the patient.

If a theology of Christian pastoral care is to have any real validity, it must find its roots in the person and work of Jesus Christ. Peter (1 Peter 2:1) tells us that Jesus, by his own suffering, set the example as to how to cope with the suffering of persecution. Paul and the writer to the Hebrews, along with others, develop theology that set us the pattern for service. In this chapter we will look in more detail at the example Jesus set. This is meant to be the launching pad for pastoral care theology.

There are so many outstanding features of Jesus' life that it would be improper to consider any theological development prioritized according to the place of its appearance in this chapter. Jesus keeps all things in fine balance. His theological perspectives are so interwoven that they form a whole, each in its place, requiring its own due consideration and practice.

Here we shall pursue eleven facets of Jesus' theology of pastoral care as taught and demonstrated by him. We could turn to other scriptures and see further aspects. The treatment of these dimensions of Jesus' theology is intended to be a springboard to stimulate your own thinking. They could also be termed catalysts which will be a means of developing and enriching your understanding of God and his expectations of us as people involved in pastoral care.

Theology is never static. Every new experience of life we have we should reflect upon and learn from. If one's theological perceptions are not developing, it is likely that he or she will not be suitable as a pastoral visitor to hospitals. Their God is likely to be too small to cope with the number and type of situations they will encounter. An expanding theology reveals a bigger, more wonderful God than was experienced before.

New discoveries about God provide the confidence, excitement and resources to be wise, caring, firm and yet gentle, as Christ was, in dealing with patients.

Examples of theological meditations are included in Supplement 4. Chapter 15 describes a method of theological reflection while Supplement 9 gives an exercise for such reflection.

A THEOLOGY OF ACCEPTANCE

Any cursory reading of the gospels will bring astonishment at the types of people Jesus associated with. This factor was one of the great weapons his enemies wielded against Jesus. He came basically for the needy, and in particular those who were lost and helpless in their own quagmires. Jesus himself said that he came to heal the sick and not the well. He had come not to call respectable people but outcasts (Matthew 9:12–13). This was the response to the Pharisees' questioning of his eating with Matthew and the tax collectors. The Samaritan woman (John 4) was not only a Samaritan but a woman and a harlot. His society dictated that he should not speak to her but in full acceptance of her as a needy person, he spoke directly to her about the troublesome areas of her life.

Zaccheus was a person hated by society and distrusted because of his cheating and fraudulent extraction of tax from people. It was not only because of his smallness of stature that he climbed the tree. He wanted to see Jesus and knew he wouldn't be allowed to mingle in peace on the street with the other villagers. A tree provided cover for him to fulfill his desire. Jesus not only accepted Zaccheus in front of the crowd, he identified himself with him by eating in his house (Luke 19:1–10).

In those times, an adulteress was automatically stoned to death upon exposure. Jesus, in a remarkable fashion, not only received such a woman, but sent her away forgiven (John 8:1–1). He highlighted the unacceptability of Gentiles to the Jews when the Syrian woman from Phoenicia approached him for the healing of her daughter from demon possession, but after witnessing her determined faith in him, he accepted her and her prayer was fulfilled (Mark 7:25–31).

For another example, we could turn to the man of Gadara who was banished to the cemetery because of his hideous, uncontrollable manic behavior. He was healed by Jesus. Again, although lepers were the untouchables of his day, Jesus not only cured them, he touched them, breaking the law and convention in doing so. The touching (above all the other things he did) reinforced the fact of his acceptance of them as they were. (Leviticus 13, 14, Matthew 8:1–4).

None were more despised by the Jews than the Roman soldiers, yet Jesus had no hesitation in listening to the plea from the

Roman centurion to heal his servant. He graciously accepted him and acceded to his prayer (Matthew 8:5–13).

Jesus was unrestricted and unrestrained in his reaching out to needy people, relieving them of their burdens. He did not consider breeding, background or social status. Whoever they were and of whatever faith, Jesus accepted them. The ministry of a pastoral care person means moving out to accept the patient, resident, family or staff—whoever they are and whatever their ethnic background, religion and state of need.

A THEOLOGY OF AVAILABILITY

Matthew tells us that Jesus, when told of the death of his cousin, John the Baptist, went by boat to the other side of the lake. This presumably was to escape the crowds, to be alone to grieve and no doubt to consider the implications of John's death for his own ministry. The crowds followed him around the lake, so he was forced to teach and heal the whole day (Matthew 14:1–21). At the end of an exhausting day the people were tired, hungry and had a long trek back home. It would have been easy for Jesus to have dismissed them and pursued the privacy he desired. Instead he fed that great crowd with the five loaves and two fish. Jesus, in spite of the circumstances, made himself available to the people, who had physical, medical and spiritual needs.

That availability is seen when he was moving along with a great crowd of people, healing and teaching. Jairus, the ruler of the synagogue, sought Jesus' assistance to heal his ailing daughter. Jesus could have easily said that he was too busy healing scores of people, and what priority did a 12-year-old girl have over these others? Yet he deliberately made himself available. His reach extended out to even the insignificant members of society (Mark 5:22–43). This is again exemplified when the disciples tried to prevent mothers bringing their children for Jesus to bless. He stopped his teaching, took these children in his arms and blessed them (Mark 10:13–16). The message of Jesus' life and ministry is a call for his disciples of all ages to be ready and available to all people.

A THEOLOGY OF ACCOUNTABILITY

Matthew, Mark and Luke each record Jesus' startlingly dramatic words, spoken after Peter's watershed confession of him as the Messiah. Those words, which he reiterated several times later, showed plainly how he must suffer, die and rise again. (Matthew 16:21–25; Mark 8:31–9:1; Luke 9:22–27), On each occasion, the imperative is used: "He must go to Jerusalem." The disciples tried to dissuade him (Matthew 16:22), but the determination was there. That determination may be gauged by the sense of accountability and responsibility expressed by Jesus himself in his reflection on the Good Shepherd. This is teaching which he applied to himself (John 10). The Good Shepherd is responsible for the safety of the sheep and is accountable to the owner of the sheep for their security. The Good Shepherd's accountability reaches as far as the sacrifice of his own life.

This Jesus, who must have known the extent of the suffering to be endured on Calvary, shrank from the reality of the physical and spiritual trauma to be borne. Gethsemane reveals the intensity of this struggle of Jesus (Matthew 26:36–46).

People called into hospital visitation accept a sense of accountability to God for those directed to them in this ministry. A half-hearted or indifferent commitment to this form of pastoral care indicates a failure to fully accept responsibility for the patients, relatives or staff. The maintenance of an accountability framework rescues the carer from self-pity and self-pampering. The spirit of responsibility is evident in the boy Jesus' reply to his parents in the Temple: "Didn't you know that I had to be in my Father's house?".

A THEOLOGY OF CARE

The one defining characteristic of Jesus' life is that of care. He showed compassion, concern and empathy in all his dealings with everyone. The implication and scope of this for chaplains is in his famous "judgment scene" (Matthew 25:31–46) which so clearly and specifically declares that unless we have shown true care of the remotest needy person in our society then we are not fit for God's Kingdom. The parables of the lost sheep and the lost coin (Luke 15) indicate a certain persistence in the caring until the final discovery is made or the task completed. In other words, Jesus considered the thoroughness of the care to be crucial.

Jesus was continually moved to compassion. "As he saw the crowds, he was filled with pity for them because they were worried and helpless, like sheep without a shepherd" (Matthew 9:36). The same caring concern resulted in his feeding of the four thousand. He saw that having been without food for three days they might feel faint on the way home (Matthew 15:32).

The principal characteristic of Jesus' caring ministry was this persistence in completing the task of caring. The demonic man in the cemetery at Gadara, an uncontrollable maniac, abandoned by society, found deliverance because Jesus was not repelled by his appalling state (Mark 5:1–13).

Turning again to the woman at the well, we find that she initially questioned Jesus' right to talk with her and rebuffed him. He saw her need. He broke cultural mores to meet her on her own ground. When she changed the subject, making it a religious issue, to take the spotlight off her own sorry plight, he persisted until she embraced the truth about herself and about him. (John 4:1–26).

In both these cases, Jesus saw the task of caring through to completion. The swine careering into the sea to drown provided evidence for the demonic maniacally possessed that he might have the confidence of a new freedom from the fear of demons. The satisfaction of seeing a social outcast come to a belief in him as the Messiah took precedence over Jesus' need to eat (John 4:31–34).

The provision of care for isolated, suffering, emotionally-hurting, or otherwise disturbed people was the sincere motivation Jesus evidenced throughout the whole of his earthly ministry. The first temptation after his baptism, and his repeated command to beneficiaries to tell no one who had performed the miracle on them, is sufficient indication that Jesus was not using his caring acts to manipulate people into the Kingdom. In many cases those acts bore fruit of eternal and spiritual significance, but it appears that the majority of those blessed by Jesus' caring did not pursue a deeper spiritual involvement. Jesus, out of his caring compassion, responded naturally without imposing any conditions.

That same concern, which results in action to alleviate the need, should be the characteristic of the pastoral person and the visitor. Other motives, evangelical or denominational priorities, kill the true spirit of caring. The hidden agenda becomes patently obvious to the one offered the assistance. The care of Jesus was offered out of his own reaction to the less-than-whole life experienced by others. He ministered without preconditions or strings attached. His caring action bore its own fruit.

A THEOLOGY OF SENSITIVITY

It is easy to recognize some needs. It is a different proposition to be sensitive to the other peculiar, and seemingly insignificant, needs which ultimately may be most important to the person. This singularly important gift of sensitivity is evident when Jesus restored life to Jairus' daughter. The excitement and joy of an unbelievable miracle overshadowed all sensitivity to the girl's real need. She had been starved for several days because of her condition. She was weak. It took Jesus to tell them that she needed some bodily nourishment. "Give her something to eat" (Mark 5:43).

Mary the sister of Lazarus, who may have been Mary Magdalene (Mary of Bethany and Mary of Magdala never appear together in any of the gospel events), gave a spectacular and extravagant display of adoration at a dinner in the home of Lazarus. She massaged expensive ointment worth several years' wages for an average person into the feet of Jesus. Judas' strong criticism of him for permitting that seeming waste was rebuffed by Jesus. Jesus looked deep into the heart of Mary sensitively, perceiving the force behind such a display of devotion. He saw that any rejection of that act would have left lasting hurt. Her purity of motive was sensitively applauded rather than squashed by Jesus (John 12:7).

To cite another example: One can only remotely imagine the shame, remorse and disgust of Peter when he heard the cock crow after he had denied his Master. The sensitive Jesus recognised the need to forgive and heal the tortured Peter. A patronizing response of forgiveness would have left Peter squirming more. Jesus, by his threefold demand of affirmation of love, made it difficult for Peter not to be reminded of his three denials (John 21:15–19). Without that replay of his darkest hour and without the threefold affirmation of love, forgiveness and commission to feed the lambs and sheep, Peter would have probably remained a maimed, guilt-ridden disciple rather than becoming the fierce apostle.

Jesus always delved below the surface to understand innermost feelings and observe the slightest trace of camouflaged need. Pastoral carers must ceaselessly be alert to such need, sharpening their skills of sensitivity until the other person becomes aware of Christ-like perceptiveness. Verbal and nonverbal communication, with their various subtleties, must be constantly interpreted with precision, after the pattern of Jesus.

A THEOLOGY OF OBEDIENCE

From Isaiah on through the whole New Testament, we read of the Messiah being sent by God to heal and to save (Isaiah 61:1, John 3:16, Galatians 4:4, 1 John 4:9). Jesus' incarnation was for the sole purpose of human salvation. His life and ministry were consistent with full obedience to that commission. He did not shrink from it. He held himself accountable to God and this accountability was fulfilled through his complete obedience.

As a twelve-year-old in the temple, he showed awareness of his mission (Luke 2:41–50) and sought knowledge to equip himself to obediently fulfill it. In his adult life, his disciples persistently tried to squash his talk of going to Jerusalem to die. When Peter objected at Caesarea, Phillipi, Jesus accused him of being Satan's instrument of temptation to divert him from the path of obedience.

There were so many things Jesus could have done to avert the crucifixion. He need not have gone to Jerusalem for the Passover. He could have called down twelve legions of angels (Matthew 26:52–54). It would have been easy to slip into the darkness of Olivet when he saw the crowd coming out of the city gate to arrest him. He could have compelled Judas to stay in the upper room and not report to the Sanhedrin. Clearly, Jesus had every opportunity to avoid Calvary. His commitment to his divine commission took precedence over what he knew he had to endure.

It is with the same sense of commitment that we should fill the commission which Christ has given to us to minister to those ill in bed. Paul (Ephesians 4:9–16) tells of Jesus giving to each of us separate gifts for ministry and for the smooth functioning of the body of Christ, the church. Those gifts are given in order that the ministry which the Lord has assigned to each individual Christian may be obediently fulfilled.

Without a call to a hospital ministry, the necessary gifts for such ministry may be absent. Without such a call, there can be no obedience in such service. It becomes a need fulfillment or an activity adopted merely through a sense of duty.

Obedience can only follow a commissioning such as Christ received from the Father (John 3:16). Examine the extent of the divine initiative behind your involvement in hospital ministry. Whether clergy or lay, we need to be assured that we are endeavoring to minister in God's place, in his time, and in his way, so that our ministry may be truly a ministry obedient to the divine command.

A hospital visitor is one who is called by God to enter a situation where there are numbers of hurting humanity. We are to approach them with the sense of urgency and compassion which Jesus' example set before us in sincere obedience to the divine command.

A THEOLOGY OF WITNESS

It is true that the great commission of Jesus to his church was to preach, teach and baptize all nations (Matthew 28:19–20). It is also true that he said on his ascension day that his followers were to be witnesses. Witnessing may take many forms. It may be through the spoken word. Often preaching is most effective, as we see in the way the masses clung to the teaching of Jesus. Yet it has been true over the centuries that many have been won over to Christ through merely observing the life pattern of a Christian. The thief on the cross found salvation, not through Jesus' preaching, but by observing him dying and observing his love and compassion even in death—"Father, forgive them"— "Mother, behold your Son" (Matthew 27 and John 19). The Roman centurion at the cross was able to say, "Truly this man was a righteous man" (Luke 23:47–48).

Jesus made clear the meaning of witness when he spoke of it being as "light" or "salt" (Matthew 5:13–16). A hospital visitor who walks the corridors of the institution must be seen as a light which enlightens all patients, residents, relatives and staff. The aura is one which attracts, not to the carer as a person, but to the Christ whom he or she represents. The Master's touch is spread by pastoral visitors to those who cross their path. This is effective witness which builds the eternal kingdom.

A THEOLOGY OF SERVANTHOOD

One of the major reasons for the non-recognition of Jesus as the Christ by the Jews was their failure to identify Isaiah's servant passages in Messianic context. Jesus in all respects fulfilled the servant role of that prophet. When Zebedee's mother claimed for her sons positions of pre-eminence in Christ's kingdom, he replied by stressing the role of servanthood. He said of himself that he had not come to be waited upon but to serve and to give his life for others (Matthew 20:28). The concept of servanthood in action is never more clearly seen than in the upper room where he washed his disciples' feet (John 13:1–17). Jesus proclaimed his act as an example which they must put into practice. No messenger is greater than the master.

Jesus by reason of his divine nature, had the right to live in opulence and grandeur, with a retinue to serve him. Yet his lifestyle was the opposite of this expectation. No fixed abode— today he would have been declared a vagrant. Being at the beck and call of the influential and the poor, he served them by offering them a service which no one else could provide. The lepers, synagogue rulers, army captains, fishermen, wealthy merchants (for example, Nicodemus and Joseph of Arimathaea), tax gatherers, and housewives all accepted his services without any obligation.

His servanthood was offered to all without fear or prejudice, without conditions and without fanfare. The service he offered was given to the grateful leper and the nine ungrateful lepers (Luke 17:11–19). The pharisees and the prostitutes met him on common ground (Luke 7:36–50). Whether it was spiritual (John 3:1–21) or a desperate physical disability (John 5:1–9), Jesus offered the service they needed. As the teacher supreme (Matthew 5–7; and John 13–17) or as the blesser of babies (Matthew 19:13–15), Jesus observed no age preferences. His servanthood was unrestricted—to believer and non-Jew alike. It showed no bias. It was servanthood at its most menial yet noblest. It was versatile enough to meet the smallest and the most traumatic crises of life.

It is therefore incumbent upon us to emulate this servant role. Regretfully, we can be selective in our hospital ministry; there are few of us who can claim to have never been discriminating in our servanthood. It is easier to minister to someone with whom we have a natural rapport. Yet the others with less appealing personalities or backgrounds most probably are in more need of our services than those who are well supported and popular.

Jesus set the example so that we should follow in his footsteps and be a servant of all.

A THEOLOGY OF LOVE

No look at Jesus should omit the patently obvious key to his whole life and teaching—the theology of love. We might read "for God so loved the world that he gave..." (John 3:16) and this, for the casual scripture reader, seems to say that it was all the Father's love, that Jesus just meekly acquiesced. But it took Jesus' love to see to its fulfilment. If we consider the co-equality and unity of the Godhead, then love also is equally determined. Without Jesus' full commitment to love there would have been no atonement. The whole of Jesus' ministry was a continuous kaleidoscope of love and compassion. The healings, the teachings, the acceptance of gross injustice and humiliation, and the infinite patience are all demonstrations of his great love.

The message of the good Samaritan (Luke 10:30–37) is to urge us to love our neighbor as ourselves. The Good Shepherd suggests a love that would lead to the supreme sacrifice (John 10:11). Jesus reduced the divine commands to two from which all right living would surge forth—"Love God and love your neighbor" (Luke 10:27). John's gospel and John's letters immortalize the love aspect of Jesus and the expectation that his followers will be identified through love. Love is the base and foundation of all true Christian ministry and service. Paul outlined the quality of this love to be seen in the church (1 Corinthians 13).

Love and empathy should characterize this ministry of the carer. Doing it merely out of duty removes the warmth, spontaneity and integrity from such ministry. Love provides the base on which to build.

A THEOLOGY OF CONFRONTATION

In a rather strange contrast to a theology of sensitivity, acceptance, love and care, when the circumstance required it, Jesus confronted people. Often in the life of the local church or denomination, problems, difficulties, and even schisms take place because in the early days of the dispute, appropriate confrontation did not take place! The matter was allowed to fester until a massive abscess grew and burst, with disastrous affects on the life and witness of the church. Paul (Corinthians 5:1–5) challenged the Corinthian church to deal with a church member involved in an incestuous relationship. The church's lack of courage to confront several issues caused Paul to write letters using strong language.

Jesus, called the "meek and mild," certainly did not behave like a kindly but ineffective individual when he saw wrongdoing and inconsistencies in the lives of people. His sensitiveness to what was going on deep down caused him to speak out strongly against certain individuals and groups.

The pharisees and scribes were a particularly powerful lobby which he took to task over their false and legalistic teaching (Matthew 23:13–16). We are told of an upright, honest and likable young man, a leader of his people who came to Jesus (Luke 18:18–25). Jesus could have extolled his uprightness. His honest seeking after eternal life was sincere when he approached Jesus. Yet Jesus pointed out to him his area of weakness—his love of his estate. He went away sad because he knew Jesus had put his finger on his weak spot. Jesus could confront people when it was necessary.

There were times in Jesus' life when we might feel he should have been firmer. The woman taken in adultery (John 8:1–11) is a case in point. But Jesus felt no need to press the sense of guilt and shame further. To rub more salt into a raw and open heart may be counter-effective. The confrontation came in the words, "Go, sin no more."

Lucy's condition was terminal. One of her daughters had been rebellious in younger years and had broken away from the family. Lucy did not want to see this daughter, Joan. In talking with the family, Joan said she was heartbroken over her mother's stubbornness. She felt she couldn't face the future if her mother died without a reconciliation. Obstinate Lucy, cherishing her Christian code of morality, felt Joan had disgraced God and the family.

Because of her physical distress it was not easy for me to point out to Lucy that Jesus still loved Joan even if her mother didn't. But it had to be done. I assured her that Jesus was prepared to forgive Joan. Why couldn't *she* forgive?

The reunion between those two was a very tearful one. Lucy regained a lost peace and a lost daughter. Joan was rewarded with a mother's love and a mother's forgiveness. Without the confrontation with Lucy, the sadness and heartache would not have been healed.

It is sometimes difficult for patients to face the reality of their condition. Where the attitude is out of the normal character of the person, it may be necessary to bring to bear a little gentle confrontation to restore more sanity to the relationship between the patient and other family members.

There are times when the need for confrontation on spiritual issues arises in the hospital, but visitors who feel it is necessary on every visit to bring a spiritual challenge are ignoring many other factors, such as the patient's physical condition, powers of concentration and the real need for such confrontation. Jesus did not confront on every occasion. Confrontation is a ministry which should be the result of the pastoral visitor's own relationship with God through the Spirit, who directs such a move. This will minimize the risk of rejection and maximize the possibility of fruitfulness, because the timing will be right.

As Jesus discerned when to confront, so must we seek to develop a similar gift of discernment. Notice how at times Jesus sternly, even angrily confronted, as when he overturned the tables of the money changers. On the other hand, he confronted Peter with gentle tenderness at the lakeside breakfast after the resurrection, and opened his hands to Thomas in the upper room to show the nail prints. The method of confrontation must be appropriate to the situation.

Jesus' confrontation with Peter, "Get behind me, Satan", contrasts with his action of breaking bread in the home of the two Emmaus disciples (John 24:13–35). This latter action was his way of confronting those two with the facts of his resurrection. There could have been no more effective method of confrontation in the circumstances.

Confrontation is not always a head-on clash. The hospital visitor confronts according to the persons involved, the nature of the circumstances and the possibility of irrevocable, destructive hurt. In the upper room (John 13:21–30) in light of the horrendous act of betrayal, Jesus confronted Judas with the most appealing warning.

Again, Jesus becomes our model for confrontation.

A THEOLOGY OF RENEWAL

Jesus spent himself in a caring ministry. Since he was God in human form, it is easy for us to assume that he was able to take the ministry of pastoral care in his stride, with the minimum of physical, emotional or spiritual stress.

As we study the life of Jesus, however, we see that that was not the case. Every miracle drew power from him, as he exclaimed when the woman touched the hem of his garment (Luke 8:46). Mark indicates that following the murder of John the Baptist, Jesus moved the disciples to a place where they could be alone to "rest a while" (Mark 6:31). Jesus recognized the emotional drain which they all had experienced and the need to marshall their forces physically, emotionally and spiritually.

They did not find the opportunity for the planned recuperation and retreat. The crowds followed, and then came the miracle of the feeding of the five thousand. This was another day of teaching and healing and equally draining ministry, so Jesus retired to the mountain to be alone with God (Mark 6:45–47). Six to nine hours later he joined the disciples by walking on the water (Matthew 14:22–25).

Jesus spent many hours of the early morning in prayer with God, renewing himself for the preaching, teaching and healing ministry in Galilee: (Mark 1:35–38). When in Jerusalem it was his habit to retire to the Mount of Olives each night to pray (Luke 22:39).

Genuine pastoral care saps and erodes the physical, emotional and spiritual reserves of carers, who, like Jesus, need to be restored. Without renewal, caring becomes stressful and burdensome. This can lead to burn-out and can dramatically reduce the effectiveness of the caring. Efficiency and perceptiveness become lost in the panic to cope with the number of patients, their problems and personal needs.

Burn-out does not come with overwork; it is the result of trying to function on drained resources. It is produced when the work is approached in anxiety and stress instead of in the renewed strength gained through recreational, spiritual "time off.".

Matthew describes graphically Jesus' encounter with God prior to the arrest and Calvary (Matthew 26:36–47). He made an open honest declaration of his feelings. He shrank from Calvary, he let God know what he thought of it. The communication was frank, open, intimate and spiritually acute. Jesus knew, Jesus accepted, Jesus went forth renewed and strengthened for the battle. The ministry of care continued in spite of his personal distress and anguish as he forgave his tormentors, as he blessed the dying thief and as he provided for his mother. Only a man being constantly renewed by the times spent meeting with God could have continued to persevere in pastoral care under such circumstances (John 19:23–27; Luke 23:39–42).

As pastoral workers, we need to study and follow closely Jesus' lead in this matter, treating as high priority times set aside for renewal.

There are many methods. God can speak through the scriptures as we reflect upon them. God can reveal himself and his ways as we sit and meditate. God can open spiritual eyes as we move into his natural world and sift the insights that come to us.

Some people find the writing of a daily or weekly journal a way of keeping in healthy perspective the events in which we participate.

Personally, I find that when the stress is heavy, I have to take myself aside and face the confronting issue. As I review it, I set it down on paper in a prayer-poem form. By the time the writing is finished, my whole attitude to the situation is changed. The anxiety has been diffused and I continue the ministry with peace of mind and spirit.

Each week I make time (usually on a Sunday morning) for a reflective, meditative period with God. This fills me with the awareness of our Lord's presence. Invariably it becomes the time of renewal and re-equipment for a ministry which will further draw from my spirit and strength until another meeting with him replenishes me.

Pastoral care workers in hospital work need to ensure that periods of renewal are built into their week—not just times of Bible reading and the saying of prayers. There must be an occasion when God in Christ is met and deep communication is experienced. With the intimacy of such renewal encounters as a basis, ministry to people in need becomes an occasion when such people are able to feel that Jesus is coming near to them also.

This theology provides a positive approach to pastoral care. It enables the pastoral visitor to have confidence in:

A *Relevant God,* who is flexible in responding to the needs of his people;

A *Compassionate God,* who cares for the whole person—body, mind and spirit;

A *Compelling God,* to whom the pastoral visitor and his people may turn with confidence, for guidance, wisdom and strength;

A *Suffering God,* who shares humanity's sufferings;

A *Patient God,* who bears with our imperfections and stumblings as we try to serve him;

An *Encouraging God,* who picks us up, comforts us and sends us back into the fray with greater enthusiasm.

In Supplement 7 an effort is made to bring this theology into practical perspective because the pure application of a theology may always be distorted or exploited as a manipulative tool, both by the carer and the one to whom care is offered. In hospital ministry this is a real possibility. Work through the issues raised, making relevant applications to your own situation.

SUPPLEMENT 4—THEOLOGICAL MEDITATIONS

A) A chaplain reflects

Lord! Did you really make this world?
Did you really make us a little lower than the angels?
Was the Psalmist wrong?
Was he living in a different world from the one I live in?
He said that you put all things under the control of
    human beings.

In these last twenty-four hours it hasn't been true.
At least for countless people it hasn't.
I've encountered ten of those in my corner.
A husband axed to death by his wife.
She made three attempts at self destruction:
electrocution in the bath,
overdose of pills
and slashed wrists.
All failed for this unhappy, middle-aged woman.
Another thirty-year-old wife used a knife.
Her husband was bleeding from three wounds.
A bullet was expertly fired into another's heart.
It was clean and quick.
Why would a twenty-five-year-old man do this?
Six sick and sorry failed drug overdoses—
physically saved this time, but
what about the next attempt?

Except to be with relatives to comfort
And provide an awareness of your presence
My efforts have seemed so meager and fruitless.
Is this what you made the world to be?
Is this all you intended your servant to accomplish?

Thank you, Lord, that Jesus came and wants to give LIFE!

Thank you, Lord, for those who have discovered you through a chaplain.

Thank you, Lord, that I am a mere instrument of your spirit.

Let me continue to be such a tool to such people. Open those still living to respond to you.

b) A chaplain's prayer

It's been a heavy weekend on duty.
An unusual weekend it cannot claim to be.
In this moment to stop for coffee
Is the opportunity to stop and reflect.

Seven sailors were enjoying a good time in a sailor's way.
Now two are dead, four are in the hospital.
The driver is facing manslaughter charges.

The wedding guests are from three continents.
The bride and groom are standing weeping.
They are at the bedsides of an African and European guest.
The unassociated victim from Asia in the other car is only
    thirteen years old.
We wait the doctors' decision on brain death.

A little three-year-old was resuscitated nine weeks ago.
The fall into the pool left her in the water too long.
Nine weeks in a coma and today she drew her last breath.

At sixteen it's too young to be told the news.
"There's no more treatment!"
The doctors will speak these words to him tomorrow.

She is a beautiful twelve-year-old just developing.
The family expect her to blossom into a lovely woman.
What will the fall from the horse do to that future?

The battling survivor of a bone marrow transplant,
This afternoon she's struggling for breath at forty.
An active Christian of forty-one took an overdose,
Her depression was due to an unresolved grief problem.

Patients and families in each case have needed my care.
It's been a long weekend. I'm exhausted.
How effective have I been? Have I displayed your care?

Has my Savior got the credit for this weekend's work?
Yes Lord! It was good to conduct chapel service.
I told them that you are our perfect friend,
You will give us your Holy Spirit.
When we have your Holy Spirit then we are able to cope—
In health and ill-health, in heartache and joy;

These people who have crossed my path this weekend.
May they ask, seek and knock
Until they receive, find, and are open to your Spirit in
their lives.

C) *The joy of sharing*

It's late at night,
I've just been around to Accident and Emergency.
It was sad to see this thirty-year-old.
She overdosed on drugs prescribed for her today.
Then there was the invalid pensioner who was finding life hard.
I was able to quieten her a little.

Next I experienced the joy of sharing.
A full-time member of staff has a school age family.

She's been feeling the tension between work and home.
The financial strain that forced her to work no longer
    bares its teeth.
A part-time job would be ideal,
Particularly one involving the midnight shift.
You've been listening to her, Lord.
She is faithful in her prayer and communion with you.
She acknowledges your provision of her present job.
This week it was suggested that she apply for a new vacancy.
It was for the one job she saw as suitable.
More than for anyone it was tailored for her present needs.
In her act of sharing in Christ, she asked, "I want you to pray
    for me and this job.
"I've got confidence that God is working this out."
Her eyes appeared watery as she spoke.
Springs of joy in God were bringing tears of gratitude.
It was infectious. You WERE with us.
My eyes filled like hers.

When our hearts are full of God's nearness,
When his assurance floods our lives,
When we share with others our blessings,
Our spirit of joy fills their lives.
Their lives, too, become a hymn of rejoicing.

I suspect, Lord, I'm guilty of denying others.
I do not share as much as I should
My thanksgiving, praise and gratitude to you.
It can open the gates of blessing and fellowship.

The joy of sharing is unbelievably rewarding
To the person sharing and to the one receiving.
Help me to be more unashamedly open in my sharing.
Use that sharing for the spiritual advance of others.

SUPPLEMENT 5—EXAMPLES OF PATIENTS' PRAYERS

The first night in hospital

Tonight, Lord, I feel I am a different person. I can't do as I please. A lot of my independence and freedom have gone. It seems as if I'm a child again. That's not a bad thought to end the day on, a child dependent upon a father. You are my Heavenly Father. That is how you would like it. In sincerity that's how I would like it. Let me sleep tonight comforted in this relationship.

Before an operation

Lord, in a little while I'll be operated on. I have moments when I feel a bit scared. I know I have a good surgeon. I need a peace and assurance that is beyond me. Please be with me so your peace and assurance may be mine.

An exhausting day

It's been a gruelling day today, Lord. I feel dopey and exhausted. I'm lost for words. You understand how it is and I love you for it. Just stick close by until I can talk more with you. It gives me strength and encouragement to know you care for me even throughout the night. Thanks for seeing me through today.

Receiving a bad report

What a blow I've been dealt today, Lord. I feel devastated and shattered. I'm lost. I don't know what to say or even think. My plans, my family, my friends, myself—well—just everything are all part of this turmoil. I want to cry. I am angry at the unfairness. Yet I want to tell my family I love them and need them. Deep inside I am so horribly alone, empty and helpless. Lord, look upon me. Lord, come to me as I cry to you. Fill me, Lord, with your understanding. Grip me in your love that I may come to grips with what is happening.

After an operation

Father, I still feel groggy and sore. Yesterday was a big ordeal although I didn't know much about it. Today I feel relief, it's over now. I have a deep sense of gratitude for your loving care and concern shown through all that the doctors and nurses have done. Help me to show my appreciation by my sharing of your Spirit with them.

Irritable

Dear Father, I've felt a bit irritable today. Maybe it's my condition or the treatment or all the tests I'm having. It's not making it easy for the staff or the other patients.

Forgive me, Lord, and just give me that patience and tolerance I need at this time. Help me to be more understanding tomorrow. A good night's rest will be helpful for this. Better still, a consciousness that you are with me all day tomorrow. May it be so, dear Savior.

Encouraged

Oh, my great God, it feels good to be walking around again. I still get tired. It's hard to concentrate for long. These moments when I can think about you and talk with you make things seem so much brighter. In normal life I say I'm too busy to speak with you. May your Spirit together with mine allow me to make the most of this time. Just the thought of your forgiveness, your love, your companionship gives me new purpose. Thank you for this.

Fearing the unknown

Lord, I'm in hospital and the cause of my being here is still a mystery. Tests—a long stay—a short stay—an operation? I'm in the dark. Is it serious? Is it nothing to worry about? I don't know and I'm worried. I think of the family, my job, my other commitments. Oh, my God, what is it? I'm here to find out. May the doctor's skill and equipment be adequate to give an answer. When I hear the verdict let me be able to accept it. Help me to make the most of my life from here on in. Teach me much in these days of the unknown.

Full of regrets

I've got time to lie here and think, Father. It seems as if my past comes rushing back in spurts. Strangely they're about the unpleasant areas of my life. I'm seeing them differently now. Some of the things I did and didn't do have hurt family, friends and strangers only too often. It distresses me when I think of them. Lord, forgive me. Where possible I would like to right those wrongs. Armed with your forgiveness show me how to do something about it even while in here.

A prayer by a patient for relatives

As I lie here, Lord, I'm not thinking about myself all the time. I sense that this hospitalization is tearing my family apart. Perhaps they know more about my condition than I do. Again, they might be just overwhelmed with the most pessimistic outcome. Lord, they may be just facing reality. Some of them are heartbroken. There's little I can do except put on a brave face. I love them, each one, and don't like seeing them this way. You are the God of comfort: come alongside of them just now. They are finding this a heavy load. I plead with you to share it with them. Add patience to their spirits also.

Full of self-pity

My power of concentration seems to have vanished. It should be a good opportunity to meditate and think, especially about you. But I cannot. It's probably the treatment and the constant ward activity. It has been a crisis and I've done a lot of self-pitying. I've concentrated on myself. That's not your way, is it? Forgive me, Lord, and enable me to lift my thoughts beyond myself.

Denying facts

Lord, many people have been around me today. I've told them everything's going fine. I'm believing almost the opposite of what the doctor told me. I'm not facing the facts. I'm hearing what I want to hear. It means that deep down I'm frightened. Lord! "Being brave" is not the answer. Oh! Help me, Father to understand the implications of my condition. I need to think quietly and to sort myself out. I believe, Oh God, your presence will help me to do just this so that I may be best able to help myself, my loved ones and the staff caring for me.

News of discharge

I'm going home, that sounds good. Father God, I'm grateful for this hospital, for all its staff. They've been thoughtful, tender and so willing to help me. Through their treatment and care I'm being discharged. Through them you have provided so much for my recovery. To you I offer my thanks. Such praise will seem hollow if I do not seek to love and help my neighbor more than I did before. May such a love overflow my life in service to others as I am able.

Recognizing blessing

Hospitalization isn't the best experience, Lord. I find it hard to take the pain, I don't like it. Yet you have known pain too. When I think of the sufferings of Jesus, it makes me feel ashamed. I want to love you more and this hospital experience is helping me do it. I'm beginning to realise that hospitalization can bring its blessing. Please help me discover more of this blessing. You work in wonderful ways.

Improving

It's great to be alive. I didn't think that last week. Each day I'm getting stronger. The old pain has gone. It's wonderful. I'm beginning to make plans for what I'll do when I get home— happy thought. I sense a danger here. I'm likely to become too self-indulgent and demanding. You've stood by me and given me strength during these days of illness. When I've been depressed, angry, irritable, frustrated or anxious, you've been around. Turn my thoughts and plans, Oh Lord, to things positive and helpful. I've received much. May I start reaching out to others also.

An uncertain diagnosis

Father, this whole illness of mine is quite mystifying. The doctors are puzzled. They can't tell me what the problem is. To date tests are inconclusive. I'm up in the air. Sometimes I'm full of high hopes; other times I'm pessimistic and fed up with myself. Some would say that I've lost my faith. It's not that, Lord. It is just the impatience of uncertainty. I know that you'll see me through. I know with your help I'll cope, whatever they discover. Your strength will be my strength, your courage, your love will be my confidence until we meet face to face at the appropriate time.

When overwhelmed by weakness

I'm just lying here, Lord, just feeling all-in. It's hard to raise a smile when staff or visitors come. It's an effort to lift my arms. My legs feel like pieces of lead. My mind would have difficulty even in working out the date. My concentration has gone. I want to talk with you. I start, then I drift off. I just can't help it, Lord. You know how it is and I am so grateful you are an understanding God. In my weakness I raise my plea to you. Look upon me, now. Assure me of your continuing love. Touch my weak body, mind and spirit with your spirit, as I struggle with the doctors' help to come out on top of my illness. Give me relaxation now which will promote the healing I need.

Thanksgiving for a new baby

I can't believe it, Lord! We have a brand new baby. I know I'm prejudiced, my baby's beautiful. My heart is just overflowing with joy. I do want to say thank you for being with us through the pregnancy. It is never easy but your help and strength comforted and supported us all the way. This new life gives us new and greater responsibilities. We have to guide and lead this little life into adulthood. In these days it is an awful responsibility. As we thank you for our addition to the family so we cry to you in a different way. Give us wisdom and understanding to be the best parents possible. May our child grow up to recognize and worship you as God and Savior.

For a sick child

My heart and mind, my emotions and thinking are jumbled and confused. My child is ill, close to death. My children are my most priceless possessions. Harm them and you harm me. The doctors are doing their best. The nurses are marvellous. The therapists are excellent and gentle. I couldn't ask for better attention. Yet there is one thing more I need. It is you, oh Lord. Come and hear my prayer. Save my child. May your soothing spirit come upon my child's body, giving peace and your life deep within. In my helplessness I cling to you and plead with you for my child. Hear my cries—mend my shattered heart—calm my tormented mind—may your peace find its place in my breast.

Cry for help

Oh God my Lord, I am beyond what I feel I can stand. Help me in what lies ahead. Strengthen my faith in you and myself. Give me confidence in those who are caring for me. Forgive me. Let your peace grow in me, your love comfort me and your presence encourage me.

A midday prayer

The day is half-gone, Lord. I've dozed, I've seen the doctor. I have no energy, I can't think. Time is just idling by. It is so unlike me and I don't like it. Oh Father, help me to see something positive for my stay here. I pray that the doctors may give me the right treatment. I do want you to strengthen me in body, mind and spirit. Come close to me and bless me with your calming, peaceful presence.

Before special treatment

I'm to commence special treatment today, Lord. Will it help me? Will I have side reactions? The doctors have said that it should be successful. I pray that it may be. I look forward to being rid of sickness and weakness. Today I have a great hope that I may be healed. Give me a new picture of a better and more useful life after this treatment. This is possible, Oh my God! If we can tread the days ahead together.

A prayer by relatives for the patient

It's difficult to sit by and watch like this. I willingly would swap places but that's not the way it is. I do pray that pain may be eased. I don't know how best to pray. Do give relief. Lord, I pray that my love may be evident. Let me speak with more than lips. My touch, my presence, my eyes, my tone of voice—let them all echo my love, assurance, and peace that his/her days of illness may be an experience of my support and comfort. Above all, Oh Lord, may he/she turn to you for spiritual strength for all needs.

Rewrite these personal prayers, expressing the patient's own feelings, as your prayer offered on behalf of the patient. This is an important exercise to develop your ability to pray an "incarnational prayer."

SUPPLEMENT 6—EXAMPLES OF VISITORS' PRAYERS

In the hours before death (for an active believer)
Thank you, Lord, for *name* and his/her hope in you. We thank you for all *name* has meant to so many people. At this moment when *name* waits for the call into your presence, we pray that he/she may be filled with your spirit. May the comfortable feeling of your love and peace fill *name*. May the two of you feel the closeness of each other as your blessing rests upon *name*.

In the hours before death (for a person generally disinterested in religion)
Father, at this time when *name* faces the unknown, we pray that *name* may reach out to you, your spirit reaching down, his/her spirit reaching up until you both find each other. Even in the final hours (days) upon earth may *name* discover an intimacy and peacefulness not experienced before. We pray, Lord God, for the warmth of your presence to settle upon *name* as he/she discovers you in greater truth. May such peace and blessing be *name's* for eternity.

With angry patient (a) (an amputee after an accident)
Dear Lord God, you seem so high, mighty and far away from *name* just now. He's only young. He's just starting out to know and understand what life is all about. Now, he's lost a leg and a hand. He is angry at you and depressed. *Name* feels you could have protected him better. Help him to express that anger to you in his own words. He needs to be honest with you. I pray for him, Lord, that you two will understand each other and that *name* with your help will fight his way to the top. Give him courage and determination and a trust in you, in Jesus' name.

For another angry patient (b)
Lord! *Name* has every right to feel angry at what has happened. *Name* has a lot of living to do yet. He/she has dreams and plans

to fulfill. It looks as if they are all smashed to pieces. It is not fair. It doesn't seem right. *Name* would like to call you a few names. He/she thinks you could have stopped it. Accept *name's* anger in all its strength. Be patient and understanding with *name* just now. I want to leave *name* in your care. Be gentle and kind to *name* at this time. Amen.

N.B. To go beyond this in prayer in these circumstances, when God appears to the patient to be unfeeling, would stimulate anger against you.

For an active Christian fighting to live

Name has often expressed anticipation at the great joy of meeting you face to face. The race has been faithfully run. Crown *name* with this greatest blessing of all. *Name* is waiting to hear your call. We give *name* the freedom to let go and be with you. We commend his/her spirit to your love. We thank you for *name,* for the love and blessing received by many throughout his/her life. Accept *name,* O Father, in Jesus' name.

N.B. The name of the person is frequently used in these prayers. It reinforces in the patient's mind (often short in concentration) that this prayer is for them and thus their concentration is kept active. Any feeling of abandonment is dispelled.

SUPPLEMENT 7—JESUS—
A THEOLOGICAL MODEL

A theology of acceptance

Name the type of people you find hard to minister to.
What are some of the traits that turn you off people?
What needs to happen for you to be able to accept them?
Are there times when confrontation and withdrawal are necessary? (Cite examples from your own and Jesus' ministry.)

A theology of availability

Being called out of hours or when you are about to go home—what does it do to you?
Can availability lead to burn-out?
Have you a fear of burn-out?
Availability may be the tool to lever a pastoral worker into being overused. How would you avoid this?

A theology of accountability

Clergy and pastoral carers are generally individualists and free-lancers. We develop our own strategies and methods of working. What criteria can your group list as ways of measuring accountability?
Quality of care, number of people offered care and self-care are the three elements of accountability.
In a scale of 10, set out your priorities for these three.
(e.g. Quality of care 7, Number of People 2, Self-care 1.)

A theology of care

From Jesus' ministry and his parables, we hear his call to see the caring ministry through to completion. In an institution it is difficult to follow up.

How concerned are you to ensure an ongoing ministry?

What are the factors which make referral back to the community difficult?

How have you handled negative responses from patient, resident or relatives in the past?

How often does duty or responsibility cloud your sense of caring?

A theology of sensitivity

To see, to perceive, to read between the lines when a person is in crisis behavior is evidence of sensitivity.

Are there experiences in your own life that enable you to be more sensitive? (see e.g. Nouwen's *The Wounded Healer*).

Patronizing and caring are unrelated in quality.

To what degree are you aware of it when you become patronizing?

Discuss the evidence of patronizing behavior.

In what ways may sensitivity skills be sharpened?

A theology of obedience

The success of Jesus' ministry hinged upon his obedience to the call to be the Messiah. It is easy to make excuses as a carer and avoid certain awkward situations or to allow some personal activity to encroach upon our obedience to a challenge or to just routine ministry.

The gifts for pastoral care have been given to be used in obedience to the call and appointment. Sometimes appointments are made without there being evidence of a strong sense of call.

Examine the reality of your call to pastoral care service. To what extent do your own feelings or personal desires interfere with or disrupt your obedient (conscientious) functioning as a pastoral person?

A theology of witness

The obligation to witness is binding upon the followers of Jesus. In the hospital setting fulfilling the role of being "salt" or "light" has significant differences for each type of patient.

Identify and evaluate the effectiveness of your perceptions of witness in your hospital ministry.

A theology of servanthood

Service and servanthood are repeated themes in Christian circles. Church members see the minister as their servant without any serious consideration of their own servanthood.

A sense of service or servanthood may be in stark contrast to your fellow professionals' attitude to their work. Have you experienced friction in the team because of your attitude to your involvement?

A servant philosophy may lead to a pastoral carer being exploited by other staff. Is there a point when the carer begins to limit willingness?

When does team harmony versus patient or resident well-being become an issue to be faced?

Is this a spiritual or merely an ethical issue?

A theology of love

The one word which is eminently Christian is the word "love." Hospital care is a ministry of caring through love and sharing God's love in Christ.

In your contact with some of the seemingly unlovable characters of this world, how are you able to overcome any prejudice you may recognize in yourself?

Discuss the quality, depth and significance of caring love.

Share your concerns about under-involvement and the possibilities of over-involvement in particular relationships.

A *theology of confrontation*

Confrontation, at times, results in broken relationships, misunderstandings and animosity. Confrontation need not have disastrous consequences. Confrontation can be for the good.

Are you too confrontational? In what ways can you control and soften your urge to rush in and confront?

Your passiveness binds you, preventing you from confronting people. List several opportunities you have lost when confrontation was necessary. Write down possible conversations that have been successful in each case and discuss these with other workers.

A *theology of renewal*

The current popular cry is "Who Cares for the Carers?"

In most cases the carers are left to care for themselves. Self-care in reality is based on self-motivation for renewal. True renewal allows time and space for physical, emotional and spiritual re-creation in appropriate measure.

What are your methods for achieving your physical, emotional and spiritual renewal?

The means of spiritual renewal vary from person to person. Our needs, our personality, our mental and spiritual abilities differ greatly.

Share both your unsuccessful and your successful attempts at renewal.

For Clergy Visiting Hospitals

CHAPTER
11

Know Yourself

As an ordained minister, the expectations put upon you in a hospital are those of a professional person. As a professional, your dress and sense of decorum may be compared with senior medical officers.

The respect of staff for a visiting member of the clergy has to be earned in these days because of inappropriate behavior, dress, and in some respects, insensitivity to both patients and staff by a few. Confidence in the clergy has waned in recent years.

You will encounter and hopefully will become more involved with patients, staff and relatives, at a deeper level than the lay hospital visitor or pastoral carer. Having read the earlier chapters, there are now some big questions for your consideration in preparation for your hospital ministry.

"How would I cope emotionally in the many types of situations that occur?" Your feelings and the patient's feelings are the essential elements to be understood so that your care may be accepted, be valid and valued.

"What is my attitude toward my own death?" If you have not confronted and considered your own inevitable death, it is not possible for you to adequately empathize with another facing death.

"How do I reconcile many of the injustices of life seen in the hospital?" Hospital experiences frequently bring the carer face to face with challenges to faith.

"Am I able to deal with this situation or should I call in someone more skilled?" To try to counsel or answer a patient's dilemma when it is beyond your expertise can do irrevocable harm.

These four questions must be addressed if it is your desire to do the greatest good for patients and relatives.

Where you stand as a clergy person visiting a hospital is the fifth important point to be addressed. It is answered when you understand your position.

KNOW YOUR POSITION

Your position as an ordained person, or religious, is a special place within the church and its community. Many of the warnings issued to pastoral counselors and even psychotherapists apply to pastoral care workers. Like pastoral counseling, hospital pastoral care is relational. Switzer's phrase applies: "It is being a person to and for another person."[1] The questions which we are going to address in this chapter deal with the carers' abilities to be in touch with their own selves.

The psychoanalyst Robert Carkuff, suggests the need to be aware of what is going on within the carer at any given moment in relation to the patient[2]. The importance of being able to communicate calm and not confusion at the bedside and know what you are doing encapsulates what Carkuff is saying.

Communication, therefore, involves intellectual as well as emotional meanings: thus meaning and feelings are the positive aspects of being a person to and for another person. Meaning and feelings are affected by our attitude and stance toward the patient.

One of the aspects of the relationship likely to be in evidence during the first visit to the bedside is that visiting clergy are accorded a certain status by the patient, who also has certain expectations of them. If the visitor clings to that status role and maintains a position (however slight) of superiority and of possessing the oracle, then that relationship of "to and for the person" will not be achieved. Unfortunately many clergy and even lay pastoral workers view their position as a symbol of power and the patient is left feeling inferior.

What should happen is that the patient sees not a symbol of power but a symbol of reality, the reality of being human and of being a human who reveals and relates to the reality of God. In seeing this the patient does not become dependent upon the symbol of status and position. Rather the reality of God, seen in the person of the pastoral carer, becomes the focus.

As a pastoral carer, your position enables you to bring reality as a human being and the reality of a living God who is concerned for, loves, and is reaching out to the hospital-confined person through you. This is done by giving patients due respect. They have a right to receive this as human beings made in the likeness of God, as you are. The paths the two of you have trod may have varied. Your backgrounds may be different. Your interests may be poles apart. Your outlook on life may conflict with theirs. Nevertheless, they deserve your respect as an equal human being. In this, your visit begins to take on meaning and the patient begins to respond to the caring feelings you are exhibiting. Respect and confidence are thus established.

That respect will come out in the degree to which you genuinely accept that person and desire to draw near. Any lack of respect will declare itself in shallowness or patronizing condescension in your bedside encounter. It needs to be repeated frequently: like a child, a patient is most perceptive to insincerity and "do-good-erism." The latter often provides the motivational impetus for pastoral care workers.

In urging you to "know your position," I suggest you tackle this by searching for the answer to the questions: "Am I sincere in my functioning as a pastoral hospital visitor or just role playing? "Am I seeking greater status and recognition by offering myself as a hospital visitor? Am I meeting a need of my own to be needed? How important is it to me that the bishop, minister or fellow priest acknowledges my hospital ministry in church business meetings and church bulletins?" Remember Jesus did not expect to get enthusiastic notices from the Sanhedrin.

Invariably in the hospital it is not the ego-projecting pastoral care worker who gives the acceptable care to patients and relatives. In times of pastoral need the staff will even cross denominational barriers to summon a proven pastoral care person.

The spirit that Jesus demonstrated when he hitched up his cloak, took a towel, a basin and water and washed the disciples' feet is the spirit with which clergy and visitors to hospitals should gird themselves. We can talk about humility and humbleness. It does not come from knowing we are humble, for that is a contradiction. It was Micah who said that we must walk humbly with our God. As Sheila Cassidy[3] points out, it does not mean that we do this by ritualistically or slavishly fulfilling all the expectations of the church. It is not a code of behavior but a "stance before God." It is not a case of doing the right thing before God but rather of fulfilling your pastoral ministry with God beside you. Your attitude by the bedside should be the constant thought that the God who made you and the patient equal is alongside. To know ourselves and our position as a human like other humans is the stepping stone for productive care in the hospital scene.

KNOW YOUR EMOTIONS

Any hospital chaplain who takes his or her task seriously will admit that chaplaincy is more emotionally, physically and spiritually draining than any parish-based role. The average chaplain has more crisis encounters of the most traumatic kind in one month than the average clergy person would encounter in twelve months or more. The ratio increases with involvement in the team at a trauma center. The hospital pastoral carer must expect to experience exhausting and draining relationships with some patients, their relatives and even staff.

Personal experience proves that unless there is a degree of emotional involvement in the case, the shallowness outlined above will be evident. The patient or relatives will not be given due respect. But the degree and nature of the emotional involvement is critical if you as a carer are to survive or the patient is to develop personally through the relationship and the hospitalization.

If there is insufficient understanding of your own emotions under the sheer weight of the trauma, the injustice and the unfairness of the case, your irrational emotions can gain control. In writing on "pastoral care to the disabled" Jessie Van Dongen-Garrard warns of the development of strong emotional bonds leading to the *manipulation* of the carer by the disabled person [4]. The same can be applied to seriously ill patients and their relatives. Feelings of dehumanization, the loss of the patient's dignity and independence, and the helplessness of the relatives may tend to make the patient try to regain some power or influence over others. The pastoral carer, representing the ever-loving God, becomes the prize target for such control. Manipulators use self-pity and guilt to compel the healthy carer to perform in a "gentle Jesus meek and mild" acquiescence to their whims or those of the relatives. Non-compliance results in accusations of hypocrisy and the falsehood of Christianity or melodramatic scenes of helplessness, pain, despair and depression to shame the visitor into response. Once you succumb the first time to such a play, it is very difficult not to yield again. The emotional net is increasingly and at times imperceptibly being tightened. Any attempt to break free brings on an explosion, which often produces renewed and stronger efforts by the visitor to regain the apparently lost confidence of the patient.

In fact the confidence in the relationship was lost the first time the minister acceded to the manipulation. You must be aware of where your emotions are leading in order to avoid such a situation. An early firm stand against any manipulation results in accepted if unverbalized respect for the depth of character of the carer. The dangers of manipulation were illustrated recently in an extreme case, a suicide attempt. The woman concerned had had an accident and the patient's minister and his wife became a sincere support team. They helped her in every way. When they realized how manipulative she was, they made efforts to reduce the dependency. This was interpreted as rejection, and a serious suicide attempt was made. The suicide note named the minister and his wife as being responsible.

The unanswerable question "Why"? in part expresses anger at the perceived injustice even though it might be the result of a self-inflicted condition. It also is intended to elicit pity and sympathy. It is a play upon the emotions of the visitor and often the "why," after receiving the right response, evinces stronger expressions of anger—at the hospital, its doctors and nursing staff. More often, however, it is against God. Sometimes the pastoral visitor, being seen as God's representative, bears the brunt of the attack.

It is easy for the visitor to be emotionally disturbed at the unfairness of such a tirade. This often results in a counter-attack defending the institution, God, the church and self. The more frequently you respond in defence, the more the patient is indulging self-interest and self-pity. It also reveals that you are not in control of your emotions.

Remember it is not your place to defend the institution. God is big enough to defend himself more ably than you can. As for yourself, look at Jesus before Pilate and Herod—he remained silent before his accusers. The more you try to defend, the more respect you are losing. It is good to draw the anger out. Accept it as the emotionally acceptable way of relieving the mounting inner tensions. In some circumstances you may take some satisfaction in that you have helped release the safety valve and let the patient get rid of some steamed up stress. An emotionally charged defensive counter-attack may result in your needing as much support as the person you went to minister to.

Patients respond emotionally to what they see of your emotions. Awareness of your own emotions and, where necessary, reducing the intensity and frequency of the visits should be considered. Often when inoffensive backsteps are made, the redirection of anger allows a more positive acceptance of the pastoral care being offered.

Attention seeking is the key that turns the manipulative wiles of the patient. You are fed a number of complaints about the staff and their perceived inefficient handling of the patient. It is easy for you to become incensed at these apparent deficiencies in patient care. Representations then might be made on behalf of the family and patient. All too quickly you can become embroiled in some heated exchanges. The staff naturally resent the accusations. When the patient is disgruntled, it is wise to remember that he or she may be trying to restore some sense of personal dignity and authority. The picture may be considerably distorted.

Calmly enquire from the hospital staff exactly what happened without becoming too excited. This will bring a helpful and co-operative staff response, one that will develop their trust in you. They may be able to fill you in on some of the patient's idiosyncrasies which will help you to understand better. Keep in mind that a patient often behaves out of character when under the influence of illness or medications. The need to remain emotionally calm and ascertain facts before taking action on the patient's behalf or sometimes on the staff's behalf is very important.

It is unnatural not to be emotionally moved and then involved with the family group at a deeper level, when the circumstances surrounding the patient and the nature of the illness are particularly tragic. It is possible for a pastoral care person to find themselves accepted and integrated into the family in crisis within a few hours, providing emotional support. Your own emotional commitment and the demands of the family upon your emotional and spiritual resources become exhausting to the point of draining those very resources. If you in empathy are moved to sobbing, confusion and guilt begin to develop in the minds of the family and even the patient, which can be harmful and negative for all concerned. It may cause them to restrict their own expressions of feelings. The balance expected from the carer is not there and the scales are tipped towards emotional chaos for the family. Pastoral persons who do not know their own emotions and how much of the traumatic they are able to absorb should not be providing ministry to those experiencing trauma and tragedy in the hospital.

There was a child under two years, who had had brain surgery for a tumor. The chaplain shared the bedside vigil with the distraught parents. Several weeks after the surgery the child died. Weeks later the mother expressed an unusual observation. She intimated that the most comforting experience was the care of the trainee nurse as she laid her son out. She said that from that she knew the staff loved her son and that they really cared for him. That trainee nurse did her job with tear-filled eyes in a professional and dignified way.

Visiting clergy, unlike the chaplain or that nurse as well, are not fulfilling a professional role if their feelings are out of control. They must act with a warm empathetic spirit in a dignified manner. The patient and relatives need to feel the comfort that comes from the presence of a warm, caring person who is emotionally stable yet feeling with them in their pain, struggle, sadness and loss.

KNOW YOUR MORTALITY

Hospitals are institutions where both acute and chronically ill people are treated. Chronically ill people are seldom facing an imminent life threat. Such a danger may arise if an unexpected complication occurs, such as a heart attack or internal bleeding. Chronically ill patients are expected to receive treatment which will stabilize their condition enough for them to return home. An acutely ill patient has an active, virulent condition which may or may not pose a threat to their mortality. A pastoral visitor must be prepared to meet a patient in any sort of condition.

It is relatively easy to visit a chronically ill patient. It is a different matter when the patient is heavily sedated with pain-killing drugs, receiving chemotherapy or radiotherapy or both, or who is aware that it is just a matter of time before they bid their last farewells to their loved ones and close their eyes in death.

To pay regular visits to a dying patient, noting the obvious deterioration, can be extremely distressing for the visitor, of course. The whole feeling of helplessness, the inability to do or say very much to relieve the discomfort and pain of the patient is bound to affect the visitor as well as the family. An abhorrence of the dying process and death increases with each weary, agonizing, drawn-out emotional day. If as a visitor you are overwhelmed by this cloud of despondency, then the possibility of providing a supportive and positive ministry to the patient and family fast recedes.

The patient and family are expected to be more emotionally involved than you are. They are the ones asking you the question "Why?" They are struggling to find some meaning in the pain, suffering and death of this person they love. Irion suggests that human beings encountering death must find a link to meaning.[5] How does this death fit into the broader plan? Such a quest expresses the need for insight and reveals the fear, guilt and abandonment being experienced.

As the "God-person" on the scene, you are expected to produce some calming panacea. When you are not able to assist, the frustration, despair and torture is increased, with some anger being directed toward you. In current times the charismatic movements' emphasis upon healing has tended to promote a concept that all illness is evil or that it is divine retribution: death is punishment for sin. Some doctors up until this ninth decade of the century have largely felt that a death was a failure of their practice of medicine. The greatest of our cultural myths is that death is unacceptable. Many Christians still persist with this attitude.

As a church pastoral visitor you must have some understanding of what death is all about. In the presence of dying and death our own feelings are stirred. A shaky philosophy of death will make you the one needing to be led: a situation of the blind leading the blind at the bedside.

Pastoral care becomes most helpful when meaning is drawn out from the patient or family, rather than your imposing meaning upon them.

One of the dangers facing any caring person is identification with the one dying. Two ambulance officers brought in a seven-months-old child who had just died from Sudden Infant Death Syndrome (SIDS). I noticed that they were both quite distressed. On enquiry, I discovered that one officer had had a two-months-old child die. His child would have had her fourth birthday that month. The other officer was picturing his own twelve-month-old baby in that position. Both were severely stressed by the case. It was necessary for me to spend time with them before their next summons to duty.

It is highly probable that the dying patient makes you think of a special person in your own life. Age or some special characteristics of face, mannerisms, voice and so on, become the catalyst for such a reaction. This is negative unless you have developed your own understanding of death and its ramifications. In other words, you must be comfortable with the idea of your own mortality.

Because of your acceptance of the appointment by the church, the dying person or their family expect you to be able to cope. Otherwise you are likely to transmit your own fears to those present. Their expectations of you are that you will bring the comfort, strength and the resources of God. Discovering that you are not in possession of these gifts they would be confused, finding that their religious shield against panic and despair is also unreliable. Without such resources they are likely to plunge deeper into confusion. The disappointment becomes complicated when you endeavor to extricate yourself from your embarrassment by suggesting a scripture reading and prayer, or start talking about having faith or about the Lord knowing best. This subterfuge is not acceptable to the distressed and anxious patient and relatives. I reiterate that unless you are comfortable with your own dying, your integrity as a pastoral visitor is at high risk.

When Irion speaks of hospice staff members, he is equally referring to church pastoral care persons:

"They have developed sufficient understanding of their own mortality, so that they do not have to be defensive in their vulnerability. They can communicate comfortably with patients and families about death. They are less tempted to engage in the conventional diversions from discussions of death. This sets a tone that is very liberating to hospice families..."[6]

Dying patients and their families are face to face with two fundamental human facts: death is a universal condition—all die; death is personal—I am dying. The crisis of grief engraves these two facts into their lives. The truth of these two facts peals forth an ominous foreboding. Initial grief seldom sees any optimistic element but usually wallows in the pessimism of the hurtful loss. You are thrust into the midst of people coming to grips with these two ideas. Their ability to cope also depends upon the interpersonal relational dynamics within the family and their own prior resolution of their personal attitude to death. Even so their subjective involvement in the dying creates tensions between rational acceptance and emotional denial.

If you are a pastoral carer who has not worked through your own feelings about death, you will be sucked into this tension because you will be unable to view the case objectively. Very quickly you will find yourself over-involved and over-identifying. Switzer[4] warns that you will feel the pain so deeply that you will incapacitate yourself.[7]

Similarly, Switzer points out that the alternate reaction will be to protect yourself from the pain, isolate yourself emotionally so as to render yourself incapable of offering care and communicating empathy.

Before becoming involved in hospital ministry, preparation for death, dying and grief is essential. This may be done by picturing your own death. Whether it be by road accident, heart attack, stroke or cancer, the mind should be allowed to run wild with fantasies of such scenes. Imagine yourself (that is, your spirit) detached from your body; looking at your dying experience, being at the funeral, watching the committal and the friends and relatives. This is a serious engagement and should not be entered into lightly (see Supplement 3).

Should you engage in such an exercise with little awareness of your own ultimate physical death or deliberately repress any reflection upon your own mortality, it will prove difficult to sustain the fantasies. The images will lack detail and there will be little emotional response. Subsequent contact with a patient or grieving relatives is unlikely to produce a feeling-response of genuine empathy. The exercise is of little value unless there is a willingness to face the issue and let the emotions honestly emerge.

There is also an opposite response, in which there is an emotional reaction which overwhelms the person. The anxiety level rises to the point of hindering the completion of the fantasy, leaving a blockage of the development of the emotions. Fear and an inability to get death out of the mind ensues. Again the ability to help a dying person or their relatives is evidently not possible. Such a carer is not stable enough to handle the situation.

The writing of the last two paragraphs was interrupted by a telephone call from a leukemia patient. This patient has several times defied doctors' prognostications and survived seemingly irretrievable conditions. Chemotherapy and a bone marrow transplant, with their very serious side-effects, have had Cathy struggling for life many times. She is now enjoying improved health. An extended lay pastoral counseling course is keeping her occupied and active.

The phone conversation described a recent dream. In it she was visiting her hematologist who told her that she had come out of remission. Such a report she knew was like hearing the judge passing a death sentence, yet Cathy reported that she had no adverse reaction. She was not frightened at the news. She was comfortable with the thought. In the dream she smiled at the doctor and said, "That's all right. We'll start again." She was aware of life and the likelihood of death. It did not produce any anxiety. Even though she would be leaving two young children, she had confidence that her God was with her and death was not to be feared. She was not denying the reality of the tightrope of life along which she was walking. Cathy had worked through her own mortality and was comfortable with it and her God.

These are the three likely responses to contemplation on your own death. If your response is either of the first two, then you need to see some competent colleague or bereavement counselor who will be able to help you to come to grips with your own feelings about your death. If you are in the last group you will be aware of, and will be able to contend with, the varying pressures and feelings of such circumstances.

It is wise to remember, however experienced you may be in dealing with the dying and death, that you will be draining yourself of physical, emotional and spiritual reserves. Your theological perceptions of death, the dead body, and the future life are under constant attack and must not be taken for granted. They need to be reviewed and talked about with colleagues who are able to understand. This theological reflection may take place when you are debriefing with your spiritual director or other special confidant or with a group who meets regularly to monitor your pastoral care ministry.

It is wise for some form of consistent supervision or debriefing to be undertaken. This will help to restore the physical, emotional and spiritual resources that need regeneration periodically. The natural consequence of pastoral care to the dying and seriously ill is constant reflection upon life and death matters. Such ministry, if it is worth its salt to the carer, will see a developing, changing and maturing theology. Any person who is not growing in theological perception is theologically stagnant, and that stale theology is reflected in the neat, pat and trite pontificating on rights and wrongs that unfeelingly emanate from the mouth of such people. The church should reconsider the credentials of these folk for pastoral care work of any sort. We find them rising to the defense of God on the slightest provocation instead of allowing the Holy Spirit to calmly direct the antagonist's mind to a more considered understanding.

The more one reflects and adjusts to the concept of personal mortality, the more the theology matures, the more practical and useful the ministry becomes and the greater the confidence carers have in the God they represent.

KNOW YOUR FAITH

A pastoral ministry in the context of terminal illness,
demands much of a man,
for it necessitates not only a wealth of psychological stability,
but also a securely grounded faith."[8]

Carlozzi is writing for the ordained clergy and chaplains. Nevertheless what he says applies to all men and women who are official pastoral visitors to the sick and dying. He describes some of the situations the pastoral person encounters. Be warned that many patients (and relatives might be added) grill God's representatives with questions concerning death and the future life. The patient's theology may be based on folk lore as popularly and often inaccurately developed from the stories heard in Sunday school. This theology may be at variance with the patient's present condition. The patient going through the dying process interprets his or her own experience, posing a real threat to the pastoral carer's own ability to offer appropriate and intelligent answers. Then there is a temptation to baffle the patient with theological clichès. Unfortunately the pastoral visitor frequently goes away with the smug feeling of having completed a duty by presenting the gospel to a dying person. The theology presented is confusing, unintelligible, often irrelevant to the patient's needs and at variance with his or her experience, leaving the patient angry and further distrustful of the church.

The question of a differing theology poses a real threat to many clergy visitors. Denominationalism until recent years meant a theological intolerance between the churches, each denomination believing they had the monopoly on all truth. Their interpretations of scripture each believed to be the most accurate as taught by Christ and the New Testament writers.

In hospital visitation it is inevitable that we will be called to minister to people who differ from us in our thinking. The hospital is not the place to correct or dispute the theology of a patient or their family. A dying person and the family members are too concerned over the illness, or may be too affected by medication and pain, to concentrate on a debate of any depth. Our objective should be to allow the person to experience God's peace. When a person is striving to discover that closeness with God through the way they know best, our understanding God will honor their sincerity. He will reach down to them.

Often a patient has shown clear evidence of being aware of the Lord's peace, blessing and presence in their lives merely through prayer linked with a desire to receive that peace. Repentance and confession have not been acknowledged responses or do not appear to have been the avenues of the new relationship with God.

God working in ways different from your customary expectations could pose real problems between you and the patient if you have not come to grips with such issues. Accepting and encountering people who experience God differently from you provides a challenge to your knowledge of God and your own faith.

Where clergy find themselves embarrassed by their inability to cope with the anxiety and frustrating questions of faith they develop what Carlozzi calls the "ecclesiastical defense syndrome."[9] Bowers identifies five common ways in which clergy cope with this syndrome:[10]

"The defense of set apart-ness"—ordination becomes an impregnable barrier which shields from any threats personally to position, to theology or to the church. Patient and family feelings, attitudes or remarks hold little value in comparison to ordination and its status.

"The defense of ritualized action"—the pastor is able to use the sacramental role of offering reconciliation, the Eucharist or anointing as if it was the only requirement of pastoral care for visiting clergy.

"The defense of special language"—ecclesiastical language, theological words and books, such as liturgical manuals, the scriptures or prayer books, are used to fob off and squash any issues raised by the patient.

"The defense of special attire"—clerical dress such as the collar, cassock and so on, are used as a symbol of the closeness between the wearer and God, implying that his or her word on religious matters should be accepted without further ado.

"The defense of business"—this provides the ideal excuse for not being available for long involvement with the difficult issues the patient or relatives are likely to raise. A quick pastoral blessing discharges the responsibility. The needs of other parishioners are mentioned to explain the short visit.

These defenses do not accord with the theology of pastoral care outlined in Chapter 7. They do, however, highlight the insecure faith of the clergy who behave in any of these ways. Pastoral workers must develop a personal theology or faith. Hospital encounters take you out of the sheltered Christian circle to where the fears of the real issues of life are faced. Hospital visitation brings you to real life traumas and heartaches which challenge your basic Christian belief. You are called upon to reappraise your understanding of how God works and what you really believe. Too few Christians have had their faith forged on the anvil of true living. Most Christian beliefs held by the person in the pew are second hand. Hospital visitation should develop in you a practical, experienced faith.

Remember that our personalities, our backgrounds, our intellectual developments and our sub-cultures differ. God, therefore, reveals to us truth in the measure that we can understand and develop. The theological stances of workers in the same church team may differ. They will be able to meet the needs of different people. We must be sensitive as to which patients the Lord would have us become more deeply involved with.

I had difficulty in engaging in a deep ministry to a certain patient who rather arrogantly boasted that she had been cured by the laying on of hands at a healing service (see Chapter 14). Her attitude belied any spiritual experience. Even when the evidence of a deteriorating condition was blatant, the confidence in the healing remained and even a few days before her death, the family denied the real situation. As chaplain, I was unable to effectively minister to the family or the patient. It was impossible to talk or pray about the impending death. Their comfort came from clinging to New Testament texts on healing and on those who would support their beliefs. I tried to remain a friend and a presence.

In such cases, a post-funeral letter may be the more appropriate way of offering ministry and support. I had to accept the disappointment and frustration, acknowledging that ministry is not possible to all by the same person. I had to support this family as much as I could in spite of their theological position, recognizing that to weaken or undermine their faith would have been to destroy their coping ability in the circumstance. They needed all the emotional and spiritual stability possible.

It would have been so much more comforting all round to succumb to the temptation to pray for miracles, to confirm in prayer the healing and to be the sweet person saying what they wanted me to say. By praying for the Lord's peace to be theirs, for the coping strengths to be given, for the warmth of the divine love and presence to be felt, and for them to honestly share their feelings for each other, I presented positive, realistic concepts for them to attempt to reach. Only time will tell whether the spouse will accept my understanding God or develop entrenched bitterness against the deceiving God represented for him in those healing texts. The post-funeral letter still remains unacknowledged twelve months later.

Privacy and confidentiality laws prevent church visitors from moving indiscriminately from bed to bed. To do so leaves the visitor and the hospital open to litigation if the patient objects. However, there are occasions when contact is made with people not of your own church or of no definite religious persuasion. The latter are occasionally known to be like a terrier to a postman. One sighting and they bark and attack the heels. They are often people who have had unpleasant earlier experiences with the church. They attack the system, priests or clergy, and lay church leaders and delight in raising theological red herrings.

These red herrings have been carefully honed by repeated attacks upon unsuspecting church people. Some of the arguments will appear irrefutable. Their logic seems sound. Running counter to your own beliefs, they may raise doubts about your own faith. That is good if it sends you back to do a bit more reading, study, prayer and thinking. Your own faith consideration is important for your spiritual health.

It is wise to recognize that red herrings are meant to cover real issues. Engagement in counter attack should not be considered. Rather the visitor's mind should be considering the best way to draw out the hidden issue. A question like, "You've had a nasty and unpleasant encounter with the church earlier in your life?" This type of question has often let the cat out the bag. The whole and sometimes sordid story floods out.

The issue is not really a faith issue at all. It is a basic church action, or official church position. Often it is the action of one priest, or prominent lay leader and his cronies. It is prudent to openly admit that in any human organization there are some who ride on an ego trip and mess things up. We do not disband a police force for the sake of the odd few bad police.

Let it be stressed again, where our theology is not properly formed, our defensive streak rises to the fore and we are blinded to the real issues. We become side-tracked and get lost, to the detriment of the patient.

Theology and faith are never static. Our theology should be always growing and maturing. Every new experience of life can be used to develop a new understanding of God and of the meaning of life. This is only possible when we can slip away quietly and reflect upon the events. That time of meditation is an appropriate time for God to speak to us through events, revealing otherwise unrecognizable insights. Such discoveries are exhilarating and God-confirming. For greatest benefit it is best to use pen and paper when you start recounting the scenes and dialogue. Such appraisals of recollections are good for stabilizing faith and are encouraged. Chapter 15 and Supplement 9 cover in greater detail this method of theological reflection.

KNOW YOUR SKILLS AND LIMITATIONS

Chaplains are part of the specialized professional therapeutic team working within the hospital. They are expected to have undertaken Clinical Pastoral Education or other supervised pastoral counseling training to develop the specialized skills for this profession. This earns them a place alongside doctors, nurses and other health workers in the total care of the patient. They are often in consultation with the other team members in protocol for the patient. In fact, the distinctive role of the chaplain is fast becoming recognized as an essential requirement of the hospital program.

In Australia, chaplaincy and pastoral care departments are now required for hospitals to be accredited by the Australian Council for Hospital Standards. The Australian College of Chaplains has been established to set standards of chaplaincy and to encourage efficiency and competence among chaplains.

Competence is expected of hospital chaplains by hospital administrators and other professionals, but Campbell rightly cautions against too much emphasis on competence. The danger is that the trumpeting of skills tends to place the stress upon counseling at the intellectual level. It then becomes not pastoral care but counseling. In contrast, much so-called pastoral care by church visitors is offered at the emotional level. Responses to the patient are dependent upon the degree of awareness and control over the personal emotional involvement in the case. Campbell suggests that pastoral care depends to a greater extent on the immediacy of our bodily presence than on counseling techniques"[11]. He wrote his book "Rediscovering Pastoral Care" out of concern at the way pastoral care had moved off at a tangent and was concentrating on counseling techniques, becoming more and more involved in psychotherapy. Pastoral care is functionally different from pastoral counseling, although there are areas of integration.

In fact if we take Campbell's point of pastoral care as "embodied care, care incarnate" for our focus beside the patient, our counseling techniques no longer dominate our thinking. They become a natural part of us. Without a technique consciousness we combine in an unobtrusive way our skills and expertise with our natural human caring, which reaches out and identifies with the patient and the family members involved.

Switzer presents a neat diagram relating pastoral care and pastoral counseling:[12]

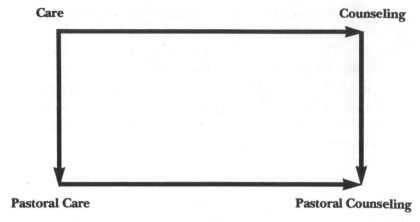

DIAGRAM 1

This is a simple depiction of what Campbell understands of the position.

This, I feel, is inadequate when chaplaincy, parish pastoral care and pastoral counseling are all considered. The following may be more relevant to the situation:

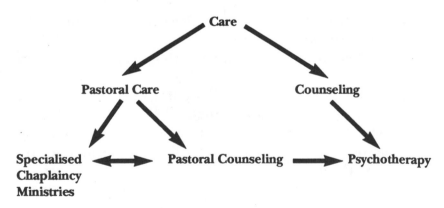

DIAGRAM 2

A caring heart may lead a person into either pastoral care or one of the many forms of counseling services, including social work, telephone counseling and welfare work. Pastoral care involves both clergy and the laity. From pastoral care the development is toward pastoral counseling or specialized chaplaincy ministries. The former may include specialized marriage and family counseling, clinical psychology, stress management, crisis counseling, and so on, with a distinctive spiritual and pastoral ethos. The latter includes any of the specialized forms of civil chaplaincies such as prisons, juvenile institutions, general hospitals, psychiatric hospitals, industrial chaplaincies and others. Here additional knowledge in bereavement counseling, adolescent psychology, home management, medical procedures etc. may be called for. In these types of ministries the needs that the chaplain has to meet are many and varied. Pastoral experience as well as additional training are essential. Theory and practice must be integrated into the patient/client relationship.

In the hospital scene, some cases are straightforward medical or surgical disorders requiring the supportive presence of the pastoral visitor. There are many patients whose reason for hospitalization is more complicated by having some emotional involvement. A woman in her thirties who, as a child, experienced rejection by one of her parents had severe asthma attacks prior to that parent's visit. Some of those episodes were severe enough to necessitate her admission into the intensive care unit.

Another evidence of the effects of early childhood deprivation is in the skill of the patient to manipulate spouse and children into feverish attention by showing severe physical pain symptoms which the doctors are unable to diagnose. After the display of attention has been achieved the pain mysteriously disappears. Those pain episodes occur at the most awkward and inconvenient times for the family when their plans are likely to be most seriously affected.

Psychiatry is continuing to uncover data which reveal that social patterns, and childhood and adolescent social experiences are the cause of many psychiatric, personality, emotional and medical disorders. These disorders sometimes culminate in hospitalization.

There are few lay pastoral workers equipped to engage in therapeutic dialogue with such patients. The ability to discern manipulation, transference, or dependency strategies would be minimal. If visits are stopped completely when an uncomfortableness is experienced in the relationship, this may aggravate feelings of rejection, isolation, and worthlessness, or the feeling of being evil. Acknowledge inexperience to handle the situation and ask, "What can be done?" Knowing when to refer to someone with more training and expertise is an essential art to master. The ability to recognize the appropriate time for such referrals is a matter of perception, to be gained with experience.

Keep diagram 2 in your mind. It will help you to keep a balance in your caring, enabling you to remember there are others with the expertise to handle situations for which your training and experience are inadequate.

There are times when people with special life experiences may be called in. A youth minister might be appropriate for an adolescent; the Sudden Infant Death Syndrome Association (S.I.D.A.) for a cot death is a normal referral. Where a child has died, the parents might be informed of Compassionate Friends' activities for bereaved parents. Parish clergy will often ring a chaplain where there are unresolved grief issues. A woman may not desire to discuss her situation with a male; so a suitable woman confidant is selected. A serious psychiatric disturbance will often be noted by nursing or other staff who will make the necessary referral.

Where a referral has been made, a pastoral worker should not try to deal with the same problem. Your method or words may counter the efforts of the specialist, thus confusing the patient. Less frequent visits to the patient will indicate your diminished role without causing the patient to feel rejected.

SELECTION OF A LAY
PASTORAL TEAM

An honest recognition of personal skills or acceptance of limitations is possible where the person has the necessary character traits and the training to be able to identify a situation and the needs to be met. There are few with sufficient innate gifts for this. Switzer[1] includes hospital visitors and home visitors of the sick among crisis counselors when he warns pastors:[13]

> Careful and enlightened selection procedures are absolutely crucial. The public asking for volunteers could be disastrous, unless the pastor has the procedures and is willing to suffer the consequences of a rigorous evaluation and screening process with the result that some of the people will have to be told that they are not acceptable for the program.

Any minister appreciates how people can be deeply hurt when informed that they are not good enough. So often the spirit is very willing but the talents do not measure up to the enthusiasm. A dampening of the spirit, unless handled prudently and graciously by opening other doors for the candidate, may lead to turmoil. And this too, can pose problems...

From his knowledge of the personality, maturity, responsibility, willingness to accept training and supervision, emotional stability, and available time of various members of his flock, the minister should select a suitable team for training for hospital and lay pastoral ministry.

Carkuff refers to other specific characteristics necessary for a lay pastoral carer:[14]

> Sincere regard for others, tolerance, and ability to accept people with values different from one's own, a healthy regard for the self, a warmth and sensitivity in dealing with others and a capacity for empathy.

All of these should be carefully considered before asking a person to accept lay pastoral training. The "healthy regard for the self," particularly the word "healthy," should be underscored. *Healthy* stands opposed to egocentric. *Healthy* recognizes strengths and weaknesses. *Healthy* does not include self-aggrandizement, the fulfilling of personal, social, emotional or religious needs.

Many volunteers for lay pastoral ministry who display self-confidence often have an unhealthy regard for their self-image. They may be so filled with their self-ascribed gifts that they are unable to hear what anybody else is trying to tell them. In the effort to satisfy their own need, they have to keep on proving to themselves that they can rescue those they visit. They must show themselves to be knights in shining armor.

It requires training, adequate training, to develop lay people who are able to be aware of the real needs of the patient or relative. That training should include role playing and supervision, the supervision to be by analysis of verbatims (written accounts and evaluations of pastoral interviews), audio cassettes or video taping of pastoral encounters. These programs are most successful when there are no more than four or five trainees to a trainer.

It is important to observe that it is often the trained person who is more ready to refer a patient or family to a more experienced or specialized counselor.

THE PARISH CLERGY AS VISITORS

If it is important for lay pastoral care workers to be trained and to have a healthy awareness of themselves, the same is true of members of the clergy. Ordination does not necessarily make a man or a woman a good person at the bedside. From the days of the early church Paul spoke clearly concerning the spiritual gifts of the church leaders. They were diverse, being given to different people for different yet important ministries. Paul speaks of some being apostles, prophets, teachers, miracle workers and healers (1 Corinthians 14). Similarly in the ordained ministry today, some are administrators, preachers, educators, youth specialists, counsellors, street workers, pastoral carers and so on. A parish minister is not expected to be perfect in all areas of ministry. Hospital ministry may not be your forte. A "healthy regard of the self" will be big enough to acknowledge it.

Such a recognition makes the decision to refer to another more skilled in hospital caring easier. It eliminates any sense of jealousy or failure. Concentration on the gifts given is readily accepted by any spiritually-adjusted congregation. Efforts at providing an unrealistic facade of competency in the hospital will bring about the undoing of both patients and the clergy. It is a mistake to try to be what one's spiritual gifts do not cover.

Acknowledging one's areas of competence and efficiency is healthy. To perceive a need and refer a patient or their family members to another more qualified person enhances the perceived integrity of the minister or priest.

NOTES

1. Switzer, David *The Minister as Crisis Counsellor* p 17.
2. Carkuff, Robert *Helping and Human Relations* p 184–187.
3. Cassidy, Sheila *Sharing the Darkness* p 65.
4. Van Dongen-Garrard *Invisible Barriers—Pastoral Care with Physically Disabled People* p 120.
5. Irion Paul. *Hospice and Ministry* p24.
6. Ibid p 53–54.
7. Switzer, David *The Minister as Crisis Counsellor* p 137.
8. Carlozzi, Carl G. *Death and Contemporary Man* p 53.
9. Ibid p 57–58.
10. Bowers, M.K. et. al. *Counselling the Dying* p 67–68.
11. Campbell, Alister V. *Rediscovering Pastoral Care* p 16.
12. Switzer op. cit. p 16.
13. Switzer op. cit. p 273–274.
14. Carkuff op. cit. Vol. 1 p 8.

12

Competence and Empathy

A pendulum swings between two extremes. Pastoral care to the hospitalized also swings between the extremes of caring which a pastoral person has available:

- The emphasis on competence, skill and professionalism and
- The need for personal involvement or empathy.

The hospital is a highly professionalised institution in which the patient is surrounded by people trained to high proficiency. The church's representative is one who comes in the name of the gentle, understanding, caring Jesus. Pastoral care in the hospital ideally is able to span the two above extremes so that the patient experiences both confidence in the skills and perceptions of the visitor and a feeling of closeness, warmth and sensitivity to his or her plight. Gibbs observes that the pastor "will combine the competency of a professional with the compassion and care of a fellow mourner and offer himself to those who grieve."[1] The pendulum must swing.

Special information, special training and special skills are the requirements of professionalism. Henri Nouwen[2] suggests that pastoral care uses these without letting them dominate, but rather with the intimacy generated by a close communication with God. "Beyond professionalism" is the theme.

I understand Nouwen and Gibbs to be saying that the full swing of the pendulum is to be made from professionalism to personal involvement if pastoral care in hospital visitation is to function appropriately.

This chapter aims to look at four special qualities. One at each extreme of the pendulum sweep: competence and empathy; the other two on the downward sweep of the pendulum, one on each side: awareness/sensitivity and sincerity. Let us take a fifth, in the median position of the swing, "compassion" or "care." True care is the result of the use of skills and the sharing of empathy.

COMPETENCE

Credentials, knowledge and an accepted status within the institution or the church can lead at times to an arrogant, aggressive professionalism. Many a time a registrar or resident medical officer has come barging in when the chaplain has been in the midst of praying with the patient or dealing with issues pertinent to the patient's wellbeing. Ignoring the chaplain, this doctor interrupts and talks to the patient. The chaplain excuses himself and waits to speak with that doctor a little later. The usual procedure, however, is for a professor or other consulting specialist to excuse themselves and seek permission to enter or to go away to see another patient until the chaplain has finished. A registrar or resident who barges in is using their professional status to assert their perceived right to have their own time and their own way. No doubt they are very competent in their knowledge and practice of medicine and in the fulfillment of their role. However, their professionalism is blinkered if they do not see the value of the other professional in the same team. At the stage of intrusion the patient may have been on the point of cathartic acknowledgment of the diagnosis.

True professionals respect each other's spheres of competence. Doctors perceive that the patient has other needs that the chaplain may meet. The chaplain on another occasion may invite the doctors to continue their rounds uninterrupted, making way for them. That is professional etiquette in the hospital. Competence includes assessing the needs and priorities of a patient within a professional team.

However, competence refers more to the manner in which the patient and/or the relatives are treated by the carer. It applies to the efficiency with which the knowledge, training and skills are utilised. The extent to which the carer is able to use those professional skills in an unobtrusive, reassuring, non-threatening way is the measure of successful pastoral care at the bedside.

A skilled pastoral care person will have spent many hours in training: reading, presenting, being supervised and being challenged in groups. That training will have alerted the trainee to all kinds of behavior and personality traits shown by people. Methods of handling and caring for the sick would have been demonstrated and explained. Undoubtedly Rogerian counseling would have been underscored. Rogers' contribution to pastoral care methodology is unquestionable, but problems arise when reflective responses dominate the interview. The patient becomes aware of the carer's training techniques and begins to feel uncomfortable. Often patients request not to see that pastoral person, or social worker again. The feeling of being a patient under scrutiny for psychiatric labeling, even by a priest or minister, is very threatening, arousing suspicion and mistrust. The important part of pastoral competence is the ability to utilize techniques learned without obviously or offensively showing them during the conversation.

Theology, ethics, crisis and bereavement understanding, personal self-awareness, mutuality, transference, confrontation, hope, guilt, feelings and emotions, stress and anxiety, and communication are areas which have been pored over both in class, in groups and privately. Granted that use develops confidence, fluency and comfortableness in ideal hospital visitation, the versatility of the pastoral carer's training is broader than that of some other health care workers. The religious component is something which others are not called upon or expected to use.

Carkuff's[3] advice to ministers involved with a crisis situation suggests 3 Rs for them to consider. They are particularly applicable to pastoral carers:

- Right
- Responsibility
- Role

The *right* of the helper to intervene in the life of another involves more than acceptability to the patient; the access you have to them through your church position, or the fact that you know them is not enough. Your right to be there depends upon your competence to deal with the patient. You must be in a position where you are functioning at a higher level of efficiency or are more able to function in the areas of concern than the person who is requiring help.

Once the right to intervene in the life of a person has been established and accepted, the *responsibility* for such intervention has to be accepted. There are those who opt for pastoral care ministry because they have experienced some of the traumas life offers. They come into pastoral care with many of their own personal issues unresolved and with no clarity in their own mind as to how to cope. Pastoral care offered for purposes of self-fulfillment is likely to add to the distortions in the other person's life. There is a responsibility to bring support, comfort, strength and personal uplift to the patient and relatives.

The *role* of pastoral workers involves a commitment to do all that we can to alleviate anxiety and distress, promoting a wholeness of mind and spirit. This may in some measure provide relief for the physical body. It is a role which offers something positive. The question for the pastoral carer then becomes, "How well am I going to function in order that the other will benefit?" It must go beyond spiritual benefit alone. It must have beneficial effects on the whole person.

In order to be able to continually do this in the role of pastoral carer, we must be contributing more than we receive from each bedside or other encounter. It means that we must ever be seeking ways and means of balancing and recovering. We do this by seizing every opportunity available for training by other professionals, by accepting some supervision of our ministry, by being involved in growth groups and continuing the process of developing self-awareness. Pastoral care in our fragmented world is not only necessary, it requires competent and efficient personnel.

While pastoral care has been practised by Christ's followers since the time he was on earth, human life has become much more complicated. Technology, higher living standards, education, multicultural influences and environmental pollution have removed mankind from the simple, more predictable lifestyle of the hunter-gatherer or the agriculturalist. Pressures upon the modern human in the global society produce complex distortions of human life and its needs. In the field of medicine there is a mounting identification of disorders of body, mind and spirit which is encouraging research to help minimize their effects. People in ministry need to keep up with research in pastoral care and counseling in order to be able to provide the required support and understanding in the most efficient way.

The large number of books on pastoral care, the establishment of Departments of Pastoral Theology and Practice, and field supervision in the curricula of seminaries, international congresses in pastoral care and pastoral counseling, and supervised clinical pastoral education programs are all indicators of the growing awareness that pastoral care is a specialized ministry requiring special skills.

The degree of your competence in such ministry will be seen in your acceptability to staff. Staff observe your approach to patients. They also get feedback from the patients themselves. When the staff feel that they can trust you with their patients, their co-operation and willingness to call upon you to help with other patients become increasingly evident. It takes time to earn such confidence. Competence is also reflected in the way you approach and respect staff in their various roles.

It is not possible to deal with all the aspects of "competence," but as an example, we shall look at one of these qualities to demonstrate the type of responsibility accepted when people volunteer for pastoral visitation in hospitals.

AWARENESS AND SENSITIVITY

During hospitalization individuals face many threats to their personhood. Our cultural perception of "person" is seen daily on television, in the printed media, heard on radio and observable almost everywhere. Most advertising reinforces this cultural conditioning about physical perfection and health. Barbie dolls and Superman emphasize to children a stereotypical physical beauty and prowess.

Illness threatens this image and helps produce the feeling of being less than human. Patients are conscious that their body is not able to do all that it is expected to do. There is a sense of loss of identity because we identify people by what they can do. Their sense of self worth faces serious threat. Sometimes the feeling of regression to childhood dependence makes the patient uncharacteristically demanding. Perhaps the biggest threat is to personal security. These threats have been considered to some degree in "Patient in Crisis" (Chapter 7).

The threat can be strengthened by the treatment the patient receives from staff, relatives, other visitors and pastoral workers. Various conspiracies may be formulated by well-meaning doctors, relatives and pastoral visitors who are meant to help and protect the patient. These may involve the awareness levels experienced by the patient and others. Glasser and Strauss in the late 60s identified four types of awareness and the effects they have on the patient. They are:

- Closed awareness: others know—patient does not know;
- Suspected awareness: others know—the patient suspects;
- Concealed awareness: both know and conceal the knowledge;

• Open awareness: both know and openly share.

In the first three, a "conspiracy of silence" is operative.

Closed awareness

A diagnosis has been determined. The relatives have been informed and often instruct the doctor not to tell the patient. Some of their reasons may be valid (for instance, the patient is a worrier who gives in to panic very easily). The protection of the patient at that stage may be a valid concern. However, there is difficulty in maintaining the masquerade without people becoming involved in lies and deceit.

It must also be recognized that the patient may not want to know. During a weekly round of a surgical ward with the senior surgeon, a social worker raised an issue. Mr. Smith had inoperable lung cancer. His wife knew. He didn't. Mrs. Smith felt she couldn't carry the burden alone any longer and felt her husband should be told. The surgeon suspected that Mr. Smith could not face the facts. The social worker was requested to see if Mr. Smith wanted to know what his condition was. If he gave a positive indication, then he was to ask the surgeon the next week on rounds. If he did not ask the doctor, the social worker was to prompt him by saying, "Mr Smith, isn't there something you want to ask the doctor?"

Mr. Smith did not ask. He did not want to know. The knowledge of what was actually wrong with him would most probably have destroyed any quality of life in his remaining days. Support under these circumstances cannot deal with the real issues, yet is very much needed by the patient.

Suspected awareness

This situation is different from closed awareness. Patient "A" wants to know. He suspects but is unsure. When the doctors make their daily rounds, "A" seems to have ten ears, interpreting the worst even in the inflections of voice. Many a time have patients had to be reassured that their assumptions were wrong. They are suspicious, accusing doctors and staff of covering up. They continue looking for clues and treat everyone with caution, as a conspirator.

The danger in suspected awareness, when the condition is actually serious, is that doctors, relatives and visitors are under a strain lest they let something slip. Patients detect this shackling of communication, which only strengthens their suspicion, escalates their fears and shatters any hope. Their emotions are continually oscillating. As time passes, despair and depression begin to dominate.

In yet other cases patients may suspect and not want to know. Let it be said again, at least eighty percent of patients know when they have a serious illness.[4] In these situations the less the patient knows about the prognosis, even the side-effects of the treatment, the better they are able to cope. There is less likelihood of their fretting and apprehensively anticipating the next development of the disease. They are able to relate to visitors in a more relaxed way.

Ability to assess where the patient is at and what should be done is one of the skills the pastoral visitor must ever keep well honed.

Concealed awareness

Here both parties are playing protection games. It frequently happens between a child patient and parents who insist that the child not be told of the serious nature of an illness. Some cultural groups leave the decision to tell the patient and members of the patient's family to second-degree male relatives (that is, cousins and uncles). These make the judgment whether family members are able to cope with the news.

The patient wants to protect the family from distress and emotional pain, as well as to protect themselves from causing such anguish of heart. Similarly, the family want to shield their suffering loved one from further heartache and fear. They feel that the mutually shared knowledge of a worsening condition and even impending separation by death would be emotionally intolerable.

The games played between the parties serve to keep a superficial air of normality in the relationship. There is a freedom to laugh, joke and make light of everything. It is when the visit has concluded that the emptiness hits home, along with hurt and the sense of isolation.

The sadness of this situation is that no real communication is possible. No sharing of feelings can be on the agenda. The tension of bottled-up emotions bites deeper. Yet for some it is the only feasible way of relating, particularly when the parties naturally keep their feelings to themselves and are normally introverted. Visiting clergy, by being alert to this situation, may be able to release the valve and allow expression of the pent up emotions.

Open awareness

This is the ideal, when both the individual, and all others involved, know what is happening and is likely to happen. It allows unfinished tasks to be attended to. Where relationships have been strained, attempts can be made to facilitate reconciliations. Reunions with past friends and infrequently-seen relatives are arranged. Freedom to grieve and cry together before the separation is mutually therapeutic. Honesty, openness and trust characterize most communication between the parties. The patient's burdens may be shared.

However, open awareness may be disastrous. It can block communication because of discomfort in the presence of the patient, embarrassment caused by not knowing what to say or do, or fears of experiencing the same kind of illness. Particularly if it is an hereditary condition, personal fears are aroused. Open awareness may cause a fall in the frequency of visits to the patient. It is hard for visitors to always try to be strong for the patient and not break down.

Why has awareness been singled out for special attention in discussing the skills required of pastoral care workers? The reason is that it highlights the need for acute sensitivity as to what is going on with the patient, the family and the staff. An insensitive pastoral visitor may reveal what the patient is not ready yet to accept, or may highlight the family's conspiracy of silence, or may even pass on as fact the conjectured condition of the patient as discussed with the relatives or staff.

As a chaplain sitting in on staff clinical meetings, it is possible to know more than the patients and relatives. A safe approach is to ask, "What has the doctor been telling you?" The patient is given the opportunity to be as open or as closed as desired. The cue is then given as to how far the conversation may proceed in discussing the implications for the patient. It also indicates the degree of support of which the patient is in need.

Unless there are critical reasons for making an ad hoc decision to alter the particular awareness type being engaged in by the patient and others, the pastoral visitor should not do it without consultation with family and the hospital team. A weakened heart condition, of which the visitor knows nothing, may be the reason for the non-disclosure of the real facts for the present. Added anxiety from such knowledge could predispose the patient to another stroke.

Sensitivity comes with training and experience. Your own ability to be aware of what is going on and your competence to discuss the situation with staff and relatives before any change of direction, are important for supportive and helpful pastoral care.

Let us now move to the other extreme of the arc of the pendulum swinging through competence, skills and professionalism to the need for personal involvement or empathy. This is the swing from the head to the heart, from the clinical to the emotional.

EMPATHY

Over the last three decades there has been a radical change in nursing education attitudes to the relationships nurses should allow themselves to have with patients. Prior to this the edict was inflexible: "Nurses do not get emotionally involved with patients." Nurses today are free to develop friendships with patients and their families. The reason for the strength of many of those relationships is that the nurse has become emotionally involved with the patient. Support has been offered beyond the call of duty as a nurse. They have shared tears at the appropriate moments. They were not tears of panic or hysteria; they did not affect the judgment or professional efficiency of the nurse. In fact they showed a heightened perception of the needs and feelings of the patient and relatives. These nurses have revealed a depth of empathy with the patient.

Empathy is a big word in pastoral care circles. It is often used and little understood. While centered in the heart, empathy has an in-built sense of objectivity. A heart response alone creates the distortions encouraged by subjectivity. Such behavior at the bedside may leave both patient and visitor in the same state of teary depression, wallowing in the misery of hopelessness. In this case no hope, comfort or strength is being offered to the patient. This is the type of situation earlier nursing administrators tried to avoid with their bans on emotional involvement.

Empathy is the ability to enter into and share the feelings of another person whether they are positive or negative reactions to life's situations.

It is easier to share the rejoicings of a patient whose biopsy results come clear of any malignancy than to share the feeling with patients whose results are positive of cancer. Yet the caring visitor must be able to enter into the emotions of the patient in both types of situations.

Most chronically and acutely ill people with a significant bodily disorder find difficulty in communicating the real feelings and experiences of their illness. They suppose there is no one who understands what they are going through. In some respects that is true because each person, each condition and each response to treatment is unique. It may not be possible to understand all that is going on. It is, however, possible to understand in substantial measure and so give the patient the freedom to be open and expansive about what are unique experiences.

Carkuff differentiated between two levels of empathy: a "primary level" and an "advanced level" of accurate empathy.[5] In the first he saw the visitor communicating his or her understanding of what the patient was experiencing and feeling. In the second the visitor goes deeper, identifying motives for the feeling of which the patient was not consciously aware.

Egan takes up Carkuff's distinctive levels in his own way:

Accurate empathy in general. A person is accurately empathetic if he or she can:

1) *Discriminate:* get inside another person, look at the world through the perspective or frame of reference of the other person and get a feeling of what the other's world is like; and

2) *Communicate* to the other this understanding in a way which shows that both the *feelings* and the *behavior* and *experience* underlying these feelings have been picked up.[6]

Empathy does not stop at the understanding and feeling level. You may feel in measure the hurt and anger of a mother who is waiting for news of her young son knocked down by a speeding, drunken driver at a pedestrian crossing. Empathy includes the ability to accurately communicate to that mother your understanding of her feeling. Then, knowing you understand and are feeling with her, she pours out more of her own anguish as she describes the lovable and the naughty qualities of her little boy who may not survive. Your eyes fill as her tears flow. You have a lump in your throat as you share those moments or hours or days of crisis with her. She is able to drop her inhibitions with you, though perhaps you were previously a little-known acquaintance or maybe a complete stranger.

PRIMARY LEVEL ACCURATE EMPATHY

The visitor tries to let patients or relatives know that he or she has some understanding of what they are expressing about themselves.

Tony has been diagnosed as having multiple sclerosis or some motor neuron deficiency condition. These are long-term, slowly crippling and paralyzing diseases. The patient says, "I've been such a physically active person. It will feel as if I'm a prisoner in my own body. I'm scared. It's too claustrophobic."

A pastoral visitor could respond in several ways:

Visitor A: "Cheer up, you'll adjust quickly to a new lifestyle."

Visitor B: "At least you know what it is and the doctors will be able to help you."

Visitor C: "They've got so many groups and things going for people with your condition. You'll find it won't be that bad."

Visitor D: "You're down in the dumps with the news. We all think the worst when we are told something like that."

These are typical of many responses by pastoral visitors and others to patients in such circumstances. They reveal that the visitor is not hearing and understanding the deep fear and panic being experienced. They also declare to the patient that the visitor is uncomfortable with the situation and does not want to face the real issue. The visitor sees the purpose of the visit as being to relieve the feeling of doom and cheer up the patient. The above replies only depress the patient more, driving the fears and sense of hopelessness deeper. Patients in those situations sense that they are not being heard and conclude that no one will understand. This results in a bottling-up of the feelings and a reluctance to air them in the future.

An appropriate primary level accurate response might be:

Response i: "It is a dreadfully frightening prospect. It must seem as if you've been sentenced for a serious crime you didn't commit, and you're being shoved into jail for life."

Response ii: "You were such a sporting type. For this to happen to you is devastating. It'd be stifling, suffocating and frightening."

Response iii: "You must feel more than scared, even trapped, angry, shocked, bewildered."

Primary level accurate empathy in these examples has been communicated because the patient now knows:

a) the visitor understands that the patient is feeling scared and trapped; and

b) the visitor understands the experiences underlying these feelings.

Responses i and ii illustrate this understanding by referring to the jail analogy and the patient's love of sports. Response iii gives evidence that the sudden cutting off of sporting activities must have generated anger, shock and a lot of questioning. The added indication is given that the carer knows the patient has deeper feelings than those expressed and is free to express them.

ADVANCED LEVEL ACCURATE EMPATHY

Primary level empathy interprets what the patient or relative states or expresses. Advanced level accurate empathy probes into the implied, unsaid or vague feelings which may be indicated by any non-verbal messages which the visitor notes.

The multiple sclerosis patient is a young man in his late twenties. He is married with two young children. They have moved into their own house and face a substantial mortgage commitment each month. On the first visit by a pastoral carer, the matter of the house is mentioned several times. Paul, the patient, remarks, "It's a lovely house. All new curtains and blinds. Sheila made the curtains herself and they look good. I helped to hang them. I've just finished landscaping the ground. The lawn's coming on fine and the spring annuals are beginning to bud. It's going to look a picture. All the hard work has been worth it."

Paul is not complaining. He seems very pleased with his new house. Advanced empathy probes the remarks.

"You've worked hard and you've been too tired to do other more pleasurable things. Do you wonder whether it is all worth-while if you have to give up your job? It would be tragic if you couldn't keep up your mortgage payments after all the work you've put in."

This is probing the feeling that the house is really a disturbing problem to Paul.

A remark like this to a real patient caused the patient to break down, as he had refused to take out any insurance on the house for such an eventuality. He was devastated because he condemned himself for not protecting the future security of his wife and children. He felt he could not forgive himself. Advanced empathy was able to draw him out.

Our patient, Paul, did not overtly state his fears. The response elicited from him was an indication that he really felt understood, also that there was something else going on inside which was not being brought into the open.

Empathy is being able to perceive and understand the implicit as well as the explicit indicators that the one in need is flashing. Empathy goes beyond the heart.

Pastoral care today may err on the side of being too skill orientated, too psychological and too professional. The pendulum must make a full swing from head to heart.

SINCERITY

On the return swing of the pendulum from the responsive feeling and emotional giving of the carer, the perceptive patient is searching for clear evidence of a particular quality of caring. The filled eyes, the choked throat, the sense of anger and frustration shared with the patient must look genuine. Where involvement is due to a desire to be where the action is, or to feel needed, or to raise one's credit rating, it will be quickly identified as such by the patient. Pastoral care offered without sincerity or genuineness is not true pastoral care.

Appointment, ordination or consecration as a minister, priest, sister, deaconess, chaplain or pastoral care visitor carries an inherent danger. It is an official task. It is a job to be done. There are certain expectations to be fulfilled. The mission or role of hospital pastoral carer may become paramount and the patients or relatives secondary. The position of carer may swamp the needs and the person of the patient. Some of the flaws which are evident in this emphasis on the role have been seen in "Beware of Temptations" (Chapter 8). Basically, pastoral visitors are prone to the accusation of lack of sincerity or genuineness.

The role-centered hospital visitor may have attended courses or pastoral care preparation groups and so have an idea of some of the skills needed, but genuineness reveals the humanness of the visitor. It provides evidence to the patient that some, if not most, of the feelings being shared are mutually experienced. The willingness to tear away the role mask, and be open and appropriately self-revealing, deepens the relationship in a helpful way.

This is contrasted with the sweeping remark, "I know just how you feel". As people respond differently to a given set of circumstances, so no two people in the hospital scene can fully understand each other's physical, social, emotional and spiritual situation.

The above remark savors of feigning understanding.When such statements are offered, efforts may be made to justify them by a long-winded recital of another case recently experienced. The tone and manner of this center-stage thrust belies any sense of true empathy.

Gerald Paul[7] attacks the hospital visitation program that adopts the psychological assumption "to reduce reality to 'just me and you.'" He recommends his practice of going in and talking about nature and bringing community news. He continues, "By encouraging an outpouring of self-pity, we reinforce the alienation of our hospitalized parishioners. It is better to take charge and bring the bigger world to the patient's smaller one. By doing this I escape the needless doldrums imposed on me every time I give a 'poor, poor me' wretch the reins...I used to stress hospital visitation as a one-to-one relationship between pastor and parishioner. How wrong I was!"

Note his use of "I" in the quoted passage. It is difficult to see any sign of genuine interest and concern for the patient's bewilderment, grief and sense of despair, or hopelessness, in it. To talk about nature and be bright and cheery in some circumstances is likely to bring on a severe depression.

Sincerity allows patients the freedom to be natural, to express themselves openly, to develop a trust in you that reveals previously unmentionable events and thoughts. Providing that freedom may mean that another carer is chosen to be the chief confidant. If you are sincere you will accept the patient's choice without personal hurt. Richard Soulen suggests that caring about your own integrity (genuineness) "helps the patient to care about his own." He postulates that sincerity is contagious.[8] Your sincerity will help the patient to be free to be sincere.

Priest in the same book indicates that the greatest gift we can offer to the dying is ourselves—"honest, open and unafraid."[9] To be with another in the midst of personal anguish is to offer the gift of humanity. In offering ourselves we are offering the real me—the genuine me, spontaneous, non-defensive, consistent and attentive.

That real me makes possible a deepening relationship in the crisis. It establishes a pattern of positive, helpful and searching communication. It avoids manipulation of a captive patient into dying "a good death" or compelling the discharged patient to live "a reformed life." It becomes relevant to the family as well as to the patient where possible. The real *me* who has a close relationship with God radiates the God-likeness—which may lead to an appreciation and need for ritual and/or sacrament.

In discussing the methods of crisis counselling, Switzer[10] sees genuineness as "both the means and the ends of counseling." Sincere people are aware of themselves and the experience of the patient. They are able to communicate that awareness to the patient. A person who lacks this quality is out of touch with their own feelings and are unable to articulate them to another person. Consequently, negative vibes are transmitted to the one being visited.

For all the emotional involvement, all the use of techniques, unless the pendulum encompasses sincerity, the visit most probably will be of little value apart from the surface talk about nature, the birds and the trees and perhaps the delivery of a cheery smile.

The pendulum in its swing from the heart end back to the mind passes through that all-important median position, care, the point from which productive and blessed pastoral care emanates. Any bias toward one side or other of the arc restricts the effectiveness of the hospital visit. The median is the point where competence and emotion with their intermediate strengths combine in exercising a ministry of care. This is the ministry with prospects of blessing, uplift, comfort and presenting humanness, sensitivity and peace to those struggling to find meaning and to understand the prevailing mystery in their lives.

CARE

Jesus, we saw earlier, is the outstanding model for pastoral care. There are those like Gerald Paul who dismiss the need for training and for any understanding of human dynamics in the variety of life's experiences. Others would suggest responding with the natural emotions that you feel as you face the hospital scene. They will point to Bethany where Jesus wept over the death of Lazarus, or was it over the grief and distress of Mary and Martha? Nouwen writes of a New Testament expression used only twelve times and only in relation to Jesus or his Father.[11] The word is translated as "to be moved with compassion." The root word is "entrails of the body." We today speak of "gut feelings." The deepest and most intense emotions were considered by the Greeks to reside in the bowels, hence the phrase, "bowels of compassion."

The word "compassion," as Nouwen points out, comes from the Latin words *pate* and *cum* which together mean "to suffer with." Nouwen continues:

Compassion asks us to go where it hurts, to enter into places of pain, to share in the brokenness, fear, confusion and anguish. Compassion challenges us to cry out with those in misery, to mourn with those who are lonely, to weep with those in tears. Compassion requires us to be weak with the weak, vulnerable with the vulnerable, and powerless with the powerless. Compassion means full immersion in the condition of being human.[12]

Jesus, in the passage instructing us to love our enemies (Luke 6), concludes with a command "to be compassionate as your Father is compassionate." The New International Version weakens this word when it is translated as "merciful." We must consider "compassion" as an essential characteristic of the caring person toward any sufferer. Are we to see it as a heart, empathetic, gut feeling response?

Jesus is asking us to enter into a relationship with others, as God has done with us. We are called to walk the same path as Jesus. He was certainly moved deeply as he saw suffering humanity. He was emotionally involved.

Jesus also said that we are his disciples if we love one another, if we show compassion, if we sit where our neighbor sits.

As disciples, as pastoral care workers, the word discipline is relevant to us. "Disciple" comes from the word discipline. Without discipline we cannot be disciples. Without discipline we become merely followers. Pastoral care involves the discipline of knowing what to do, how to do it and when to do it. If Jesus had been ruled by the heart at the time of Lazarus' death, he would have been in Bethany four days earlier. He perceived the wisdom of delaying his entry so that Mary and Martha and the disciples would learn so much more about him and his future resurrection. His heart did not dominate.

Two dangers for the emotional and empathetic carer are over-involvement and over-identification. When there has been a very traumatic case, or a long-term patient and death is imminent, it is prudent to call staff together to talk out their feelings about the patient's death. These are times when tears are shed. Personal identification by staff may be with the patient or a family member, or a friend as the dying patient. Freedom to talk it out has enabled staff to care more effectively for the patient during the last hours. These sessions bring involvement and identification into perspective.

Pastoral care workers sometimes are so guilty of over-involvement and over-identification that they smother the patient and the family, often denying them the privacy they need at such a time.

One clergyman became so involved that reason went out the door during the eulogy at the funeral service. The deceased, who was killed while driving a car intoxicated, was a wife-basher and an objectionable character. The eulogy painted him in idealized terms in order to make it easier for the wife. She was told he was now the perfect husband waiting in Heaven to welcome her as the perfect bride. That is not pastoral care. That is undisciplined emotion.

We are called to be disciples of Jesus with his discipline. We must follow the example of his use of wisdom, of knowledge and experience of human behavior, with the discipline of spiritual preparation. After the feeding of the five thousand he went to the hills to pray. After a Sabbath of healing and preaching, he rose early in the morning to pray. Pastoral care in the hospital requires the preparation and balanced use of heart, mind and spirit.

It is at this median point of the pendulum's swing, that the spirit of God is able to weld together the mind's knowledge and the heart's feeling. The living God will use this knowledge and feeling to provide the right care for the person or persons to whom you are called to minister at a particular point of need. This is pastoral care.

Carlozzi warns that

... the man who is spiritually dry internally can offer nothing to those to whom he ministers, except, perhaps, his own despair, lack of trust in God's goodness, and the burden of his own personal inadequacies.

On the other hand, an effective and responsible pastoral ministry demands of the Pastor a disciplined and secure faith in God through whom he derives confidence and trust in his own abilities.[13]

A pastoral carer becomes the incarnate presence of Christ's love to the patient or relative.

R.E. Buxbaum, an American chaplain, in an unpublished paper, titled "The Protestant Ministry to the Dying in the Hospital Setting", says:

> ... Even God could not communicate his love until he did it in person...In the same way we cannot communicate the fullness of God's love until we become incarnate.

It is in this that we demonstrate that we are Christ's disciples, and are able to offer the care of the master shepherd who is in us, motivating us and using our discipline of mind and heart. In this we are showing that we are not merely disciples of the behavioral sciences, or of emotional responses, but that we use the full range of qualities which a disciple of the living Christ possesses.

"Be compassionate as your father is compassionate." This is the care that pastoral visitors to hospitals, as disciples of Jesus, are called upon to minister, mirroring God's love in all that we do.

NOTES

1. Gibbs, C. Earl *Caring for the Grieving* p 173.
2. Nouwen, Henri J.M. *Creative Ministry* pp 60ff.
3. Carkuff, Robert *Helping and Human Relations* pp XI–XIV.
4. A statement at a public lecture conducted by E. Kubler Ross in Sydney in 1979. This has also been confirmed by my own experience in hospital ministry.
5. Op.cit. Vol. 1.
6. Egan, Gerard *The Skilled Helper* p 76ff.
7. Paul, Gerald W. *Ministry* p 4ff.
8. Soulen, Richard N. et al. *Care for the Dying* p 78.
9. Ibid. p 56.
10. Switzer, David K. *The Minister as Crisis Counselor* p 75.

11. Nouwen H. J. M. *Compassion* p 16.
12. Ibid. p 4.
13. Carlozzi, Carl G. *Death and Contemporary Man* pp 60–61.

CHAPTER

13

Why Suffering?

Any regular visitor to a hospital will inevitably be asked the question "Why?" "Why me?" That question involves more than the Kubler-Ross explanation of it as a response of anger. Fundamentally it is a theological question. The question is not one that the patient alone faces. The pastoral visitor, time and time again, will also ask, "Why should it happen to him or her?" or "Where is God in this?" What is at issue here is the problem of evil.

It is difficult to condense into one chapter whole books on the problem of evil and suffering. As long as there is human life, it will remain a contentious issue.

Schilling maintained that there are three main approaches to the subject of suffering.[1] The first is that of *the sensitive thinker*, religious or otherwise, in his or her philosophical approach to the world. This person is keen to understand human existence. He recognizes the contradictions in the world of good and evil.

Some of these thinkers see the universe as uninterested in good and evil and therefore for them there is no point in maintaining that there is a problem. It is here. It happens. We can't do anything about it. Others simply admit there is "some principle of order, a generative force, or a blind purposeless vitality." Some force developed the universe aimlessly or purposelessly, they say. A third approach by these sensitive thinkers is that there are possibly two cosmic forces, one the protagonist of evil, the other of good. Another extension of this thinking is that there is one reality with two sides, good and evil.

The second group are the *atheists*. Some researchers say that a large percentage of atheists were denied opportunities to grieve the loss of a significant loved one in early childhood. The unresolved bewilderment and suffering could not find reconciliation in a God of love they were told about. The extent of evil and suffering observed in natural forces and people's inhumanity to people and the obvious injustices meted out to good people, confirms atheism's stance.

The third group are the *theists* or *religious believers*. As we know, suffering provides the greatest source of confusion in religious believers' thinking. The Psalms echo repeatedly the psalmist's searching for the answer as to where God is.[2]

Epicurus as recorded by Lactantius (who died c. 330 AD) is cited by Schilling as proposing four possibilities:

- God wants to remove evil but is unable;
- He is able but unwilling;
- He is neither willing nor able;
- He is both willing and able.

The last is the only option for a believer. Augustine asked the question in his Confessions:

Where, then, is evil and coherence and how crept it in further? What is its root, and what is its seed? Or has it no being at all?...Whence is evil?(V11:5)

Augustine maintained his emphasis upon the almighty power and perfect goodness of God. He saw God as a mystery that human minds were unable to comprehend.

Thus we see that from the early days of the church, the problem of evil has been an issue still unresolved. Yet as pastoral carers we must ourselves look at the issues involved.

The question also can be posed "Is the problem of evil and suffering a creation of Christianity?" For the Muslim it is no problem. It is believed that everything that happens in a person's life was determined by Allah in the first forty days after conception.

It is my experience that an Arabic Muslim in the last stages of cancer will interrupt his own and the chaplain's conversation every two minutes or so with the words "Hum Dullah" or "Thanks be to God." He is praising God for each experience of discomfort. He does not question or object to his physical pain. He does not want Allah to feel he is ungrateful or complaining his lot.

Richmond writes:

> The problem becomes more acute through the New Testament's affirmation that the nature of the God revealed in Jesus is love...Christianity has a problem in attempting to reconcile a God with an inherently loving nature who maintains some sort of control or influence over the created world on the one hand, with the very evident and contradictory existence of evil and suffering present in that world on the other.[3]

Richmond highlights five problem areas for many Christians:

1) Faith in God is supposed to protect those who believe, but the Book of Job shows otherwise.

2) Those who live righteous and unselfish lives should live free of suffering. Yet look at the lives of the apostles after Pentecost. Throughout history saints have suffered.

3) The presumed innocence on the part of the one who suffers is confusing. This is exemplified in seeing small children suffer and die from lukemia or a brain tumor.

4) The relative lack of meaning in the suffering being experienced is bewildering. Where is God?

5) The random nature of suffering causes questions as to God's goodness or omnipotence. Why do some people suffer more than others?

How we speak about God, therefore, becomes of critical importance when a person is suffering, or a relative is angry and grieving over a loved one who has died. The big question is "How can I say anything of faith-value to this person at this time?" As Kubler-Ross says, quite obviously it is "inappropriate to speak of the love of God" at a time like this.[4]

At such a time pastoral visitors may feel inadequate, embarrassed, yet feel they must maintain the Christian flag and that they must do something. The tendency is to rush to defend God. Remember, God is big enough to defend himself, without us barging in prematurely, as Richmond says:

> Sooner or later, the time comes for us to begin to set tragedy in the light of the Gospel. Assuming that we have acknowledged the presence of doubt and the feelings of alienation that accompany it, we can begin to move meaningfully toward an interpretation that can facilitate healing". [5]

As a hospital visitor, it may be that you will not be the one available to do the follow up. The important thing to remember is that initially you were the God-presence there at the time of doubt. Because of you they became aware that God had not forgotten them. Perhaps there may be someone else who will be able to bring to their lives order out of chaos, meaning out of confusion and peace out of the turmoil of the heart. Nevertheless, you must develop your own theology of the problem of suffering.

As I have already observed, efforts have been made to come to grips with this problem of evil. The German philosopher Liebniz (1710) coined the word "Theodicy."

> A theodicy is an attempt to vindicate the justice and righteousness of God in ordering or permitting evil and suffering in his creation.[6]

In the next few pages an attempt is made to set out briefly some of the arguments in defense. Perhaps they may be called theodicies, which have been produced over time.

SUFFERING: A MYSTERY

When people ask "Why?" the safest and most trust-building response is to answer honestly, "I don't know" and perhaps at a later stage to say, "There are many things that happen to us to which we will never find the real answer in this life." You are being honest. Suffering *is* a mystery.

Such an answer is much more helpful and less destructive and depressing than remarks like, "God has a purpose for everything," or "It must be God's will and we can't do anything about it."

Schilling[7] sees two values in the "I-honestly-don't-know" response: it encourages an acceptance of the mystery, which in turn results in knowing that individual testing is in the hands of a god, gods, or unknowable powers over which we have no control. Schilling would have been clearer, I believe, if he had simply stated that in accepting the mystery of suffering, a person can move in the direction of naive fatalism.

Contrariwise, the acceptance of this mystery may be taken as indicating a greater trust in God. It may be a quiet trust. The story of Job presents us with a classic example of a continuing, even a growing trust in God. Job[8] in simple faith is resigned to the fact that if one accept's God's blessing one must also accept evil. Even before the restitution of his prosperity, Job[9] was able to tell God that he knew God could do all things and admitted that he—Job—had spoken about things he did not understand, things which were too wonderful for him to know.

Resignation, simply saying "It is God's will," does not accord with the concept that God is love. It does not allow the person to really get to know God in his fullness. Tucked away in the mind are unanswerable reservations. This type of acceptance virtually lays the charge in the subconscious that God has perpetrated evil. It may be argued that when this is the case there is deep down an ambivalence between loving and hating God. The possibility of an intimate relationship with God is minimized.

There may be some logical explanations as to why the suffering occurred. Was it a drunken driver? The carelessness or negligence of the sufferer? A young British woman in her thirties suspected she had cancer. She received medical advice that surgery was necessary, but she put it off for twelve months until she could visit her mother in Australia, where the surgery would cost less. She suffered considerably. The surgery could not remove all the cancer, and a caesium implant did not kill the remaining cells. She died some months after returning home, leaving a husband and children.

Accepting suffering as purely a mystery may be a way of escaping facing the real issue. Yet for many, particularly those with a less enquiring, analytical or probing mind, this account may suffice for them to maintain a measure of mental and spiritual peace. We cannot be the fountain of *all* wisdom. When our own wisdom falls short or we do not know all the facts of the case, or the data is confused, it shows proper wisdom to admit that we don't know.

DUALISM: NO SOLUTION?

We have referred to the Book of Job. Job opens with a dialogue between God and the devil. The Bible, both in the Old and the New Testaments, unmistakably declares the presence of evil. John's vision on Patmos describes the ultimate defeat and demise of the evil one and his cohorts. With the rejuvenation of the occult in our day, demon possession and the spirit world are being more and more talked about as a reality by those who dabble in these areas.

There are obvious forces of good and evil in this world. We almost seem to be able to dichotomize the world's functioning as seen in war and peace, love and hate, tenderness and violence, care and indifference, support and manipulation, selfishness and unselfishness.

This has caused at least two hypotheses. The first arises out of biblical concepts, that there is God and there is Satan. Ancient religions and mythology see these as two ultimate forces or gods, functioning antithetically. The Bible portrays one supreme being, God, and sets the devil or Satan as a principle or being thwarting and frustrating the activities of God.

The second postulation discussed by Sontag[10] in 1970, suggests that there is good and evil both within the divine. In the world, that evil is actualized.

Sontag offers no real solution. He only compounds the problem of suffering for the one who is feeling its tragic load and the acceptance of the biblical presentation still does not provide answers as to why God does not act. It has been suggested by many theologians that as we are open to God's guidance and direction, so we are also capable of being seduced by Satan; thus evil and suffering are experienced.

It is not possible for the pastoral visitor to say to a young terminally-ill patient that Satan has wrought this havoc and that ultimately God will rectify it all. This prompts further questions, such as "Why didn't God stop him? Why can't God act now? How can God love me and let this happen?" An answer leaving such unsolved questions without providing any real hope opens the way to atheism.

Dualism offers no real comfort for the sufferer, it only provokes deeper and more profound imponderables.

SUFFERING AS PUNISHMENT

The ordinary person frequently exclaims "I haven't done anything to deserve this!" It is a part of the cultural background of some of us to believe that we will be punished for our sins. The Old Testament belief that the sins of the fathers are visited upon the children to the third and fourth generation has remained engrained in our philosophy of life. This was interpreted to mean that the offspring are punished for three and four generations. What they actually mean is that the consequences are felt by future generations, for example, family vendettas. The psychological and other mental disorders that arise from neglect or rejection in early childhood have their repercussions on the way grandchildren are handled by their parents.

The idea of punishment was seen in the questions asked of Jesus when he healed people deformed from birth. "Who sinned, this man or his parents?" (John 9:2). A Muslim woman had an abortion after bringing up ten children in a two-room house. Nineteen years later, she was diagnosed with cervical cancer. She automatically assumed Allah was punishing her in this way for the termination of the pregnancy.

In many cases, search as we may, we can find no justification for the nature of the suffering in the quality of life lived by the sufferer. The devastation of the spirit of a person, of high Christian living standards, who is suffering the impost of the guilt inflicted by the "punishment theory" is great.

Natural disasters such as major earthquakes, man-made disasters such as a bursting dam, or a jet airliner crash can in no way be attributed to the ethical quality of the lives of the dead, wounded or surviving.

In some cases the individual may reap the results of his own actions. In modern times there are those who contract AIDS , by sharing drug needles for example.

The general principle which affirms that all human suffering is due to sin and therefore is punishment, flies in the face of our knowledge of God.

SUFFERING AS TESTING

Paul's rationale for God's not granting his request for the removal of the thorn in his flesh, was that it was to keep him from conceit and pride. It probably made Paul more God-dependent and tempered his ego. To use this as an example of God causing an ailment in order to make him a more effective missionary is stretching the point.

Such testing as God's instrument for personal growth is one of the theodicies identified by Schilling. Schleiermacher put forward the concept that the universe provided the scenario in which the imperfect human beings God created and placed on the earth could respond to God's graciousness and salvation. According to this theory, God created an imperfect human race, open to suffering in order to receive God's resources to make them whole. Evil and suffering are in this view essential for human recognition and acceptance of God. This is hardly tenable when we consider the suffering of Christ, the God-man.

If it were merely God testing or punishing us with a particular illness or disease, why then did he permit his instruments of testing or punishment such as the black plague and smallpox to be virtually eliminated?

The other aspect of the "testing theory" is that suffering such experiences supposedly produces the best characteristics in us. Suffering is said to enable us to understand life and what other people go through, refine us so as to make possible an otherwise impossible rate of personal growth.

While it is true that significant strides in personal development are possible through evil endured, there are also as many, if not more people, who are left broken and in despair. The unequal distribution of hardship and tragedy, particularly as seen in third world countries, places further strains on the credibility of such a God, for these people would understand little of the need for personal growth. It is difficult to see any purpose in what is often aptly described as needless suffering.

SUFFERING AND FREE WILL

One of the distinctions of Christianity is formulated out of the story of the fall. God gave us the right to decide issues for ourselves. One cannot work in a trauma center without being aware that many of the physical disasters encountered are due to the abuse of this gift of freedom, given to us by God. Few road accidents are caused by mechanical failure. Most can be attributed to selfishness, impatience, carelessness, overtiredness, error of judgment, aggression, distraction and so on.

There are, of course, many cases of evil which we would have to be very imaginative to explain as products of a free-will decision.

In those cases which are attributable to the misuse of human free will, it is not possible to directly place the responsibility on God. Questions like "Why did God create us as he did?" or "Why did God give us freedom such as exercised by Hitler and Stalin?" open up much broader theological issues.

THE CONTINUING SEARCH

Depending upon your theological preferences, you may be inclined to use some of the above views about suffering. In doing so you must always consider the background the family comes from. If they are of reformed church background, the emphasis will be on the sovereign God who is in control. Others will stress the mystery, while some will want to stress free will. Recognize that there is no one adequate explanation. Whatever line you take, see that it is one which will satisfy the patient's own theological position if you are desperate enough to want to provide answers.

The search for a solution to the problem of evil will continue. Richmond follows the school of thought known as "Process Theology." Both the Revised Standard Version and Today's English Version produce as an alternative reading of Genesis 1:1 "When God began to create the universe". It was a *beginning* not a *completion* of creation. In creating the human race God created us as free beings not in a stereotyped mold but with the capability to:

> ...determine what sort of persons we will become. In order for us to develop fully our potential as persons, it was necessary to place us within a stable environment that inherently contained conditions that constantly challenged us to take part in God's creative activity of making the world a more human and humane place.[12]

Thus the universe and humankind is in a process of becoming. This is in line with Carl Rogers' theory. We will never actually arrive and reach our full potential until beyond this life. God made us free to love, to create, to follow freely the divine pattern. David Griffin applies this to the problem of evil:[13]

If God has always worked with materials that were not necessarily in a perfect state, and which have some inherent power to deviate from God's aims...there is no reason to infer that cancer, polio, tornadoes and earthquakes exist because God wanted our world to have them.

This implies that God, in creating humans as he did, imposed limitations upon himself. God loves us. Love leaves itself vulnerable. God's vulnerability reached its weakest on Calvary, yet it is in that weakness we see God's greatest strength–the greatness of God's love. Paul says that God's strength is made perfect in weakness. Paul sees his own vulnerability as his point of strength. He here sees himself in this process of becoming.[14]

The argument against this is that in our struggle in this unpredictable world of immature humankind, with its suffering, injustices and agony, we ask "Where is this God?" Both Old and New Testaments tell us where he is. God is agonizing with us in our gropings, experiencing our frustrations, begging, urging and pleading with us.

The agony of watching us resulted in the incarnation, the crucifixion and the resurrection. That is, where God is alongside us. This is the approach which we can offer the patient or family to whom we are ministering. Richmond gives six reasons for its acceptability:

1) *It is scriptural*
Jesus says, God's work is incomplete and on-going (John 5:17). Paul affirms it (Romans 8:21ff).

2) *Trials lead toward maturity as sons and daughters of God*
Produces strength of faith and balanced character (James 1:2–5). Endurance produces character and hope (Romans 5:3–4).

3) *God comes near to us*
As the suffering servant (Isaiah 49:4; 50:6; 53:3–12) understanding what suffering is (Luke 22:44; Matthew 27:33–54).

4) *God is with us now*

In the form of the Spirit (John 14:26–27, Acts 1:4, 5 & 8), inseparable from the Love of God in Christ (Rom 8:35–39).

5) *Suffering is natural and God frees us to identify with the suffering of others*

6) *Suffering can be the result of a life lived in faithful obedience to the gospel*

For instance in the life of Bonhoeffer and the martyrs of all ages.

If the patient is struggling with the question of "why", if there is a search for a peg to hang guilt on, if the adrenalin is pumping because of anger, the last thing that is needed is talk of God or life's goodness, of trust and faith or of some unknowable reason. If we can acknowledge that creation is still in the process of becoming, then we are able to admit and acknowledge the imperfect; we are able to sit and listen, accepting the expressions of anger, doubt and guilt. We are open to the patient's feelings and are not defensive or threatened. Nor do we pose a threat which stifles openness in the patient.

In the hospital we do not suddenly put on a mantle that sets us up as an authority above all and all-knowing. Our task is to come with our own frailties, imperfections and unanswered questions. We come as a fellow human being in all our humanness. We come imagining ourselves in their situation, feeling our own hurt, and through it releasing them to share more deeply. To come with our tidy pack of "Here is the answer" cards is not the way to hear what they are asking and what the real problem is.

In accepting and sharing the pain of others, we incarnate our faith in the God who stands with us in their suffering, sharing their burden.

The problem of suffering, seeking an answer to why something is happening or where God is in this, becomes less important as the patient or relative *knows* we hear them and sense their hurt and pain. The love of God incarnate in us is seen by them. Involvement in debate, rationalizations and embarrassed, faulty explanations are mostly futile. Where this love of God incarnate is seen, pastoral care is being received.

These are some of the approaches to the problem of pain and suffering.

All our theodicies can sound so artificial to the one on the bed of pain or the one grieving near it, unless we have come to acknowledge our own imperfect understanding of the problem of evil. Our confirmed faith in a God who understands can come only out of our own knowledge and experience of God-in-Christ in unique life situations. Without the indwelling reality of Christ, our "explanations" will make us sound like brass and clanging cymbals. Suffering and evil will continue until the process of becoming is complete.

The recognition of our genuine concern and pastoral support will compensate for any inadequacies in our ability to make a pronouncement on the nature of the suffering being endured.

NOTES

1. Schilling, S. Paul *God and Human Anguish* (Nashville:Abingdon) 1977 p31-43.
2. Psalms 10:1-11; Ps 43:1-2; Ps 44:9-24.
3. Richmond, Kent D. *Preaching to Sufferers - God and the Problem of Pain* (Nashville:Abingdon) 1988 p19-33.
4. Kubler-Ross, E. *Questions and Answers on Death and Dying* (New York:MacMillan, 1974) p178.
5. Richmond op. cit. p113.
6. Schilling op. cit. p55.
7. Schilling op. cit. pp56-72.
8. Job 2:10.
9. Job 42:2
10. Sontag, Frederich *The God of Evil : An argument for the existence of the Devil* (New York:Harper & Row) 1970 pp129-135, 140.
11. Schilling op. cit. p147ff.
12. Richmond op. cit. pp62-76.

13. David Griffin in Davis, Stephen, ed. *In Encountering Evil* (Atlanta:John Knox Press) 1981 p101.

14. 2 Cor 12:9

14

Depression

Often a nurse or nursing unit manager has called to say, "Will you see Mr. So-and-So, he's depressed after hearing the results of his tests." But when I have gone in to see the patient, I have often found him reacting naturally and normally to such negative news. Sadness, sorrow and grief are not signs of depression. They may, however, lead to depression if appropriate support and care are not forthcoming.

Depression is an "in" word in our times. There is a prevalent danger of too easily labeling a person "depressed." Many doctoral theses have been written on the subject of depression. Each generation produces new circumstances which predispose people to episodes of depression. Research will continue into the causes, incidence and processes of depression as long as the human race survives.

As pastoral care persons it is not possible, except for special reasons, for us to devote time to an intensive study of the subject. However, it *is* necessary to have some basic knowledge of depression. In hospital and post-hospital visitation, depression is likely to be encountered from time to time.

WHAT IS DEPRESSION?

A good starting point is to digest Fairchild's statement: "Clinical depression refers to the slowing down of the whole organism—emotional, intellectual and physical—and not to mood alone."[1] He sees the complexity of the depressive state. Mitchell, in contrast, defines depression as a mood. He sees it as combining "a sense of being down in spirit, low in energy, having a sense of loss, hopelessness and uselessness."[2] It implies apathy and pessimism. It comes after a disappointment, a loss and sometimes spontaneously without apparent cause. He associates anxiety with depression. Anxiety can arise simultaneously with depression or be sparked off by the depression.

Mitchell not only sees depression as a mood, he identifies it as an experience, such as losing something valuable, or an attitude to life, for instance not coping, and as an illness. We are more concerned with the latter and shall explore depression from a different perspective in more detail than Mitchell does. He sees depression as mostly a state of mind which results from something that has happened or is happening to a person. He sees it as an illness when the depression affects "bodily and mental functions." This view implies it is a coping ability, it switches off from life and its environs until the broken-down bodily and mental functions are able to be put right again.

Here we see two men from different disciplines, Fairchild the pastoral theologian and Mitchell the psychiatrist. Fairchild is seeing the whole person: emotion, mind and body. Mitchell is mind-oriented in his approach.

Perry and Sell help us to clarify the scene when they distinguish three kinds of depression in ascending order of severity.

- *Normal depression* manifests itself as "lack of energy, negative self image or a sense of hopelessness." A clear cause can be identified. It becomes abnormal when it persists and there is no relief.
- *Neurotic depressive reaction* sees a lingering sadness, guilt, lostness, emptiness. This is often associated with helplessness, hopelessness, despair and suicide; happiness and joy are not possible.
- *Severe depression* or *severe depressive behavior* is evident when it becomes extremely disturbing to others and requires institutional care.[3]

Scott Peck supports the first of the above points when he writes:

> ...depression is a normal and basically healthy phenomenom. It becomes abnormal or unhealthy only when something interferes with the giving-up process, with the result that the depression is prolonged and cannot be resolved by completion of the process.[4]

Mitchell would classify them only as depressive reactions and depressive illnesses, the latter including manic-depressive psychoses, recurrent depressive illness, involutional melancholia and senile depressions.[5] We should recognize that abnormal depression is generally accepted as being beyond the capacity of the average pastoral care person. Over-involvement with such patients can lead to manipulation, counteracting medical therapy, and compounding the state of the depression.

Wise, an early writer, uses the word "despair" and not the word "depression". He provides an understanding of it from the religious standpoint.[6] His thesis does not cover all aspects of depression; as a mental health chaplain, he sees the situation from the pastoral visitor's perspective.

Wise postulates that "megalomania and despair spring from the same root—the failure to find an absolute that gives balance and significance to the relative." If Wise were writing in the 1990s he would probably use the word "depression" along with "despair." How can we interpret what Wise is saying? A person becomes depressed when in searching (their God?) for purpose and meaning to events in their lives, they draw a blank. Doubts that a supreme being can help them leave them in a state of despondency, without hope and without a God to rescue them. Depression enshrouds and consumes the mind. The depressed see the reality of their situation of pain, suffering, rejection, weakness and dependence as dehumanizing. Neither God nor any "ism" has shown any ability to relieve or provide hope. Faith in whoever or whatever has been shattered. In today's so-called non-religious Western society, the God-concept is often absent or very faint. The following definition may be relevant:

> A depressed person is one whose faith in whoever or whatever has been shattered and who sees no way out, or any hope for the future.

These are the possible types of depressed persons one is likely to meet in general hospital ward rounds. The more serious cases of depression, of course, are likely to be found in the psychiatric ward, and some senile depressives may be met in the geriatric ward.

IDENTIFYING DEPRESSION

Since depression is a mental health condition, it would be wise for us, first of all, to have some idea who mentally healthy persons are. They are described by Jahoda as having six basic characteristics. Although these were listed over thirty years ago, they are still widely accepted.

Mentally healthy persons:

i) Are able to acknowledge their own feelings and have a sense of personal identity.

ii) Have a sense of direction, provide their own motivation and can make independent decisions.

iii) Are resilient to emotional stress and are not overcome by their own emotional involvements, fears or guilt.

iv) Are realistic, seeing things as they are rather than as they would like them to be.

v) Can appreciate the feelings of others.

vi) Have appropriate emotional responses to new situations.[7]

In depressed persons we should expect to see breakdowns in some of those characteristics. In fact there are a wide range of departures possible in a person suffering from depression, some of those reactions being different in two people under similar criteria. Fairchild offers a broad list which may serve our purposes:

- *change in appetite and eating habits;*
- *insomnia or sleeping too much;*
- *low energy level or constant tiredness or boredom;*
- *feelings of inadequacy or guilt;*
- *decreased effectiveness at school, work or home;*
- *decreased ability to pay attention, or to concentrate and think clearly;*
- *social withdrawal from groups and friends;*
- *loss of interest in and enjoyment of sex;*
- *restriction of involvement in pleasurable activities;*
- *physical and mental slowing down ("psychomotor retardation");*
- *irritability;*
- *being less talkative than usual;*
- *pessimistic attitude to the future;*
- *tearfulness, crying; sad facial expression;*
- *recurrent thoughts of death or suicide;*
- *loss of interest and motivation in activities formerly considered important.*[8]

Perry and Sell cite Job, the oldest book in the Bible, as fitting a description of a depressed man, listing seven indicators.[9] I have chosen to add another eight.

Extreme sadness	Job 3:20; 6:2–3
Desire for death	Job 3:21
Sleep disturbance	Job 7:4
Pessimism about life	Job 14:1
Helplessness	Job 3:26
View of life as worthless	Job 9:21
Physical signs of distress	Job 17:7; 16:8
Loss of appetite	Job 6:6–7

Hopelessness (despair)	Job 6:11; 7:7; 17:1,15
Weakness of body and resolve	Job 6:12–13
Anger	Job 7:17–19
Loss of self-esteem	Job 9:21
Fear of suffering	Job 9:28; 10:19; 17:6
Bitterness	Job 10:1
Sense of rejection	Job 19:13–20

These two lists of observations will provide a good working basis for recognizing such a condition when it shows itself in a patient.

Having raised the issue of depression, the big danger is that you might be so preoccupied over depression you could interpret everything you see in terms of a depressed state. There are "near relatives of depression" which Fairchild warns us about.[10] He suggests that sadness, sorrow and dejection may be the normal reactions to unpleasant news or happenings in a person's life. Grief responses are not signs of depression unless they are unresolved (compare Scott Peck [11]).

He describes anxiety and depression as being frequent bedfellows, resulting in "anxiety depression." Anxiety is not depression. A significant loss of self-esteem, if unchallenged, may create an anxiety generated and sustained by uncertainty. Uncertainty dominates anxiety, but helplessness and despair pervade depression. An element of hope is clutched at by anxiety; depression, instead, is linked to hopelessness.

Boredom produces apathy and emptiness. Weariness from lack of interest makes living tedious. Stimulation can stir a person out of boredom. When there is no such response, and boredom is unrelieved, then depression may develop: life has no meaning or usefulness.

This raises the question, "Who is likely to develop depression?" Let us not forget that a mentally-healthy person is less likely to develop abnormal depression, although he or she may show some normal depression signs for a short period in certain stressful circumstances.

THE DEVELOPMENT OF DEPRESSION

In avoiding the title "Causes of Depression," I have sought to avoid becoming involved in theoretical conflict. Volumes of research material have been devoted to the nature of the cause of depression. There are two main lines of thinking: one emphasizes the psychosocial factor; the second sees biochemical imbalance as the major causative influence. As Fairchild warns, *"the Pastor...should never forget the body-mind-spirit unity that is presupposed by scripture."*[12] Jules Bemporad observes that the clinician must consider the biological factors, just as the chemical researcher must recognise the effect of significant life encounters on the patient.[13]

In reading you must assess the bias of the writer and make allowance for any imbalance detected. For the purposes of this book, the emphasis will be more toward matters the pastoral care worker in a hospital should be aware of, that is, the development of depression because of the reason for the hospitalization and the resultant psychosocial effects. It is beyond the scope and expertise of this book to consider the biological and chemical causes. Nor is it the area into which the hospital visitor should venture.

We are concerned with the depressed person in hospital. Perry and Sell state "depression can occur because of an illness or tumor."[14] It is puzzling as to why they isolate tumor. Any reason for hospitalization has potential for the development of depression in the patient.

Mitchell tells us that organic (physical) causes of depression "may have psychological and social consequences and vice versa."[15]

He lists the major organic causes:

Traumatic —head injuries, operations and damage to or loss of valued parts of the body.

Infective —influenza, encephalitis, hepatitis, peritonitis, etc.

Cardio-Vascular —non-fatal stroke, thrombosis, heart attack, hemorrhage.

Hormonal —biochemical and glandular changes: post-natal, menopausal, thyroid deficiencies, etc.

Epileptic —unpredictable mood changes or violent alternations of behavior (psychomotor epilepsy) in lieu of fits.

Degenerative —for example, due to hardening of arteries in later life.

Pharmacological —prescribed drugs may induce depression, e.g. blood pressure medication, contraceptive pill, etc.

Depression as already noted is often associated with low self-esteem. Self-esteem may be associated with an inferiority complex at not being as good at school work, sport, or other skills as others in the peer group. Sometimes rejection by a significant other is a cause of this sense of worthlessness and unacceptability. Frequently in depression there is an underlying burden of guilt, which is exacerbated and distorted as the depression develops into what is called "pathological guilt feelings."

A father may have had an obsession to have a son. He was blessed only with daughters. The youngest daughter has the frustrations of the father meted out to her when she is not able to do the things a son would do. She is made to feel guilty that she is not a boy. She is constantly cited as a failure because she is not her father's dream son. From an early age she develops a guilt complex because she feels unwanted. The worthless feelings and guilt are reinforced with almost every sighting of her father until depression is entrenched and the guilt is pathological.

LOSS

Both outside and inside the hospital, the one element that is consistently observed in depression is the sense of loss. Loss produces a disabling of a normal or anticipated life-style. This is no more keenly felt than when parts of the body are unable to function and adjustments have to be made to living patterns. A person may not be able to cope with even the thought of not being physically whole. The negative effects of the handicap become paramount in the mind.

The loss of a limb, speech, sight, hearing, a vital organ, or the impairment of any of these means that the same form of activity cannot be undertaken in the same way with the same dexterity. The ability to fully participate with peers and their schedules is seriously affected and may result in a withdrawal from the group. Change of employment, and unemployment, are of course serious factors to be taken into consideration. When physical mobility and function is affected in this way, with no loss of mental capabilities, the reflective process has the capacity to lead the person into depression.

For the pastoral visitor, it is possible to sense a loss of faith. My repeated experience has been that some of the most ardent church workers facing the reality of organic losses, or even terminal prognoses have been among those who have fallen into irretrievable depression. The sense of being abandoned by God after having served him diligently was overwhelming. Or else they manufactured evidence of their unfaithfulness to God.

It would be legitimate to reproduce all of the fears outlined in "The Patient in Crisis" (Chapter 7) here, because any one, or a combination of many, of these fears may contribute seriously to a depressive episode. Guilt and unfinished business are two key elements which become catalysts for depression. In these, fantasy magnifies and distorts the sober facts. The depression becomes deeper as the ingenuity of the troubled mind weaves its exaggerations into the fabric of the loss or losses. Fear can bombard the patient with all forms of possible and impossible combinations of complications, difficulties and impending traumas, pains and hurts and forms of loss.

The signal loss which applies to all depressed people is the *loss of self-esteem*. The effect of all the other losses can be seen in the loss of all recognition of self-worth. Fairchild speaks of negative internal conversations to which severely depressed people cling.[16] These conversations concern the following themes:

- *I am, and will remain helpless;*
- *I am losing my mind;*
- *I am alone responsible for my present condition —I am not angry at anyone;*
- *I am lonely and rejected by others because I am worthless;*
- *Things won't ever work out for me.*

Many additions could be added to Fairchild's themes, for instance:

- *Everything that is worthwhile is always taken from me;*
- *I am ugly —nobody would want me;*
- *I'll never be a man (or a woman) again* (since the operation/accident).

The negative attitude of the depressed person is the dominating feature, increasing the depression. As the losses are viewed negatively, the self-esteem plummets, the incentive for motivation is destroyed, and the mind opts to be passively dependent.

The "primary triad" of a depressed person's thought patterns identified by Beck is enlightening. The first of his three concepts is *the pattern of interpreting events in a negative way.* The events taking place around relatives and friends and their actions are viewed as being personally destructive, denigrating, dehumanizing and depriving.

The second pattern views the self in a *negative way.* It is a self-derogatory appraisal. All others present, or referred to in conversation, are assessed as being superior to the person depressed.

The third pattern *views the future in a negative way.* The pain and the suffering will never end. The fracture will not heal properly. I'll have to use a walking stick. A transplant will never work on me. God can never forgive me. The patient cedes no possible grounds for hope.[17] Thus the past, present and future are and ever will be bleak, dark and unhelpful.

INTERNALIZED ANGER

From a very active, often creative life, a patient is incapacitated in hospital with so much still to achieve outside. Deadlines for work, or exam dates have passed by unfulfilled. This is a bitter blow to the ego. Even though uncontrollable, it is failure. The accident may have been caused by the other driver while drunk. Enough to make anyone angry! The depressed person sees the failure to complete the task as a reflection upon the self; therefore the anger is directed into self-reproach. The image of the self has been shattered.

This loss of self-image is always irrational. Bitterness that is unexpressed though justified often indicates an internalization of anger and resentment toward the self. The situation is exacerbated when the victim is a member of a church who has adopted the church's negative attitude to anger. The hostility is driven inward, enhancing and deepening the depression.

UNRESOLVED GRIEF

An area which has been rarely identified in relation to depression is unresolved grief, which occurs when adequate opportunity for grieving the death of a loved one, maybe some years before, was not allowed.

It may be a wife who lost her husband through illness or accident. With several children to provide for and nurture, she saw herself as the one who had to be strong for their sakes. Her normal grief reactions were repressed in the mistaken belief that she had "to be able to cope."

As a chaplain I have often discovered that the patient's depressive signs were due to the death of a much-loved sibling, parent or grandparent, who died up to forty years earlier, in pre-adolescent years. Being so young at the time, it was thought that they could not understand. The lack of opportunity to say goodbye to their loved one or to take part in the normal funeral and family gatherings compounded the hurt the child was experiencing. The fact that they were excluded from the scene and no one, not even the parents, offered them comfort or allowed them to share tears together, added fear to the depression.

The parent of the opposite sex may have died or been separated from a young adolescent. This is a time when a young person's attachment to the parent of the opposite sex is strong. Few are able to sense the depth of feeling experienced at such a loss at that particular period. This lack of understanding by others does not permit the free expression of grief emotions. Remarks such as, "You are a big boy now. You can look after yourself," indicate that the youth can manage without a mother. These are barbs which pierce deeply into the young person's heart and mind.

"Your mother has suffered a great loss; now you have to be her support," is often said to an adolescent whose father has died, or "Well, lad, you have to be *the man* about the house now." Such remarks are unfeeling and place undue expectations upon the grieving youth so that the grief feelings are again repressed. Similarly, adolescent girls can be insensitively rushed into household management. By becoming defacto housekeepers and mothers, they find many of the normal teenage experiences are denied them. Their grief is also repressed.

A threat to their own life, or the hospitalization of another loved one, resurrects in their minds the death of the one for whom true grief expressions were not permitted. Patients or relatives may want to work through that grief but would perhaps consider it a stupid notion to remember back so long. The fear is that nobody would understand. So again, the past and present griefs are pushed aside from the conscious and allowed free reign in the subconscious. Thus depression begins to paralyze the opportunity to bring the real issue to the fore. Depression is like a massive fog which prevents the person from clearly seeing the issue needing to be tackled.

So, unresolved grief of yesteryear is often the overlooked factor when dealing with the depressed person. It is so frequent in my experience that every reasonable effort (while respecting propriety) needs to be made to understand family background early in the developing relationship with a patient who is showing signs of withdrawal.

SOCIAL FACTORS

Depressions may arise because of social factors, particularly broken relationships. Close bonds between people, whether they be between family members, student friends, lovers, business associates or others, have significant effects upon the way we function. Many of our aims and purposes in life and living are interwoven with other lives. When a relationship is broken, there is a yawning gap which can never be filled in the same way, a void in part of the person's life. The breakdown, with future reconciliation seemingly out of the question because of the great hurts, projects itself as rejection.

Rejection is one of the causes for the onset of depression, linked with loss of self-esteem. Many cases of depression brought on by breakdown in relationships are accompanied by psychosomatic illnesses.

Julie had had a rapid weight loss over the previous five months. In spite of an adequate diet, the weight loss continued until she was hospitalized. After three weeks in hospital, with all the tests proving negative, the medical specialists were baffled. They were on the point of discharging her. She and the chaplain started talking about what she would do when she went home.

Julie: "I'll be going to my sister's wedding in three weeks."

Chaplain: "That's something to look forward to. What's the fellow like your sister is marrying? Do you think she's made the right choice?"

Julie: (An outburst of sobbing.) "He was engaged to me and broke it off to go with my sister."

The loss of weight started from the time of the sister's engagement. Seeing the man in the home with the sister several times a week kept alive the reality of the rejection, causing Julie's withdrawal from the family. Loss of appetite and loss of weight were significant indicators of the depression.

With Julie's permission I notified the medical team and the course of her treatment took a new turn.

FEELINGS

Each and every person has feelings. Without them we would not be able to function as adequate human beings. Our gregarious nature would be non-existent if we viewed everything in a clinical or mechanical way. Feelings are vital and necessary for us.

It may be an obvious statement yet it is worthy of attention. Feelings are neither right nor wrong. It is what we do with them that matters. Some marriages break down because of an inability to demonstrate feelings. Others fail because the negative feelings expressed are too destructive. Good marriages thrive on the mutual sharing of warm positive feelings.

Two people are involved in a gross injustice perpetrated by a third person, which brings tremendous sorrow and heartache to a family. Both are furiously angry. One talks out the anger with a friend and engages in some strong, straining physical activity. The second fumes and boils over what has happened until the anger erupts and a murder follows. It is what these two different people did to cope with the anger that is important.

Feelings need to be expressed in a helpful way. Being humans, our feelings are often the result of being too close to the parties and the incident concerned. Being subjectively aroused, feelings tend to make us become irrational or clouded in our perception. It is in the expression of those feelings that they can be seen from a more logical standpoint.

Not only must the feelings be expressed, they must be identified. How often we encounter a red-faced argumentative person who shouts, "I'm not angry." Failure to admit, identify and work through negative feelings is a stride down the track to depression.

There are many other possible causes for depression which are not directly or indirectly due to the hospitalization. They may be long-standing, severely depressive conditions which need expert handling by qualified specialist personnel. Recognize when you are getting out of your depth and propose a referral to someone else. A little knowledge can be dangerous if strictly applied. It is therefore unwise here to step into the more psychological and psychiatric aspects of depression.

PASTORAL INITIATIVES WITH THE DEPRESSED

"The recovery of hope by despairing persons is a primary goal of pastoral care."[18]

Hopelessness is a major characteristic of depression. The healing of that hopelessness and restoration to wholeness is the role of pastoral care. Hope is paramount in all healthy living. If this is true, then a depressed person cannot expect a return to health until hope is again in perspective.

It is easy for the Christian pastoral person to provide a picture of hope in the future with God. *Pastoral care offers hope within the context of present reality*—hope in the midst of suffering, pain, disappointment and hurt. The pages of the Bible are scattered with floggings, exiles, defeats, shipwrecks, murder, illness, a cross and a tomb. It speaks of an empty tomb, of deliverances from prisons, as well as the truth, "my grace is sufficient for you."

Hope is not the pie in the sky held dangling for the despairing to reach up and try to grasp. Hope generates awareness of possibilities perhaps different from what one had planned for life. Hope is not wishful thinking. The unrealistic nature of false hope only increases the depression when the glow becomes dim and is finally extinguished.

To the patients for whom active treatment has been abandoned, all the doctor's words of hope for a cure, your talk of asking God for a complete healing, or encouragement to think of going home or back to work—even if siezed upon by the patient—will eventually be hurled back at you in mistrust. God and the church will be cynically ridiculed. Future pastoral care to these patients and the possibility of a spiritual ministry in the dying stages are annihilated.

The pastoral visitor must distinguish between hoping and wishing, as Pruyser differentiates them:

> One who hopes is concerned with attitudes and global benefits such as life, freedom, deliverance, salvation; the one who wishes tends to focus on specific things: money, rain after a drought, expensive birthday presents, the death of an enemy. The hoper tests reality; the wisher engages in magical thought...The hoper says, "Now I see through a glass darkly...," while the wisher cherishes his room reservation in a heavenly motel.[19]

Goal-setting is mostly not appropriate for a critically ill depressed patient. As Fairchild says:

> The kind of hope needed by the depressed person enables him to say "yes" to life, to believe that it is always possible to imagine another way to go. Such hope sees reality as open-ended and having resources as yet undiscovered and untapped. Certainty may be lacking, but he has the courage to act "as if" it existed.[20]

Paul had good reason to feel depressed. His woes were numerous. His rejection by the Corinthian church hurt. His many narrow escapes might have caused him to react with "What's the use?" Yet he could write to the Philippians (4:11–13) that God was able to give him all the strength he needed to face any and every circumstance that came his way. He did not ask for significant change in those circumstances, only the ability to cope. He wrote this after exhorting the church to always rejoice, asking God to supply their needs, assuring them that God would keep their mind in peace.

Presenting hope as the initial pastoral initiative with the depressed is not done in the sense that there is a sequence for handling the depressed; (there may indeed be times when the hope mode increases the depression). Rather it is to emphasize to the pastoral worker that the development of hope is the goal. More specifically, the pastoral carer must have the faith to believe that in Christ it is possible to have hope in resources yet untapped. The patient who has been so bruised by a careless, uncaring world must have demonstrated to her or him that you, the carer, are really caring, unquestionably sincere, and motivated by Christian love. This must happen before a glimmer of hope will begin penetrating the depression.

Sincere caring may include just being there, offering nothing. Hope is often engendered merely by the patient's realizing that there are in fact caring people in the world.

THE ROLE OF THE VOLUNTEER CARER

Ross Mitchell is a psychiatrist working with an English charity caring for the mentally ill and handicapped, whose main task is to relieve mental distress in the community.[21] The organization uses a number of volunteers in their program. Mitchell makes some terse points which are applicable to pastoral care to the depressed and on which we could expand a little.

The role is basically that of a friend. The depressed person is needing some stability, reliability and genuine care. He or she is like a snail who has gone into its shell out of fear. It is extremely wary when it ventures out; testing everything it sees and hears. The slightest doubt and it's back into its shell.

Mitchell sees a friend as offering to the patient three things: a *listening* ear, *companionship* and *encouragement*. The stress is on a listening ear as being far more important than advice. He sees companionship as more important than glib answers.

Encouragement is a crucial attitude for the carer. This is the encouragement needed by the patient to see the attending doctor, counselor, or psychiatrist even when feeling too afraid, embarrassed or guilty to do so. The last may be because the patient failed to attend the last appointment.

Where the carer is prone to advise rather than listen, or tries to have ready answers for each question, it is unlikely that she or he will encourage the patient to seek the appropriate health care person.

Mitchell lists a number of dangers:

Don't try too much –let the person tell you what is wrong in their own time and in their own way.

Don't take on too much –this means that you should not get involved with cases that are beyond your expertise, capabilities or knowledge. Offer simple help and comfort.

Don't lose your objectivity –it is easy to become so emotionally involved that your own personal problems become mixed up with the patient's.

Don't be manipulated –"I feel that you are the only person who understands me." You may be *a* significant understanding person. It is possible others have been told the same; it is a well-known manipulative tool to keep your attention and avoid another possible rejection. The depressed person may want to cling to you at all costs. Manipulation may be evident in efforts to make you feel guilty if you do not respond in the right way.

Don't be afraid to call in others –one of the signs of good pastoral care workers is that they are confident enough to know when to ask for help. This does not mean abandoning the patient. The patient needs the professional and the non-professional. A discreet, trusting, loving friend is extremely important for a depressed person.

Jessie Van Dongen-Garrard is a social worker with physically handicapped people. She points out that among the physically disabled there are ten times more emotionally disturbed men than in a comparative number of able bodied men. However, among women, the ratio is two to one.

Van Dongen-Garrard says that to help these people, it is necessary to be flexible, prepared to adjust to their changing moods and needs. The range of help she suggests is:

- being alongside
- helping them to express their anxiety and fears verbally
- assisting them to take appropriate action themselves.[22]

There are two stages: the hospital stage and the home stage. Pastoral care is needed to help the patient face the current situation and the future.

The skill of the carer is displayed in the ability to decide the right time to withdraw active help and yet remain available if needed. A too early withdrawal can heighten the depression since it is perceived as another dreaded act of rejection. In deciding to withdraw, the patient's games of manipulation must not be allowed to determine the decision. You determine the timing of the next visit, not the patient.

Helping is seen by Van Dongen-Garrard as stages in a continuum. Depending upon the patient's state of mental health, the type of help to be given is decided and any or all three methods may be used. They range from the authoritarian to the egalitarian relationship:

- *Active–passive relationship*, where the patients are passive and in need of such help
- *Guidance–co-operative relationship*, where advice or suggestions are offered and patients are encouraged to do something about it themselves, for themselves.
- *Mutual participation*, where carer and patient are equal partners.[23]

If Fairchild placed hope as the primary goal in helping the depressed, it is not achievable without a progression of the relationship along the full length of this continuum. When the patient is able to look you in the eye and say "let's do it", you know the depression has been worked through. Or when the palliative care patient is able to say, with a smile and direct eye contact, even through the voice is feeble, "I'm feeling at peace. I'm ready when the Lord is."

At this point we shall recall Wise's words to the effect that a person becomes depressed when in searching their religious beliefs for purpose and meaning to their life, they draw a blank. The need is for a restored relationship between the depressed and their God, this being their only source of hope.

Some sort of self-mastery is called for, but the incapacity or illness has destroyed that possibility. Self-motivation may now need to be in a different direction from the patient's previous *modus operandi*. When in full health that self-mastery involved the manipulation of the elements, or even of people associated with them. The debilitation and restriction of the illness make such manipulation impossible now. Hence an increasing loss of self-control develops. Rehabilitation must be pursued through the world of the inner self, of attitudes, of understanding of both self and surroundings.

For people with severe brain damage, such encouragement to gain new insights about themselves is obviously not appropriate. Nevertheless, your presence most probably will provide some comfort and assurance. To just sit and hold hands is meaningful. However, for others attentiveness, presence and displays of genuine interest help to restore some sense of self-worth: "If I weren't worth something, they wouldn't spend their time with me. These pastoral care people must consider me to be of some value. I should try a little harder."

Acceptance becomes the keynote of such visits. Acceptance stands in contrast to rejection. It is the uplifting factor to providing some relief from the depressive state. The response to you will eventually turn from a sullen, downturned face into a smile. It will come if your presence is reinforced by your words of encouragement and news of the outside world of common interest. To treat them as defenceless, dependent children, fussing over them in a patronizing way, further deflates their spirit.

Acceptance is not possible for some pastoral visitors because of their prejudged bias concerning the cause of depression. As Baker[24] points out, until recently the Christian community carried many misconceptions about people who had abnormal mental health, such as:.

- Truly spiritual people do not become depressed.
- Depression is a sin.
- Depression is a result of sin and guilt.
- Increased Bible reading and prayer will cure depression.
- Depression can never be used by God as a means of personal growth.

If the hospital visitor holds to any of those fallacies, she or he will not be able to help a depressed person. Someone else should be allocated to visit the patient. Such wrong assumptions are likely to be picked up by the patient, either verbally or non-verbally, and will only do further damage.

It may be confidently reiterated that all of the above beliefs are fallacious. In many cases, the opposite is the case! Bible reading and prayer with a depressed patient often only internalizes anger against God even further. A discontinuance of daily prayer and Bible study for a period may be advisable. Preaching, too, can actually entrench the depression, particularly when the preacher harps on the theme of "unworthiness in God's sight."

Depressed persons should be accepted like any other patient requiring treatment in hospital. Simply treat them as normal human beings needing a little extra understanding and care. Stimulation and the encouragement to attempt to do things for themselves are important. This begins the process of seeing themselves more positively, which all helps to build up faith and hope—a faith in God and in fellow human beings. A hope that all is not lost for the future.

The flawed negative self-concept that has taken over begins to change. The "You're OK; I'm not OK" perception begins to change to the "You're OK; perhaps I'll be OK." It will take patience—much patience—to persevere until it is acknowledged that "You're OK; I'm OK." Along the road to this goal, we must hear, share with, walk with, and cry with the patient—all at appropriate times.

There is another approach, depending upon the patient's response to you, and the acuteness of your awareness. Instead of trying to draw them out in conversation, express your willingness just to sit silently and hold the hand. It is harder and shows much greater sensitivity in caring than maintaining a dialogue which may further tire the patient.

Practical evidence of real care may be demonstrated out of hospital by seeing that the patient's family are not burdened with meal preparation, lawn-mowing, washing and ironing and other chores. These tasks need not be done by you. You may organize other members of the fellowship and it is wise to consider these helpers who are willing do such seemingly mundane jobs as part of the pastoral care team.

Please note that manic depression and other severe depressive illnesses have not been considered here as such cases should be dealt with by psychiatrists or trained psychotherapists.

NOTES

1. Fairchild, Roy W. *Finding Hope Again: A Pastor's Guide to Counseling the Depressed* p 15ff.
2. Mitchell, Ross *Depression* pp 9–13.
3. Perry, Lloyd M; Sell, Charles M. *Speaking to Life's Problems* p 109ff.
4. Scott Peck, M. *The Road Less Travelled* pp 72–73.
5. Mitchell op. cit. pp53–54.
6. Wise, Carroll A. *Religion in Illness and Health* pp 143.
7. Jahoda, M. *Modern Concepts of Positive Mental Health* p 143.
8. Fairchild op. cit. pp 15–16.
9. Perry & Sell op. cit. p 108.
10. Fairchild op. cit. p 12–14
11. Scott Peck p 196.

12. Ibid. p 18ff.

13. Arieti, Silvano; Bemporad, Jules *Severe and Mild Depression: The Psychotherapeutic Approach* p 54.

14. Perry and Sell op. cit. p 109.

15. Mitchell op. cit. pp 45–50.

15. Fairchild op. cit. p 25.

17. Beck, Aaron T. *Depression* pp 255–256.

18. Fairchild op. cit. p 46.

19. Pruyser, Paul W. *The Minister as Diagnostician: Personal Problems in Pastoral Perspective* p 66.

20. Fairchild op. cit. p 55.

21. Mitchell op. cit pp 92–93.

22. Van Dongen-Garrard, Jessie *Invisible Barriers: Pastoral Care with Physically Disabled People* pp 53–60.

23. Ibid. pp 125ff.

24. Baker, Don; Nestor, Emery *Depression* p 183.

Theological Reflection

The last fifty years have seen a number of developments in Christian theology, psychology and ministry. These have had radical effects upon the practice and development of pastoral care and within the church an important development has been the rise of an emphasis upon theological reflection.

Prior to World War II, Anton Boisen and the developments of clinical pastoral education put a new face on pastoral care and pastoral counseling, drawing much from the psychological approach, especially that of Carl Rogers. The influence of Jung within the Catholic sphere highlighted the need for self-awareness in the pastoral care person. The spiritual exercises of St. Ignatius provided the basis of a new surge of interest in spirituality and spiritual direction. The development of liberation and political theology in South America and Germany absorbed much from Marxist philosophy, turning the churches' attention to social justice not only in Third World countries but in all areas of human existence. The development of field education in seminaries placed importance upon theological reflection in pastoral practice.

The Center of Spirituality and Justice founded in the Bronx, New York (1980) for the training of spiritual directors is indicative of the above named changes. The center's research[1] showed that the Ignatian method of contemplative prayer and direction did not raise pertinent issues of social concern. Among their conclusions was that any experience of God is simultaneously an experience of self and an experience of neighbor. They saw each experience as intrapersonal, interpersonal and societal and developed a structure consisting of four phases.

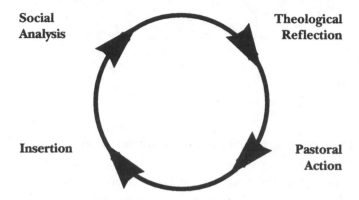

Insertion phase–This involves identifying yourself and others in the experience and each person's role and reaction.

Social analysis phase–It demands a discovery of the facts and an explanation of them, the relationships involved, the emerging implications and future possible outcomes.

Theological reflection stage–This stage contemplates the gospel values observable in the situation. How is God seen in the midst of the experience? What scriptures are applicable to the events?

Pastoral action phase–What actions may I as a Christian take to offer the compassion of God? Pastoral action, it was discovered, was strongly influenced by the quality of theological reflection.

While the above arose out a program of spiritual direction, it has admirable points for application by the serious hospital visitor. It sets theological reflection in context.

A BREAK WITH TRADITION

Reflection would be considered as rank heresy by Richard Baxter, whose work *The Reformed Pastor* is a historic classic on pastoral care, first published in 1655. Section 2 of the book is devoted to "the duty of personally catching and instructing the flock"[2]. Doctrine on theology came from the "Word." It had to be taught. It was one of the most important aspects of the Christian ministry of pastoral care. Barth's theology of the Word of God, as Campbell indicates, renewed the authoritarian declaration of theology. It was a revolt against human reflection for spiritual understanding. Theological indoctrination in Baxter's role model demands unequivocal acceptance of what is taught and eliminates any opportunity to question or identify areas of experience not matching the dogmatic. Campbell suggests that "exploration" encourages questions and searching response.[3]

Theological reflection confirms the reality of theology because it elucidates what is happening in life and God's activity in it. This enables the rediscovery of pastoral care today, where the pastoral carer becomes a companion on the same journey with the sufferer. The quality of a relationship, personal involvement and mutual trust that develops between the carer and the cared through theological reflection produces pastoral care that neither Baxter nor Barth could comprehend from their self-exalted positions. Care offered from such an aloof, dogmatic pose will produce a like remoteness from the patient.

DEFINING REFLECTION

James Conlan, Assistant Director of Field Education of the Toronto School of Theology, has viewed theological reflection and social analysis in practical terms:

> Theological reflection is the application, integration and response of our faith in and through our concrete experiences. Theological reflection is the interaction and re-creation

of the gospel in the concrete circumstance of life. Theological reflection is the current nomenclature for describing the way in which the gospel is once again made new in the life of an individual or group. Theological reflection is simply this, reflection on faith in the light of experience.

Theological reflection, as stated above, is the integration of conviction and action. Theological reflection is the process by which the believing person creates a congruence between faith and life; the goal of theological reflection is to surface and articulate one's operative theology: by this we mean the instinctive value system which guides our lives toward meaning and purpose in the light of the gospel. A person's operative theology is, I believe, fundamentally formed in the significant life experiences of the subject."[4]

Conlon stresses the need for theological reflection to be made with full awareness of the social context. In reflecting upon a hospital encounter this means reflection on the faith dimension in the light of the experience of a patient in the hospital. It respects the political, economic, social, cultural and religious background of the patient and the hospital setting.

THE CARER'S PERSONAL THEOLOGICAL INVOLVEMENT IN THEOLOGICAL GROWTH

Theological reflection includes not only what is happening in the lives of the patient or relatives, but also causes the visitor to do a little self-examination, a personal appraisal of his or her own theological involvement in the case. There are theological principles which need to be recalled by the visitor in these times. They were first put forward by Doran McCarty in relation to field education supervisors.[5]

The principle of ministry

Pastoral care at the bedside must issue from Christian motivation. Purity of heart is necessary in approaching the patient. Game playing is not acceptable, for instance bringing false hope to avoid the embarrassment of talking about the implications of dying. The use of scripture reading and prayer or the pretence of business to avoid issues is equally unacceptable.

The principle of the value of persons

Christianity, following Jesus' example, places value upon the individual person as created in God's image. In the hospital setting the patient has much of his or her dignity stripped. The pastoral visitor will enhance the patient's sense of self-worth. Manipulation of patients in their weakened physical, mental and emotional condition is anathema.

The principle of creation

God created persons to be growing, developing beings. Self-realization is part of the process intended through God's creation of human beings. The hospital can seem to be defeating, humiliating and depressing for the patient. In the midst of apparent injustice and pain, pastoral care can point out avenues along which the patient can move toward personal growth and understanding.

The principle of revelation

Revelation comes with a divine-human encounter. In the context of any human activity, including hospitalization, God's personal presence may be experienced. The pastoral care person's role is to facilitate such revelatory experiences for the patient.

The principle of incarnation

Incarnation means God with us. Incarnation means that Jesus is sharing the journey of suffering with the patient. The pastoral person is able to help the sufferer activate that incarnational relationship with Jesus. Thus pastoral hospital visitors should carefully reflect upon their own theological position in relation to the patient, applying these principles which are also motivational.

REFLECTION PRODUCES GROWTH

A striking statement by William Close, Professor of Christian Theology in Edmonton, Canada is relevant here: "Hospitals, liberation movements and corporation board rooms are now the places where theology is finding a home."[6] A pastoral person working in a hospital must be able to recognize readily the theological activity being generated in each hospital visit. Sensitivity to the congruence or incongruence of a theology with the bedside is a skill that develops through theological reflection, as should all of life's encounters. Any person who reflects upon the hospital ministry will have traditional theological concepts challenged. A Christian's theology should not remain static; it should ever be growing and developing in the knowledge and understanding of God in the context of day-to-day living. A stagnant theology based purely on imparted knowledge is possible evidence of a theologically and spiritually inert priest, pastoral worker or parishioner.

Questioning of theology through reflecting on experience results in spiritual growth. Over many years of full-time hospital ministry my own theology has developed, matured and is still providing fresh insights and perceptions of God, human beings and the universe. An openness to such growth makes religion and Christianity vital and relevant in a changing world.

REFLECTION PRODUCES
CHRISTIAN PASTORAL CARE

The key is theological reflection. This supports Michael Taylor, who presents the case that Christian pastoral care "not only transforms and supports those who care but actually informs what they do."[7] Two of the basic questions in reflection are

"What are we dealing with? and "How best can we help?" Taylor suggests that a good pastoral care discussion has taken all relevant material into consideration and has not made an impulsive, uninformed decision. Pastoral care must apply the doctrines of the church in its reflection if it is to be Christian. Theology is relevant to practical concerns and must be recognized by ministers and the laity alike. Recognition of theological involvement and an openness to theological growth in the context of the patient in hospital makes possible a positive, helpful, supportive and Christian ministry. This then becomes recognized as Christian pastoral care. It makes the difference between the caring offered by an allied health service worker and a ministry of the pastoral carer. Or, to cite Taylor again:

> Pastoral care then may become Christian pastoral care when exercised by Christians and by people sustained by Christian faith but also when the actual substance of it, what is actually done, is informed by a constant critical dialogue between the Christian and his or her Lord and the Christian and his or her community.[8]

According to Laurence O'Connell[9] theological reflection enables better recognition and appreciation of the human theological dimensions of various pastoral situations. He also sees it as enhancing the pastoral person's personal identity, and at the same time it fosters "practical effectiveness in ministry."

ACCEPTING THE RELEVANCE OF THEOLOGY

In order to reflect effectively there must be a real conviction that Christian theology is relevant to today's experiences. Taylor[10] develops a chapter entitled "The Relevance of Doctrine," in which he refers to many Christian doctrines; although they are in the past tense they are applicable to the present tense. One instance is the doctrine of incarnation: if

God is incarnate in Jesus, then we may accept him as being incarnate in us, for through the spirit he comes to dwell in us. Similarly the doctrines of creation and the fall speak of every person's need to accept the responsibility of right living in this world of God's creating.

The more one reflects upon pastoral encounters, the more proficient become the skills at applying Christian doctrine to contemporary life. The doctrine of the person of Jesus exemplifies a human living in relation with God—the human and divine at their best.

Having accepted that theology has relevance to every pastoral experience, it is time for us to look at a practical framework for theological reflection in the hospital setting.

A PROCESS FOR THEOLOGICAL REFLECTION

Recall, analysis and *strategy* would be a reasonable summation of the well-known three-phase movement. *Action/reflection/action* a model is used in many other disciplines.

I would like to take up three phases as advocated by Carl Trutter,[11] and then add another two to highlight them. Otherwise some aspects may be glossed over.

A. Detailed Picture Building.
B. Analysis for Meaning.
C. Identifying Theology.
D. Imaging or Interpreting.
E. Strategy Formulation.

This process will be demonstrated by a particular case.

Detailed picture building

Behind everyone's personal story, there is a greater story, a cosmic story that takes the many incoherent elements of our personal story and shapes them into a coherent pattern. This is the religious domain of story, the interaction between personal story and that underlying story that gives meaning to human existence. For the Christian this underlying cosmic story is embedded in the biblical account of redemption, culminating in the life, death and resurrection of Jesus. Fenhagen presents the argument that we do ministry when we enable others to see the connection or interaction between their personal story and cosmic story.[12]

Theological reflection is the searching out of the story. This means bringing the patient's personal story and cosmic story into unblurred focus. Fenhagen identifies four values of detailing the story:

a) It provokes life questions which encourage exploration and growth.

b) It invites participation in the struggle to comprehend the unknown.

c) It deals with themes of human existence, themes of bondage and deliverance, separation and reunion, life and death.

d) It has the potential for initiating us into the mystery of our own being.

Detailed picture building is the setting out of the story that the patient has enunciated. Some of it will be fascinating, some may be fantasy, some may be masked. Nonetheless, the detailed picture as told by the patient is to be pieced together as accurately as possible.

A patient had just been admitted for a bone marrow transplant, for which (at that time) there was up to a sixty percent chance of success, meaning remission. My chaplain's blazer identified me and I was standing at the nurse's station when she bounded up and said in a loud voice, for all to hear, "I'm Helen, I'm in for a bone marrow transplant. I've no need to be here because I'm cured. I've been anointed, had hands laid on me. I'm cured."

Later conversations revealed that she had been "zapped" (her word) in the spirit three times, being thrown to the floor backward each time. Helen was a young mother of four children.

My immediate reaction was that either here was a confident zealous person, who showed remarkable faith, or someone in an exaggerated state of denial. She wanted to live and believed she was going to live. Her new-found faith was to accomplish it.

My "on the run" summation at the first encounter was that I had to tread warily with her, not to alienate her by showing any scepticism about her faith and try to establish dialogue with her in order to discover the real person beneath.

Nurses at the station looked up, and raised their eyebrows at each other and me.

The following is an abridged version of the elements of picture building in the above incident:

• Record the scene, where it was, what the patient did and said.
• Provide evidence of the patient's reaction to her hospitalization.
• Record the pastoral person's internal response and the initial summation of what to do. The picture painted tried to be non-judgmental and to avoid the stereotyping of the patient.

All analysis is avoided in the picture-building stage.

Analysis for meaning

The second stage sets out to discover meaning in the encounter. Here was an unusual display of confidence for someone about to undergo a transplant. At this stage the questions are, "Why was she so aggressively confident? Was this her method of coping with her life-threatening situation? What was the nature and depth of her religious experience? Was it merely a security blanket or a genuine relationship with Christ? What were the family dynamics? Was this her own personality trait of independence and control being acted out?" By asking these questions we are analyzing what was going on in the patient.

I had to ask myself some further questions. "Why was I on the defensive at the worst or cautious at the least? As she was so confrontational, would she respond to confrontation and challenge by the carer?" Raising these and other questions with another involved chaplain helped provide some clarification. It is by the consideration of possible answers that some pattern of meaning in the patient's behavior is discernible.

Identifying the place, presence and activity of God (theology)

The pastoral person should not be satisfied with the purely analytical approach of stages one and two. That is the role of secular counselors, social workers and other carers. For truly Christian pastoral care, the search for the awareness of God must constitute the third stage of theological reflection.

In the case cited in stage one, the patient had an easy passage throughout the transplant and isolation periods. She went immediately into remission and remained so for three years before she relapsed. She then returned for a second transplant with an almost identical story of another three encounters with the Holy Spirit. Each time she was "zapped." Demons were allegedly cast out of her on the third occasion.

She died three weeks after the second transplant had been performed.

In the three years of remission, neither she nor her husband and family were active in their relationship with God or the church. The relapse forced a return to the healing services and to the woman with the gift of healing. At the second transplant, the Bible was not required as they had a computer print-out of every scripture verse containing the word "to heal" or a version of it.

The patient was a person who had to dominate in all situations. She was the pivotal force in the family. The husband and children all submitted to her. She was not interested in spiritual support from chaplains. She only wanted to hear prayers that confirmed her supposed cure. The names of Jesus or God were seldom on her lips; the Holy Spirit was named only in relation to the healing services.

Reflecting theologically on this case, I felt that the patient appeared to be setting herself up as God. Her wishes and desires had to be obeyed by God. In fact she had decreed that she was cured, therefore God had to prove her right. It appeared that she was an excellent manipulator of her husband and family by the way they attended to her every whim. The husband was constantly massaging her legs, feet and toes with cream. She showed an adverse reaction to all in authority in the hospital system: specialist, residents, nursing unit manager and chaplains. Others had to be subservient to her. She was the goddess figure who put God to the test, demanding a "cure."

Thus she actually denied herself the support and comfort of God, even at the very end, because she still insisted that she was cured, right to the time of lapsing into a coma a few days before her death.

My fellow chaplain and I felt restricted in our endeavors to minister to Helen as she dictated the agenda and closed off any other aspect we dared to raise. Efforts at confrontation were treated with scorn. She lacked a willingness to let God be in control and change her life. She demonstrated a dominant ego position in all her relationships and that egocentricity prevented her from seeing that she needed God's assistance in accomplishing a lasting remission from her illness.

The doctrine of faith was heavily in focus, but faith in what? In the woman who laid hands on her in the healing services. Doctrines of repentance and forgiveness are strikingly absent in the story. The faith was in the woman, in the evidence of falling backwards six times and so forth. God, Jesus and the Holy Spirit appeared to have a low profile in her mind.

On arrival for the second transplant Helen had remarked, "It's different this time. I've turned my back on Satan." Again the dominant "I" protrudes. The words of the song "I did it my way" came into my thoughts. This faith was also in herself. Faith in the divine seemed strangely absent; in spite of the claim of healing in a Christian service, it was as if God were an "extra" in the performance.

The salient theological implication involved here is healing. The patient was obsessed with healing or perhaps a more precise word would be "cure." The odds favored her in the first transplant but she was clearly told that the second transplant carried only a ten percent chance of survival. Her indomitable response was, "I'm cured. I don't need this transplant."

The doctrine of healing involves the healing of the whole person—body, mind and spirit. In this case it was the body which went into remission. She claimed physical or bodily healing. While in remission, apparent healing could not be disputed. Emotional healing? Her strength not only for herself but for the family also could perhaps be classified as evidence of healing of the emotions. I imagine members of the tennis club where she played following the transplant were emotionally strengthened. Her mind was firmly fixed on the positive. It never wavered.

Spiritual healing? That is difficult to assess without appearing to be judgmental, but the evidence of her speech and non-verbal behavior gave little indication of any significant spiritual healing. The scriptures were reduced to three feet of all the healing verses. They were used as something to bolster and maintain the family faith in physical healing. This does not indicate a deep spiritual perceptiveness. Moreover, there were certain words and a demeanor which indicated the contrary:

- The name of God and Jesus were conspicuously absent.
- Gratitude to God for the remission never surfaced.
- The first-person pronoun dominated in all conversations.
- She showed no sign of ever questioning her ways of thinking and acting.
- There was no church attendance during the remission or sharing in any spiritual group.

Spiritual healing, it is assumed, would have resulted in different attitudes and behavior.

Many questions are posed in theological reflection: "Where was God in this when she was displaying such strident faith?" "What was the nature of that faith?" "Are there conditions to the fulfillment of the healing ministry?" "Why aren't all people healed?" Experience, the scripture and Christian doctrine are aligned and harmonized through reflections of this nature. Christianity and theology become relevant to the patient, and to the man in the street when church leaders relate theology to real life.

Theology matures when reflection is made upon encounters in the cold, non-discriminatory, ruthless, cruel human world so far away from the cozy protective confines of the average sanitized Christian church fellowship.

Imaging or interpreting

The fact that psychology and sociology almost swamped methods of pastoral care from the 1950s to the 1980s was recognized by Alister Campbell in his book "Rediscovering Pastoral Care"[13]. He writes: "We want to discover a style of Christian caring which treats adults not as feckless sheep and which acknowledges the ambiguity of every offer of care in a situation of mutual responsibility and mutual need..."

Much recent pastoral care literature seems to have been so enamored of psycho-dynamic insights and counseling methodologies that it refers to the Christian theological heritage only in passing and then only in a functional way. Michael Taylor suggests, rightly, I believe, that there is a difference between pastoral care and Christian pastoral care.[14] He devotes a whole chapter to answering the question, "What is Christian pastoral care?" It is seen to be transformative, supportive and informative. He sees Christian theology as being intricately involved in all three aspects.

Taylor identifies cycles in Christian discipleship. The first is the active or commitment phase, followed by a reflective stage, a questioning of the action, which in turn leads to further committed action. Reflection tries to align Christian faith with the experiences of our commitment to pastoral care. This reflection informs the carer of what is actually happening, clarifying the way for future action.

Campbell struggles with the fact that values and concepts which resist logical analysis are apprehended intuitively.[15] This involves an appeal to the imagination as well as to the intellect and appears to be a step in a different direction from Taylor's and other field educators' propositions. "Images" is the descriptive word Campbell uses. Images are not necessarily logical. They arise out of the stimulation of the imagination by observable events. It is possible that this product of the imagination highlights the major impression received, overshadowing other aspects. The emphasis is upon concrete images of caring rather than on the somewhat more abstract symbols.

One of the most beautiful and descriptive images was suggested in 1968 by Heije Faber,[16] who sees the hospital chaplain as a clown. The clown experiences three tensions:

• Being a member of the team and being in isolation.
• The tension of appearing to be and feeling like an amateur among acknowledged experts.
• The need for study and training, for originality and creativity.

Faber identifies the so-called clown or fool as having to be the most professional among professionals. This is true of many pastoral care persons. Campbell[17] takes the shepherd as a biblical image of the pastoral care person.

One of the classic books of modern times, almost compulsory reading for pastoral care workers, is Henri Nouwen's *Wounded Healer.*[18] His image of the pastoral person is a wounded healer, after the pattern of the wounds of Jesus being the necessary element for human salvation. Nouwen sees the modern minister as using his wounds creatively in the care of others.

Taylor[19] examines the validity of using Jesus as our image for pastoral care. While Christian workers aspire to be like him in their caring, Taylor says that we have little to go on as to what Jesus was really like. We live in a different cultural setting. Jesus left no personal writings. The writings we have about him may have been idealistically written by his devoted followers.

The danger Taylor sees is to make Jesus in our own image. If we are a passive type, Jesus is mild and gentle. If we are aggressively oriented, then Jesus is the vigorous reformer. The difference between the conditions of Jesus' day and ours is no small factor in the matter of how Jesus cared.

We are open to error if in accepting Jesus' divine nature we conclude that he cannot be a model for us. We could easily disregard Jesus as appropriate for theological reflection in determining an image of the pastoral carer.

We must remember, continues Taylor, that Jesus *did* live in a world of human beings full of the same emotions, sufferings and experiences we encounter. Starting with this common base, it is proposed that we take the image of Jesus we have and improve on it, analyzing and comparing as we do so. The test of our imaging exercise is whether we can say that these images are really like the Jesus we know personally. Images are intended, as Campbell[20] points out, to describe that peculiar quality of care which pastoral relationships can provide.

I would like to suggest that images not be confined, as Taylor has highlighted, to the person of Jesus but also include some drawn from biblical vignettes or from biblical doctrine. Campbell[21] visualizes our being able to produce images from topics like penitence, faith, sexuality, friendship, repose, mortal combat and so on. The scope of image work is unlimited.

Let us turn to some of the images that may be gleaned from the case of Helen. Helen was so far along on her control trip that she was like the prodigal son, taking all her inheritance, confident that she could manage it herself. The father, knowing the predicaments likely to be encountered, had to wait and watch for the right moment to stretch out the hand of love and support. I faced the difficult decision of choosing between confrontation and possible rejection or waiting in anticipation of some sign of softening on Helen's part. Adopting the prodigal father's image, my choice was patience.

In this particular case, the wait was futile. Helen never released her grip on the controls. She never recognized the need to return, probably because she believed that she had already arrived. The pastoral care I offered consisted of faithfully visiting Helen, offering prayer when appropriate and waiting for the opportunity to be realistic about her physical and spiritual condition.

Let us take a non-biblical image. The setting is the ballet theater. The ballerina is playing two roles. There is a call for a quick change of costume for the second role, and in the star's dressing room the costume is all laid out. The dancer's wardrobe assistant stands in the wings to effect the change to the new role. In our case Helen is, of course, the ballerina starring in front of a packed house, the audience gasping at her skill, stoicism, endurance and fortitude in a difficult and almost impossible role. As the assistant, I wait in the wings and wait and wait. As the sole artist on stage, the ballerina appears to be ad libbing her choreography, while the orchestra plays when she should be off stage. The assistant cannot hiss for her to come off, nor is it possible to rush on stage and drag her off. The ballerina is too absorbed in her performance and the adulation it brings.

The other—and probably most important—revelation offered by the image is focused on the wardrobe assistant—the carer. It highlights the tension that I experienced, which I must have taken into the ward every time I visited Helen. On reflection, I have no doubt that she picked it up. This tension was generated by my inability to be able to run to the stage and save her from embarrassment. If this tension was obvious, then I had been erecting barriers to my ministry. In my concern for Helen, this important aspect of the image was not given the attention it should have received.

A carer needs to consider honestly all the lessons that an image offers, recognizing and admitting any personal weaknesses that are reflected.

Images that come to mind in various circumstances may be as different as an angel and a brick wall. They may be animate or inanimate, rational subjects or tangible objects. They may belong to the realms of fantasy. The Psalms provide us with numerous examples, such as a rock, refuge, hiding place, sheperd or chaff. Ezekiel sees a valley of dry bones and a watchman, while Hosea is tormented by the image of a harlot.

The master teacher demonstrated his mastery in his use of images throughout the gospels: a lost sheep or coin, wheat and weeds, a grain of wheat falling to the ground, a mustard seed, an elder brother, fishing nets, a mugged man, a basin and a towel, a yoke, a barren fig tree and so on. Our ability to understand God and his ways may be perceived through countless images of everyday experiences.

Supplement 10 is an example of seeing images in an ordinary coffee cup. Through images, God is able to speak and reveal much to us.

Imagining, then, is using the imagination in such a way as to identify the basic dynamics going on within both the person being cared for and the carer.

Strategy formulation

Through the identification of the theological dynamics involved and the interpretation of the images, strategies may be formulated to deal with the patient and his or her presentations.

In Helen's case, it may be readily seen how my decision not to confront and challenge her was part of a strategy developed as a result of such reflection and imaging. This position was to change little in over three years. It was also confirmed as the right strategy for me to follow. There will always be those times when we say to ourselves, "If only I'd done it differently." The important thing is that care was offered.

This process of theologising, using theological reflection and imaging in the same encounter, makes possible a more effective and balanced understanding. By this process, logical analysis (stage C) and intuition (stage D) become integrated, allowing practical strategies to evolve for effective pastoral care.

The importance of reflection upon pastoral ministry cannot be overstressed. By it pastoral care is turned into Christian pastoral care with greater effectiveness. Carers may need to work at their own process or follow one of the number of processes put forward by pastoral theologians and educators.

NOTES

1. O'Shea, Sr. Elinor *Spiritual Direction and Social Consciousness*
2. Baxter, Richard *The Reformed Pastor.* pp 173–256.
3. Campbell, A. *Rediscovering Pastoral Care* pp 41ff.
4. Conlon, James A. *Theological Reflection and Socal Analysis* p170.
5. McCarty, Doran. *Theological Principles for the Supervising Task* p 92-95.
6. Close, William J. *What Does it Mean to Think Theologically* p 187
7. Taylor, Michael H. *Learning to Care—Christian Reflection on Pastoral Practice* p 38.
8. Ibid. p 35.
9. O'Connell, Laurence J. *Theological Reflection and Ministerial Identyit* p 201.
10. Taylor op cit p 42ff.
11. Trutter, Carl B. *Theologising in Field Education* p215–225.
12. Fenhagen, James C. *Mutual Ministry* p33ff.
13 . Campbell, op cit pp 1–2.
14. Taylor op cit pp 19–37.
15. Campbell, op cit p 18ff.
16. Faber, Heije *Pastoral Care in the Modern Hospital* p 871ff.
17. Campbell, op cit p26.
18. Nouwen Henri *The Wounded Healer*
19. Taylor op cit pp 87–98.
20. Ibid. p 24
21. Ibid. p 25

SUPPLEMENT 8—DEVELOPING AWARENESS

Imagine yourself as the patient in each of the four awareness settings discussed in Chapter 12. Write down your feelings about each situation.

As a patient, which of the four would you prefer and why?

Allow sufficient time to adequately consider the above. Be sure to put yourself in the position of the patient. Use pen and paper to express your thoughts.

Consider the positive aspects you may discern in each category of awareness. Do you think it is always advisable to ensure that open awareness prevails?

Some cultural groups insist that second–degree male relatives (for example uncles, cousins) make the decision as to whether the nuclear family and the patient are told of the diagnosis and prognosis. How would you cope when the decision is not to tell the family or the patient the true condition? How would it affect your relating and praying with the patient?

Meet in a group with three or four other visitors, priests or pastoral care workers and discuss what you have written.

SUPPLEMENT 9—REFLECTING THEOLOGICALLY

Take time with pencil and paper to reflect on a current pastoral situation in which you are involved.

i) Detail the picture you recall.

ii) Analyze your picture.

iii) Identify where God is or was present or absent in the pictures, that is reflect theologically.

iv) What image(s) come(s) into your mind about yourself and the patient?

v) What strategy do you see for handling the case in the future?

Having written this all down, discuss with your group or with an experienced pastoral person what you have written: your observations, your reflections, your images, your past actions and your planned future actions.

SUPPLEMENT 10

Just a coffee mug

A whole truck load of clay
discharged its sticky mess.
It moved up the conveyor belt
to be battered and moistened,
to be conditioned and prepared,
to be fashioned and shaped,
into a thousand cups...
Cups with fancy handles,
cups with curvaceous sides,
cups to be patterned
in colors attractive,
cups of glazed beauty,
cups of Dresden fineness.

Some cups were flawed
or didn't conform to shape;
they were retrieved
to be re lumped,
to be re moulded
into something else.
I see myself as one like those,
to be something else, like a coffee mug.
Not so dainty, not put on show
in a china cabinet,
not to be admired
as delicate and elegant,
not to be brought out
before the genteel visitor
in the drawing room.

A coffee mug to be used by all and sundry
in the kitchen,

by the tired and exhausted,
who need a vessel
filled for refreshment,
filled for renewal,
filled for revitalization
by the hurting heart,
who needs a listening ear
over a coffee mug,
filled for reflection,
filled for recall,
filled for reconstruction
by those lonely and alone,
who need a coffee mug
to sip over communication,
to sip over companionship,
to sip over communion,
in the sharing of love and care.

An ordinary coffee mug, useful every day,
available whenever, for whoever,
I'm happy to remain just such a coffee mug
if that's your desire.

Epilogue

Having read this far, some of you will be sighing, "Pastoral care in general hospitals is not for me". It *is* a special ministry. Not all are fitted to fulfill specialized roles in the parish, let alone pastoral care in a general hospital. It is a ministry which should only be undertaken as regular Christian service after a sense of God's call to this type of task and after much prayer. If you are convinced that hospital pastoral care is God's sphere of special ministry for you, then every effort should be made to train and equip you for such a ministry.

That it is an important and essential ministry of the followers of Jesus is found in Christ's commission of his church in Matthew 25. Acceptance into the kingdom is on the basis of caring for the sick, the prisoner, the poor and all the needy of body, mind and spirit. Pastoral care to the sick must bear the hallmarks of the God whom we seek to serve. It is ministry which, in spite of its stresses, strains, and occasional disappointments, brings fulfillment, satisfaction and adoration of a God of the impossible. It draws the carer into a closer and more dependent relationship with God. It compels a more intense search of the mind and heart of God. It tests and challenges faith in God and in so doing strengthens that faith.

The chaplain and pastoral visitor in a general hospital, though at times weary and exhausted, are able to experience the soft, warm, inner glow of the Spirit's presence because this caring is only possible through the constant guidance and awareness of that presence.

In conclusion, pastoral care in general hospitals involves five responses by the carer:

Move with the hands and feet of God. Wherever we go it should be to the bedside of the one to whom God has led us. To be at another bedside is to be in the wrong place. We do practical things with the patient to whom the hands and feet of God have brought us—no more, no less. We are not out to impress by over-doing it. We are not so timid and scared that we do not do enough.

See with the eyes of God. We look beyond the surface. We read what is not being shown. Our perceptiveness penetrates the masks that hide the real fears and apprehensions. Our seeing goes beyond the human to a divine understanding.

Hear with the ears of God. Beneath the talk and sometimes stoic front, there are muted cries, cries that are not audible, yet are punishingly real to the patient or family members. These cries are not to be heard except by the ears of a God-inspired carer.

To be heard, to know you have been heard, to be open and honest and to share the reasons for those cries is healing and comforting. Hearing with the ears of God brings relief to the sufferer. It makes pastoral care effective.

Speak with the voice of God. When you are at the God-appointed bedside, when you have observed with the eyes of God and heard with the ears of God, then you are able to speak with the voice of God. God will speak through you. It is God's voice the patient needs to hear, not yours. It is God's voice that soothes, encourages, motivates, provides and maintains hope.

Love with the love of God. Not a sounding gong or a clanging cymbal, not the gift of prophecy nor an academic wisdom, not a great display of faith—it is love the patient longs to hear and to see. The kind, unboastful, calm, self-effacing and hopeful love of God incarnate in the carer is that for which the anxious and stressed are searching. The love that is willing to go to the extremes of Calvary is the love that bears fruit at the bedside.

Bibliography

Areti, Silvano, Bemporad, Jules *Severe and Mild Depression: The Psychotherapeutic Approach* (New York:Basic Books) 1976

Baker, Don and Nestor, Emory *Depression* (Basingstoke:Marshalls) 1984.

Baxter, Richard *The Reformed Pastor* (Edinburgh:Puritan) 1974

Beck, Aaron T. *Depression* (New York:Harper and Row) 1967

Bonhoeffer, Dietrich *Life Together* (London:SCM Press) 1954

Bowers, M.K. et al. *Counseling the Dying* (New York:Nelson) 1964

Brusate, Louis J. "Theological Reflection and Erikson's Development Framework" *Key Resources* Vols 1 and 2

Campbell, Alister V. *Rediscovering Pastoral Care* (London:Darton, Longman and Todd) 1981

Campbell, Alister V. *A Dictionary of Pastoral Care* (London:SPCK) 1987

Carkuff, Robert *Helping and Human Relations* (New York:Rineholt and Winston) 1969

Carlozzi, Carl G. *Death and Contemporary Man* (Grand Rapids: Eerdmans) 1968

Carr, Wesley *The Pastor as Theologian* New Library of Pastoral Care (London:SPCK) 1989

Cassidy, Shiela *Sharing the Darkness* (London:Darton, Longman and Todd) 1987

Close, W.J. "What Does It Mean To Think Theologically?" *Key Resources* Vols, 1 and 2

Conlon, James A. "Theological Reflection and Social Analysis" *Key Resources* Vol. 5 (New York: Association for Theology and Field Education)

Davis, Stephen, ed. *In Encountering Evil* (Atlanta:Knox Press) 1981

Dobihal, Edward F. Jnr, Stewart, Charles William *When a Friend is Dying* (Nashville:Abingdon) 1984

Egan, Gerard *The Skilled Helper* (Monterey C.A.:Brookes/Cole) 1975

Fairchild, Roy W. *Finding Hope Again: A Pastor's Guide to Counseling the Depressed* (San Francisco:Harper and Rowe) 1980

Fenhagen, James C. *Mutual Ministry* (New York:Seabury) 1977

Fowler, James W. *Faith Development and Pastoral Care* (Philadelphia:Fortress) 1988

Gibbs, C. Earl *Caring For the Grieving* (Corte Madera:Omega) 1976

Harlem, Ole K. *Communication in Medicine—A Challenge to the Profession* (Basel:Karger) 1977

Helm, John *Weak but Strong* (Sydney:Anzea) 1985

Holst, Lawrence, ed. *Hospital Ministry—The Role of the Chaplain Today* (New York:Crossroad) 1990

Hulme, William E. *Pastoral Care and Counseling Using the Unique Resources of Christian Tradition* (Minneapolis:Augsberg) 1981

Irion, Paul E. *Hospice and Ministry* (Nashville:Abingdon) 1988

Jahoda, M. *Modern Concepts of Positive Mental Health* (New York:Basic Books) 1958

Kubler-Ross, Elisabeth *On Death and Dying* (New York:Macmillan) 1969

Kubler-Ross, Elisabeth *Questions and Answers on Death and Dying* (New York:Macmillan) 1974

Lake, Frank *Clinical Theology—A Theological Psychological Basis to Clinical Pastoral Care* abr by Martin Yeomans (London:Darton, Longman and Todd) 1986

McCarty, Doran "Theological Principles for the Supervising Task" *Key Resources* Vol. 5 (New:York Association for Theology and Field Education)

Mitchell, Ross *Depression* (Harmondsworth:Penguin) 1975

Nouwen, Henri J.M. *Creative Ministry* (Garden City, New York:Doubleday) 1971

Nouwen, Henri J.M. *The Wounded Healer* (New York:Doubleday) 1972

Nouwen, Henri J.M. et al. *Compassion* (London:Darton, Longman and Todd) 1982

O'Shea, Sr. Elinor "Spiritual Direction and Social Consciousness" *Key Resources* Vol. 5

Paul, Gerald W. *Ministry* Vol. 57 No. 11 1984

Perry, Lloyd M and Sell, Charles M. *Speaking to Life's Problems* (Chicago:Moody) 1983

Pruyser, Paul W. *The Minister as Diagnostican: Personal Problems in Pastoral Perspective* (Philadelphia:Westminster) 1976

Raphael, Beverley *The Anatomy of Bereavement* (New York:Basis Books) 1983

Richmond, Kent D. *Preaching to Sufferers: God and the Problem of Pain* (Nashville:Abingdon) 1988

Rumbold, Bruce D. *Helplessness and Hope—Pastoral Care in Terminal Illness* (London:SPCK) 1986

Sanes, Samuel *A Physician Faces Cancer in Himself* (New York:State University of New York) 1979

Schilling, S. Paul *God and Human Anguish* (Nashville:Abingdon) 1977

Scott Peck, M. *The Road Less Travelled* (London:Arrow) 1991

Sontag, Frederich *The God of Evil: An Argument for the Existance of the Devil* (New York:Harper and Row) 1970

Soulen, Richard N. et al *Care for the Dying* (Atlanta:John Knox) 1978

Switzer, David *The Minister as Crisis Counselor* (Nashville: Abingdon) 1974

Taylor, Michael H. *Learning to Care—Christian Reflection on Pastoral Practice* (London : SPCK) 1987

Trutter, Carl B. "Theologising in Field Education" *Key Resources* Vols 1 and 2

Van Dongen-Garrard *Invisible Barriers—Pastoral Care with Physically Disabled People* (London:SPCK) 1983

Wise, Carrol A. *Religion in Illness and Health* (New York:Harper) 1942

Zima, Joseph P. *Interviewing, Key to Effective Management* (Chicago:Scientific Research Associates) 1981